"*GraceQuest* is a gripping story of one man's (and his family's) struggle with tremendous weakness and pain, but it is also a narrative theodicy—defense of God's goodness in spite of the undeniable reality of evil. . . . This is an honest and hard-hitting book about God's grace in and through tremendous loss of health and strength. Readers will find hope and help here if they are open to its message about the God-given 'strength to suffer well.'"

—**Roger E. Olson**
Foy Valentine Professor of Christian Theology and Ethics,
George W. Truett Theological Seminary (From the Foreword)

"[This work] by Dr. Rakestraw is important for pastors, church leaders, and professors who often succumb to the temptation to be one person in their public roles while functioning quite differently in private . . . Bob offers us a different model of wholeness and holiness . . . [and] an example of *healthy* personal self-reflection that is honest and open . . . What a gift this book will be to all those who read it!"

—**Wyndy Corbin Reuschling**
Professor of Ethics and Theology, Ashland Theological Seminary

"Bob has written a book which should prove of interest to readers on a number of levels . . . I say this [despite having] significant theological differences from Bob on a number of vital issues . . . [Hearing] about Bob's own faith journey and theological development is fascinating . . . [and] the book is marked by honesty and vulnerability. Bob's story of his heart problems, his heart transplant, and the struggles that mark his life are riveting and ~~~~~~ I enthusiastically recommend [*GraceQuest*]."

—**Thomas R. Schreiner**
Associate Dean, James Buchanan Harrison Professor
New Testament Interpretation, The Southern Baptis

D1293342

"This book is a helpful and serious engagement with issues of suffering and grace. . . . While the autobiographical materials are engaging and interesting, this is much more than simply an autobiography of his experiences . . . [*GraceQuest*] . . . presents important theological issues in ways that are attractive, accessible, and understandable to lay readers . . . I am not aware of other books that so deftly meld the personal experiences and theological reflection."

—**Peter T. Vogt**
Adjunct Professor of Old Testament, Bethel Theological Seminary

GraceQuest

GraceQuest

One Teacher's Relentless Pursuit of Salvation,
Spirituality, and the Strength to Suffer Well

Robert V. Rakestraw

FOREWORD BY ROGER E. OLSON

WIPF & STOCK · Eugene, Oregon

GRACEQUEST
One Teacher's Relentless Pursuit of Salvation, Spirituality, and the Strength
to Suffer Well

Wipf & Stock
An Imprint of Wipf and Stock Publishers
199 W. 8th Ave., Suite 3
Eugene, OR 97401

www.wipfandstock.com

ISBN 13: 978-1-4982-1736-1

Manufactured in the U.S.A.   04/21/2015

To Joni and Laurie
Greatly loved by their father and their Father

Contents

Foreword

HAVING KNOWN BOB RAKESTRAW for almost a quarter century, I was eager to read his autobiography. I knew him before, during, and after his heart surgeries as colleague and friend. Although I always believed Bob to be a profoundly Christian man of high commitment to Christ and the church, I know now, after reading *GraceQuest*, that he is also a suffering servant sustained by God's grace and one who wants others who suffer to know that God's grace can be sufficient even when "the victory" is not being experienced as hoped.

GraceQuest is a gripping story of one man's (and his family's) struggle with tremendous physical weakness and pain, but it is also a narrative theodicy—defense of God's goodness in spite of the undeniable reality of evil. I say a "narrative theodicy" because even though Bob knows, understands, and discusses the various speculative theories called "theodicies," his ultimate theodicy is the experience of God's good and sustaining presence in and through unspeakable and undeserved pain.

This is a book for Bob's family and friends but also for all who cry out "Where is God?" in the midst of undeserved and relentless suffering. Far from "watching from a distance" as a popular song would have it, and far from "powerless to do anything about it," as much liberal theology would have it, and far from "punishing imperfect faith" as much folk religion would have it, according to Bob's experience God is powerfully present, sustaining and drawing him closer in spite of not intervening as Bob would, of course, ideally wish.

This is an honest and hard-hitting book about God's grace in and through tremendous loss of health and strength. Readers will find hope and help here if they are open to its message about the God-given "strength to suffer well."

—Roger E. Olson

Waco, Texas

January 2015

Preface

DURING MOST OF MY lifetime I had never given a thought to writing my life story, except perhaps as a sketch of events for our family history. Following my heart transplant in 2003, however, I began to think differently. After I had sent out a number of health updates to family, friends, and colleagues at Bethel University, where I served on the Seminary faculty, I was encouraged to publish the story of my pre- and post-transplant experiences, since I had had considerable difficulties both before and after the surgery. For years I debated the value of such a book.

Long before my heart problems I had been well aware that something (Someone) far bigger than me had been watching over me, opening doors, closing doors, and enabling me to make my way through life. Some super-natural force within me—what I call the grace of God or the God of grace—had buoyed me upon and through some rough seas while filling me with a deep contentment and trust in God's goodness and wisdom. My developing intention to write about my health issues gradually broadened to become a yearning to tell my whole story, one of being embraced and empowered by the relentless grace of God through many twists and turns. I decided to relate the details of my heart problems within the broader context of my sojourn on this earth.

My specific motivation then, for writing this book, even before I put down the first word, was to give to present and future generations of God-seekers (whether Christians or non-Christians) one person's account of the grace of God in action. Because I have been helped so remarkably through-out my life by reading the autobiographies of men and women of God, some from centuries ago, I developed a strong desire to provide something of this genre for those who, like me, long to know about the activity of God in the lives of people as they perceived that activity and responded to it.

In over fifty years of reading books by Christians, those that have mesmerized me and benefitted me most in my relationship with God and my attempts at serving God have been autobiographies. (Those *biographies* that tell the person's story accurately, with both objectivity and some de-gree of warmth toward the subject, presenting both the pleasant and the not-so-pleasant, have come closely behind autobiographies in usefulness and encouragement.) If only one person—young, middle-aged or elderly— finds, through the reading of this book, some quenching of his or her thirst after God, I will consider this project to be of eternal benefit. In addition, if there is even one thing only one reader learns from my life and applies that information or principle beneficially to his or her experience, I will be doubly grateful.

Have I been totally objective and accurate in the writing of my story? I doubt that pure objectivity in a work of this kind, or in any kind of history or in-depth reporting, is attainable. We all—writers and readers alike—consider events, interpretations of events, and personal thoughts and feelings about those events from our own perspectives at the time and in the circumstances in which we find ourselves. All anyone can do, especially while telling one's own story, is to be aware of this issue of perspective and seek to be as straightforward as possible.

As for accuracy, I have prayed often for guidance in this regard as well as for objectivity in writing. Seeing that I have now passed the "threescore years and ten" mentioned by the writer of Psalm 90:10 (King James Version), have I had the necessary memory to write accurately about events and impressions over such a span of years? I surely cannot claim to be exact in every detail, but where I have been even a bit unsure I have indicated this by such expressions as "to the best of my knowledge" or "as closely as I can recall." I thank God for giving me a strong, often remarkably clear, memory to write this account of my life.

For this book I have chosen the title *GraceQuest* to highlight the activity of God throughout my life. In God's never-ceasing quest to call out a people for his name, his grace is always prior and preeminent. He sought me, who had been stumbling in the darkness, and aroused within me a spirit of searching for him. My quest, prompted by and directed toward his grace, doubles the meaning of "grace quest." The book then, is about the grace of God pursuing me and my attempts at pursuing the grace of God in response.

The three phases in the subtitle of this book unfold in the order of my quest. With great gratitude I am nourished daily by the cumulative activity of God as he works wisely and unfailingly to deepen and widen my positive experiencing of salvation, spirituality, and suffering.

Acknowledgments

WITHOUT THE GRACIOUS ASSISTANCE of certain key people this book would never have become a reality. First of all I want to thank my wife, Judy Rakestraw, and our friend, Kim Olstad, for their willingness to dialogue with me during the summer and fall of 2011 concerning my desire to write a book on suffering. After several bewildering months (I wanted to cover every conceivable form of suffering throughout the world) I was able to narrow my thoughts (reluctantly at first) to this more realistic project. Kim and her daughter Jessie Jubert graciously contributed many hours to typing the first half of this book. I am deeply indebted to them. I am grateful beyond words for Judy, who not only read and offered valuable suggestions on the manuscript as I wrote, but without whom there would probably be no book. My life and hers have been, for over a half-century, increasingly and preciously intertwined. I have been blessed by dear family members and friends who followed this effort from the beginning and offered ample encouragement along the way. I am especially thankful to Alan Padgett and Jane Spriggs for crucial help at key stages of the project. Roger Olson, the Foy Valentine Professor of Christian Theology and Ethics at Truett Theological Seminary of Baylor University, and one of the finest theologians working today, has favored me with his perceptive and generous Foreword. I benefit regularly from Dr. Olson's insights at www.patheos.com/blogs/rogereolson. Finally I want to express special gratitude to Gloria Metz, longtime faculty secretary and friend to me and to a very large number of professors, students, and staff at Bethel Seminary Saint Paul. Gloria's many hours of cheerful and highly-skilled service in bringing this manuscript to completion are the gift of a lifetime to me in my desire to extol the God of all grace.

PART ONE

Pursuing Salvation

CHAPTER 1

Early Years

Roots

I WAS 12 YEARS old and living in Penndel, Pennsylvania. Serving as an altar boy at Our Lady of Grace Catholic Church gave me access to the altar and the sacred space around it, where only the priests and altar boys were allowed. Before each mass, I would go in the private preparation room behind the altar to help the priest put on certain vestments. These were items of outer clothing that served no practical purpose, as far as I could tell, but which were part of the traditions and customs of the church.

I was no angel, however. On some mass days I would get to the room before the priest and eat some of the communion wafers and drink some of the communion wine because it was something daring to do. Because these wafers were not yet consecrated they had not yet become the body and blood of Christ. Even though I did these and similar pranks I still felt a certain awe when I was serving the priest during mass, because I thought, deep down, that God somehow was in the midst of the happenings at the altar. I did not know it at the time, but God was engaged in a steady, unhurried, grace-full quest for my heart, my soul, and my entire being.

I was born in the fall of 1943, in northeast Philadelphia, Pennsylvania, to a Roman Catholic mother (Italian) and a non-religious father (Scottish, Irish, Welsh, and English). My brother Tom was born a year and a half before me, and my sister Rosemary almost eight years after me. We three children were baptized into the Catholic faith.

Before they married, my parents learned that when a Catholic married a non-Catholic, the church required the non-Catholic partner to sign an agreement that any children born from the union would be brought up in the Catholic faith. Although my father accepted this condition, even paying for a Catholic school education for the three of us children (which was not part of the agreement), he had no personal interest in or attraction to the Catholic Church.

My parents never had much of anything, nor had their parents. As for education, I believe that my mother quit school after ninth grade and my father after eighth grade. Previous to their marriage, my father Arthur had been a kind of hobo riding on tops of freight trains and getting off to find work here, there, and anywhere he could throughout the western United States. He labored mostly at outdoor jobs, but for a while worked as a model in San Francisco (in an art studio, I believe).

He sometimes spoke about riding the rails across the continental divide, fueling the fire in me for adventure. He actually slept on the walking plank (about 12–14 inches wide) on the top center of the boxcars. He told me he lay on his back and, with his hands clasped to the plank, one on each side, he slept like a baby as the train barreled along. I had come to know my father as a man who never lied, so I believed him when he told me about his past. However, I sensed he sometimes held back from saying more, for my sake.

At the age of 14 my father left the last of his foster homes, returning 16 years later, after the Great Depression, to Chester County, southwest of Philadelphia, where he grew up. In 1940 he married my mother Mary whom he met in a taproom, after which they lived in lower-class housing in northeast Philadelphia. My father worked as an electrician and my mother as a homemaker. Prior to her marriage she had worked at Nabisco, a very large food processing company.

Trains and Trolleys

When I was quite young (about three) my parents moved to Ardleigh Street, just a short walk from Germantown Avenue. They rented a half-duplex from my uncle and aunt.

To keep our food cold we had an "icebox," which was a large upright refrigerator-sized metal storage container with a tight door. Food was placed on shelves inside and on the top shelf were large blocks of ice. The ice-man came every few days with new ice. When the man used his icepick to cut the blocks to size, we kids surrounded his truck and begged for the cool wet ice chips produced.

Behind the house there was—to my delight—a railroad. Even though there was a train station not far up the tracks, when the trains passed behind our house they were moving at relatively high speed—or so it seemed to me.

Some of them, I think, were express trains and did not stop at the station. However, every train of any speed stirred excitement within me as it passed.

As a boy growing up in Philadelphia I developed a love for railroads—everything about them. I loved the rails, the ties, the grey stones, the trestles, the engines, the couplings, the boxcars, the flat cars, the oil cars, and the cabooses. And I loved walking on top of the cars when they were parked and no workmen were around. I loved looking down the parallel rails toward the point far off where they seemed to converge. I loved when the square-capped conductor yelled "all aboard!" and then came walking down the aisle punching a hole in each passenger's ticket. I loved the rumble of steel upon steel, the mournful call of the whistle, and the Doppler Effect when the sound suddenly dropped off.

I suppose I was fascinated with trains because of their size, strength, speed, and possibly (subconsciously) because they carried people and cargo to distant places. When I rode on a train I was going somewhere special, usually to a relative's home or to downtown Philadelphia with its awesome skyscrapers blotting out the sun.

In addition to the trains there were trolleys, also called streetcars. Riding the trolley cars on the tracks embedded in the brick street surface of Germantown Avenue was not quite as thrilling as riding the trains, but it was never dull. I liked all kinds of adventure, especially being on the move. Like little children all over the world, I loved the quest: the quest for adventure, excitement, and fun experiences beyond (or in the midst of) my ordinary life.

On the Waterfront

After several years living on Ardleigh Street we moved to paradise—at least for my brother and me. My parents rented an old boathouse (one level and a very musty space below) built right next to the Delaware River, one-quarter mile south of the Tacony-Palmyra Bridge at a spot called "Lardner's Point." We could see New Jersey across the river. Each day, during the high tide, the house extended well over the river. The water came under the screened porch and allowed any boats stored in the musty area under the porch to be floated out through the wide wooden doors that opened onto the river. However, it was no longer used as a boathouse when we lived there.

Just north of our home was a yacht club, with its docks and boat slips. As time went by, Tom and I got to hanging around the docks so much that we came to know many or most of the boat owners by name. We were probably about nine and seven when we moved there, and we were in our glory, especially bumming rides from the boat owners and even being allowed to steer the boats at times.

Not only was there a yacht club about a stone's throw from our house, there was a freight-train line no more than 15–20 feet from our front door! The trains moved slowly along, and we waved to and talked with the train engineers from our tiny porch. This was an industrial area, to be sure, with a machine shop close by on the other side of the tracks and the Frankford Arsenal just downriver where military weapons and ammunition were tested. We heard the "boom" sounds often. No parents who could afford otherwise would choose to raise three children at a place like this! But we boys loved it, even the junk yard on the other side of the yacht club and the railroad trestle over the lagoon very close to the house. We climbed in and on every train car we could, and took the rough packing-crate wood to build a fine treehouse. Dad made a sturdy floor first, on which Tom and I built a two-story "fort." I even hitched a ride on a moving boxcar at least once. When a workman up the tracks saw me, he waved his hands and yelled. I jumped off and ran. I think I first rolled on the ground just after I jumped.

There was danger all around. Many dozens of rats lived in the stone retaining walls next to our house, which came out and scampered around the moist gravel every day at low tide. My father succeeded at poisoning almost all of them with Warfarin before we moved from the house. I never thought about the danger—just the adventure. I spent as little time in the house as I had to, so my memories inside are few.

I vividly remember once while I was standing in the screened porch over the river at high tide. It was dark and somewhat foggy. Suddenly before my eyes a gigantic oil tanker loomed out of nowhere, silently moving upriver to discharge its treasure. Even with the fog I could see the captain's head in the lighted cabin. I was mesmerized and felt I could almost touch the behemoth. Just as exciting was the day my brother and I got our first (and only) bicycle—a used, plain-looking, full-sized riding machine. We saved the $25 to buy the bike and took turns fixing it up, sanding it, painting it blue, and riding it. It was another form of adventure and another reason to stay outdoors.

My overall chronological memory is a bit vague about our time there, but a number of specific memories are quite clear. As I mentioned above, I think I was about seven when we moved to Lardner's Point. I distinctly remember, because the house was so small, that I slept in my parents' bedroom. One night while lying in bed I heard my parents whispering. I heard my mother saying something like, "Not now, he's not asleep yet." I knew they were talking about me so I lay very still for some time. After a while I heard some movement in the bed. Something within me was saying, "No, Mom, don't do it." I didn't know what "it" was, but Mom seemed to be resisting it. I thought it must not be right. Finally I heard my mother say, "All right Art, get it over with." Soon after, I fell asleep. My parents never had a good relationship, but the years at Ardleigh Street and Lardner's Point were reasonably calm compared to what was to come.

Hurricanes

In October of 1954 Hurricane Hazel struck hard at the east coast of the United States. It was a major storm that caused extensive damage, and when it hit eastern Pennsylvania it wreaked havoc along the Delaware River. Almost all of the eighty or so pleasure boats docked at or near the yacht club next door were destroyed by the storm. Only a few of the owners heeded the warning to move their boats to a cove upriver.

The hurricane also destroyed our rented house. Before Hazel hit with its full force the five of us were welcomed into the sturdy, cinder-block yacht club to ride out the storm. We watched from the windows as the winds and waves literally tore the roof off the house, knocked out some of the major pillars holding the house off the water, and generally blew the house apart.

After a few weeks living in a motel we rented a half-duplex on Woodland Avenue in Penndel, Pennsylvania. I was ten years old—almost eleven. The Catholic school my brother and I attended was just a half-block down the street. As I look back on my elementary school years I realize that I have practically no specific in-class memories until this new school. Here I completed grades six, seven, and eight.

Not all of my experience with hurricanes was literal. In this new location I became the class clown, especially in eighth grade. My sense of humor emerged more each year, and in eighth grade my report card usually had a "C" recorded for "self-control." The report had a section for numerical grades on the right (such as arithmetic and spelling) and letter grades on the left (respect for authority, kindness to others, and so on). The lowest grade one could receive on the left side was "C." The nuns always had one of the priests come and hand out the report cards to frighten those, I suppose, who did not do well.

I remember once in eighth grade my teacher—a very nervous nun—contacted one of the parish priests about my behavior. He then requested that my mother and I come, after school hours, to the classroom where I clowned incessantly. I remember my mother crying, wiping her eyes, looking at me, and asking, "Why do you do these things, Bobby?" As I recall, my only answer was, "I don't know." I'm sure I got a lecture from the priest but I remember none of it.

As I look back now on these three years and my lack of "self-control" (which continued throughout my high-school years, although more covertly), I suppose I was "acting out" (joking, imitating the teachers, getting the ball rolling on some extended prank involving several students—all behind the teacher's back) because (a) I was bored (I was a quick learner), (b) I liked how I could make the other kids laugh, and (c) I wanted to escape the unhappiness in our home. I also started to develop an inferiority complex over my parents' increasing hostility toward each other. I thought everyone must know about this, and thus look down on me. In addition, we did not have a car—just a junky old truck. I felt inferior about this as well.

During the years we lived on Woodland Avenue my parents' marriage worsened considerably (or I just noticed matters more). They fought verbally quite often, and I especially dreaded the holidays. Christmas was the worst of all. We practically never went anywhere as a family, on holidays or any other days, and very rarely had people over. As far as I can recall we never sat down at a meal table as a complete family. Perhaps we did, but the closest to this that I can remember was the rare holiday occasion when my father and the three of us children sat down while my mother stood nervously nearby, hovering about to see if there was anything we needed during the meal. Even at such times there was often another potential hurricane gathering strength.

Mom never looked happy and rarely managed even a forced smile. The tension between my parents was always in the air when they were in the same room and the aggravation seemed to flow in one direction—from my mother toward my father. I never saw any signs of affection or respect from her toward him, though I noticed that there were occasional desires for her from him.

No one in our home ever used the word "love." I never heard either of my parents say "I love you" to me or to anyone else. I never remember being hugged by my parents until my father hugged me when I was in middle age, and I initiated that. It was a big surprise to me, years later, when I saw that Christian people hugged one another, and even said such things as "I love you." I was almost fifty years old when another man (a fellow faculty member) said to me, "I love you." I was startled, but I appreciated it.

CHAPTER 2

Being Catholic

Altar Boy

THE CATHOLIC RELIGION WAS a major part of my upbringing. I spent five days a week in Catholic school, taught mostly by nuns. I attended mass every Sunday morning with my mother, brother, and sister. My father had no interest in the church and never came to mass with us. To the best of my knowledge, neither my father nor my mother ever asked a question or made a comment about the Catholic faith or about any religion or religious thought until I was eighteen.

During my years in Penndel, under the influence of the nuns (and sometimes the priests), I served the local Catholic parish as an altar boy, as mentioned earlier. My classroom antics apparently were not serious enough to eliminate me from this honor. I served at Sunday masses, midweek masses, and (not very often) high masses, and assisted the priests during special Lenten and Christmas services. Sometimes I would be called out of class to help serve a funeral mass or other special mass.

During the nearly three years I lived in Penndel, the subjects I studied at Our Lady of Grace School included daily catechism. As in my previous Catholic school I learned about the "one true church" (the Roman Catholic Church), the sacraments, the different types of sin (especially mortal and venial), heaven, hell, purgatory, indulgences, Mary, the rosary, the mandate to attend mass on Sundays and holydays, and many other rules.[1]

---

1. Two catechisms from my Catholic school education are *Catholic Faith, Book Three*, based on *The Catholic Catechism As Drawn Up by His Eminence Peter Cardinal Gasparri* (Washington: The Catholic University of America Press, 1938), and, used by me more than the above, *Baltimore Catechism No. 3, Confraternity Edition*, by Rev. Francis J. Connell (New York, NY: Benzinger Brothers, 1952).

I remember the solemn warnings to stay away from all churches that were not Catholic. There was a Presbyterian (or was it Lutheran?) church across the street from the school, and I remember walking by and gazing at the large, grey, somber-looking stone building from the other side of the street and wondering about these "Protestants" and their false beliefs and practices. I had a sense of fear about the place and walked on the other side of the street from it even though it was out of my way. In all of my Catholic education (seven years of elementary school with the nuns, four years of high school with the Franciscan priests, and two years of Catholic college with the Jesuits), as best as I can recall I never heard or read about the "Protestant Reformation" of the sixteenth century. If I had been exposed to this major piece of church history it surely was very little.

These were the years before the Second Vatican Council (1962 to 1965). The mass was still said in Latin, and the priest and altar boys faced the front of the church with its large crucifix attached to the wall. I had to memorize and repeat the Latin responses to the priest's Latin prayers. (In high school all students, I believe, at least at my academic level, were required to take two years of Latin—something I've never regretted since a very large percentage of English words have their roots in Latin.) I also knelt and rang the bell three times while the hosts (the communion wafers) were being consecrated through the priest's words: "This is my body." At that moment the round wafers of pressed bread became, I was taught, the actual body of Jesus Christ. The priest then placed the consecrated host on my tongue (but only if I was in the "state of grace" . . . more about that later).

I let it melt in my mouth for a few seconds, then followed the priest, with his chalice full of consecrated hosts, to the communion rail where those receiving communion knelt. As the priest placed a host on each person's tongue, I held the gold-plated platter (at least it shined like gold) under each person's chin, lest any crumbs of the actual body of Christ might fall on the floor. This was all very solemn. If altar boys (as with all Catholics) planned to receive communion, they had to fast (abstain) from all food and drink (except water) from midnight the night before, except for those with health conditions that required eating.[2] The reason behind this was that the sacred body of Christ would have an empty stomach to dissolve in.

2. While I was serving as an altar boy in the 1950s, the Catholic Church teaching on abstinence before communion was evolving, although I never knew it during those years. The traditional requirement to fast from food and drink after midnight had been changed, and the new requirement, as given in the *Baltimore Catechism No. 3*, reads as follows. "All Catholics may receive Holy Communion after fasting three hours . . . . [However,] Catholics are urged to observe the eucharistic fast from midnight as formerly, and also to compensate for the use of the new privileges by works of charity and penance, but these practices are not obligatory" (215–16).

Catholics were instructed never to touch the consecrated host. We were told of one boy who, after having the host placed on his tongue, secretly removed it and enfolded it in his handkerchief. When he got home he opened his handkerchief and all he saw was a drop of blood. This made quite an impression on us students who heard it. I never tried that.

Fear of Hell

I have written about these practices of the mass and receiving the communion (the Eucharist), and now bring up the sacraments of Baptism and Penance, because these four requirements of the Catholic religion contain the essential elements for spending eternity in heaven rather than in hell. Actually, these requirements can be condensed into two: one must be baptized into the Catholic faith and die in a "state of grace," meaning that there is no unconfessed "mortal sin" in one's life at the moment of death. After one dies in a state of grace one may still need to spend thousands of years in a place called purgatory, where the pain is exactly the same as being in hell, except for knowing that you will someday be delivered from the agony of the flames.

I received the distinct impression that very few Catholics, if any, went straight to heaven when they died. Those who did not die in a state of grace went straight to hell. Those who went to purgatory still had to be punished in proportion to their sinfulness throughout their lives. I believed all of these doctrines and was affected deeply by them.

To amplify the above, the basic requirements to secure one's eternal salvation were to be baptized a Catholic, attend mass every Sunday and holyday (unless health reasons or other emergencies prevented this), receive the sacraments of Penance and the Holy Eucharist at least once a year (during the Easter season), and die in a state of grace. These rules were quite easy to follow—except for the last. All of my morally-aware life, up to the age of 19, I was burdened with the absolute necessity of dying in a state of grace. I did not want to spend eternity in the flames of hell!

One possibility attracted my attention when I was about 13 or 14. I learned that if a Catholic attended mass and received communion nine months in a row, on the first Friday of each month, and if they were in a state of grace when they died, they would never spend any time in purgatory! Whenever they died, they would go straight to heaven! If they died in a state of mortal sin they would, of course, go straight to hell.

This was very appealing to me because it narrowed down my possible destinations at death to only two instead of three. If I completed the nine first Fridays I would go either to heaven or to hell. And if I could die in a state of grace I would avoid the flames of purgatory.

I decided to do the nine Fridays early in the mornings and obtain this very generous indulgence from the church. I suppose I told my mother about my decision and that I would not have breakfast on those mornings, but I have no recollection of her commenting on my project. Most likely she said nothing, except perhaps, "That's nice, Bobby."

Each month I made sure I was in a state of grace before the first Friday arrived. I believe I went to confession a day or two before each of the Fridays to receive absolution for my sins committed since my last confession. Each month I walked the two or three miles to the church, and attended the mass and received the Eucharist.

For eight months I followed this routine. On the ninth first Friday I overslept! I slept right through the ringing alarm or had forgotten to set it. I was horrified because I woke too late to get to mass, and that was the only mass that was offered on weekdays. I could not believe I had done such a thing! I could have started the project again, but my enthusiasm for doing so was simply not there. I was discouraged about my failure for some weeks, but gradually pushed the memory of it into the past.

As mentioned above, one was considered to be in a state of grace as long as one did not have any unconfessed mortal sin in one's life. Mortal (deadly) sin included such matters as murder (even in one's thoughts), missing mass on Sunday without an acceptable reason, any sexual sin (including not only actions, but also words and thoughts), and stealing more than the victim earns in one day.

Venial sins included everything else that was wrong, such as disobeying one's parents, lying, and stealing small amounts of money or property. In Penance (confessing to a priest), once we were kneeling in the dark box (the confessional), we began by making the sign of the cross and saying, "Bless me, Father, for I have sinned. It has been ___ days, weeks, months, years since my last confession." We then recited our list of sins and how many times we sinned each way. While it was not absolutely necessary to state venial sins, we were encouraged to do so. Then the priest pronounced the absolution (told us we were forgiven) and gave us a "penance" to do—usually something like reciting ten "Hail Marys" or five "Our Fathers"—when we left the confessional. If there was more than one priest hearing confessions, and I happened to know which priest was in each confessional box, I always got in the line waiting for the priest who gave the lightest penance. This was not necessarily the shortest line.

Going to confession was never pleasant, even though, at that time, the confessional box was darkened so that the priest probably didn't know who you were. He sat looking straight ahead, not at you. You entered the small chamber on his left side, closed the door and knelt. There was just a screen between your voice and the priest's left ear, so he might recognize your voice, especially if you ministered with that priest in the serving of the mass. It was always embarrassing, but absolutely necessary to be absolved of the guilt of mortal sins. These had to be confessed to a priest. Sometimes the priest asked for specific details about your sins. This was a very uncomfortable time!

I usually, especially in my younger years, left the altar rail, after saying my penance, feeling ready to meet God if I should be hit by a car and die on the way home. The ongoing problem, however, was how to remain in a state of grace. There were many practices I learned in school that were supposed to be helpful, such as praying to Mary, Saint Joseph, other saints, and sometimes to God (written, formal prayers, not spontaneous "made up" prayers), saying the rosary, receiving frequent communion, and adoration of the Sacred Heart of Jesus. But none of these helped me live a better life. In my case, I did them only as rituals, to somehow get more "grace" and gain favor with God.

Not everything about school had to do with religion, but the Catholic culture was ingrained in the minds of all students. Our high school held dances every Friday night in the gymnasium. There was always at least one priest present and several parent volunteer chaperones. The music was the popular rock and roll of the day—all the hits. When the student disc-jockey played "The Twist" for the first time, and the priest witnessed the boys and girls gyrating and "twisting" on the dance floor, the priest grabbed the record and broke it right at the microphone for all to see and hear. He said the song would never again be played at the school dances. There was too much sensuality and temptation in the dancing.

After the dances I sometimes went with several other students to our favorite diner. We all sat in the back and were sometimes a bit rowdy. I remember one occasion when we ordered our burgers and fries about 11:30 pm. The server brought us our food about 11:45 or 11:50. We could not eat the burgers right away, however, because it was still Friday until midnight, and we were not to eat meat on Fridays. So we each sat there with one eye on the clock and one eye on our burger. Finally about 11:55 someone said, "Oh we're close enough," and we all dove into our food. I don't think anyone felt terribly guilty.

The whole routine of fasting, mass, confession, penance, communion, holy water, reciting the rosary, wearing a "scapular" around my neck, and making the sign of the cross was all quite mysterious and meaningless, and I did these things only to avoid going to hell. I was searching for goodness—trying to be good enough to get into heaven someday. My sin—which I readily acknowledged—was a burden on my back that seemed to be getting heavier as I grew older. I had no quarrel with the Catholic Church or its teachings. Indeed, I accepted it all. But I had no power to live the life, no power to be good.

Physical Labor

After graduating from eighth grade, I had moved with my family to Levittown, Pennsylvania. My parents bought their first house, on Ruby Lane. This was in the summer of 1957 and I was thirteen. My brother Tom was fifteen and my sister Rosemary was six. My parents, who had become more and more antagonistic toward each other, now had separate bedrooms. Tom and I shared a bedroom and Rosemary had her own room. It was a two-story house, with the three of us children upstairs.

My father had started his own small landscaping business while we lived along the Delaware River, because he hated being confined indoors with the dust and grime that went with industrial electrical work. He grew up around a longstanding (and still-standing) business started and run by his father's relative. By working at the nursery he came to know some things about plants and trees.

With this knowledge and his years of outdoor labor throughout the western states, he started doing plantings and tree trimming. As early as eight or nine I started working for my father on some Saturdays and some summer days. I distinctly remember how pleased I was when my father said he would pay me fifty cents a day. My brother worked for Dad also, and we continued working for Dad during our years in Levittown.

Dad's business was always small, in that, to the best of my knowledge, he never had a full-time employee other than himself. But Tom and I were doing increasingly more of the heavy work every Saturday, some school evenings, and every day during the summer. Dad also had great part-time employees who worked for him to supplement their incomes.

The tree work became as large—or even larger—as the landscaping part of the business. Dad had excellent professional climbers, and we took down or topped some incredibly tall trees during those years, with the huge trees often growing quite close to houses, garages, and sidewalks. Some of the tulip trees (often mistakenly called poplars) were 90 or 100 feet tall. I loved handling the ropes for the climbers, guiding the limbs down slowly over the buildings and cement work. We had no "cherry-pickers" and practically never used ladders or spurs. Everything was done by ropes and belts, and most work in the trees was done with handsaws. We had no wood-chippers.

I also did some climbing, and spent many, many hours with the chain saws, sledgehammers, wedges, and axes, splitting wood. I was always slim and wiry, but could work steadily from eight in the morning until nine or ten at night. I had seen my pay rise from fifty cents a day, to fifty cents an hour, to $2.50 an hour in high school. I remember negotiating with my father over my request for considerably more. He resisted and squirmed at first, looked at me standing in the doorway for several seconds, then yielded. This was good money in those days, at least for me.

Considering the Priesthood

As mentioned earlier, I was thirteen when we moved to Levittown, where now in high school I continued my Catholic schooling. I was, of course, required to take courses in the Catholic religion, and was taught by Franciscan priests. I was learning the Catholic faith thoroughly, and at one point during my high school years I seriously considered becoming a priest. Some of the attraction to the priesthood, I think, had to do with the mystery and pageantry of such rituals as the mass and the Stations of the Cross during the Lenten season. I liked the incense and the ringing of the bells at the moment of consecration.

The more I thought about becoming a priest, however, the more I was dissuaded by the lifetime vows a candidate must take before ordination: poverty, chastity, and obedience. The vow of poverty—agreeing to live a life of simplicity with only a few essential possessions—did not bother me. I had always lived in the lower economic strata of society and had no ambitions to be wealthy. The vow of obedience entailed being willing to accept any assignment, whether to live within certain specified quarters of the rectory or monastery or following orders to move to some other parish, city, or state. Since I had grown up learning—to some extent—to obey those in authority over me, I didn't think I would have much difficulty with the vow of obedience. It's not that I was always obedient, however. Whether in school life, home life, and life outside the home, I frequently did what I felt like doing—especially if it was daring and risky.

My father, who had the will power to quit both drinking and smoking as an adult—drinking first and smoking later—said to me when I was about twelve years old: "If I ever see you smoking I'll shove the lit cigarette right down your throat." And because I knew he meant it I did what any sensible, frightened kid in my situation would do: I made sure I hid my smoking habit. Fortunately, I never smoked enough to develop an addiction. It was no big thrill, and around the age of sixteen I threw my cigarettes away. What prompted me to quit for good was the nagging of my high school girlfriend. Not because she was urging me to quit but just the opposite. I had tentatively quit smoking at one point and the girl said that because all the "cool" guys in school smoked, I should too. I told her I didn't see any reason for it, and to "look cool" wasn't much of a reason to pick it up again. So, to exert my independence, I broke up with both her and the cigarettes for good.

This girl had reminded me too much of my mother, who incessantly nagged my father to "Be like other men, Art." My father was definitely unconventional, not caring too much what people thought, whereas my mother had a strong pull to "be like other people." In this respect I did feel embarrassed often over my father's odd ideas, dress, and behaviors. But because of him I developed an unconventional streak also, which I still have (quite subdued) to this day.

Sword of Damocles

Chastity—the third vow for the priesthood—troubled me the most and it was this requirement that caused me (sadly) to give up any serious notion of becoming a priest. Chastity means to be chaste, that is, sexually pure. Since the Catholic Church teaches that any sexual sin—thought, word, or action—is a mortal sin, and mortal sins need to be confessed to a priest to receive the absolution (pardon) of the sacrament of Penance, even one impure thought after being absolved of sin plunges one into condemnation again immediately. The Catholic is then said to be living in a state of mortal sin, and if he or she dies before going to confession he will be sent to hell, from which one will never be delivered.

For me, this theology—this set of ideas about God—presented serious distress of soul. I needed to be in a "state of grace" at the moment of death, and the only way to guarantee chastity when I died was to avoid totally any improper sexual thought, word, or action. Or if I did slip, I needed to get to a priest right away to receive the sacrament of Penance. I had to get out of the pit of mortal sin and back into the state of grace—at least until I committed mortal sin again (which might have been five minutes after confession). This sword of Damocles hung over my head continually.

I felt that since I could not realistically live a life of complete sexual purity, and therefore could not take the vow of chastity with integrity (even if I did plan to run to a priest and receive absolution every time I committed a mortal sin), I would need to give up my idea of becoming a priest. I simply could not be holy enough, so I abandoned this possibility for my future. I would still struggle, I was sure, with the divine requirement of chastity, at least until I married. But to live the rest of my life not only in chastity (sexual purity—required of all Catholics) but also in celibacy (singleness as well as sexual purity—required of all priests) was beyond any way of living I could imagine.

I never thought the theology of the Catholic Church was in any way erroneous in its teachings on these matters, but felt rather that I was unable to be what I was supposed to be. At one point I even resigned myself to going to hell, because of the practical impossibility of trying to get to confession after every mortal sin. It never occurred to me at all to ask God for the strength to be victorious, or to ask God directly for forgiveness.

We never were taught that one should, or even could, approach God in personal prayer from one's own heart and mind. Prayer was always saying some kind of written prayer that was approved by the church, such as the Hail Mary or the rosary. As I look back now, I believe that this emphasis on only written, prescribed prayers blocked me from moving toward God in any personal way. It was only after I was in college that I discovered personal prayer from the heart—speaking to God directly (either silently or out loud) as one speaks to a person. My life was never the same after God introduced me to this revolutionary way of prayer.

CHAPTER 3

Humor Without Happiness

A Troubled Entertainer

COMEDIANS ARE SUPPOSED TO be troubled individuals. At least that's what I've heard. Whether they are more troubled than accountants or cooks or bricklayers I don't know. But in my case, during my latter years in elementary school and my high school years, that was true of me. Outwardly I suppose I didn't seem more bothered than any other teenager, but inwardly I think I struggled more.

I never thought of myself as a comedian, however. I just liked to have fun being myself and making others laugh. I seldom planned anything comical; I just went with the humorous flow in my mind, according to my impulses at the moment.

Because I had lived a life that was probably more adventurous, more free, less supervised, and more outdoors than most children my age, I didn't dwell as much on my inner issues as I likely would have otherwise. I was too busy playing with fire (literally), sledding down the nearby crowded, narrow, and risky "Suicide Hill" (so named because of its rough surface and nasty trees waiting to stop one's sled) from morning until well after dark, building model airplanes and ships, collecting baseball cards and comic books, and enjoying camping, canoeing, and star gazing with the Boy Scouts of America.

I was even in the CYO (Catholic Youth Organization) for a short while, when I was 12. I got kicked out because, before one meeting started, I went behind the bar in the room where the youth group met (used by the Knights of Columbus or other such adult group) and set on the bar about eight or ten bottles of beer (church property) that I had discovered and opened. As soon as I invited the other kids to come help themselves I was taken from the scene of the crime by some angry adults. I was then expelled from the youth group—told not to come back. I don't recall being very troubled by the incident. CYO was boring compared to Boy Scouts. Instead, this caper helped solidify in my mind how a sudden, totally unexpected, and outrageous prank (particularly when carried out with a straight face) can bring about interesting reactions (shock and startled laughter especially) among those present.

I don't know if my parents ever found out. They didn't know half—or even a fourth—of what I actually did with my life, and certainly not even five percent of what I thought about. Because we never sat down at a meal table, and because we seldom talked about much of anything that mattered, they really didn't know me or my brother Tom. Rosemary had more interaction with them after Tom and I left home, but that's not to say her home life was any more pleasant. Both our mother and father were troubled individuals, but I think both tried to the best of their abilities to be good parents.

I cringed often when my parents were battling verbally and loudly, especially when the house windows were open. Some neighbor or my mother must have called the police during one of these fights because one of my parents—I assume my father—had struck the other. I was in so much pain that I ran to my room upstairs and turned on my radio, as I usually did when they fought.

There was nothing quite as electrifying and diversionary as the new rock and roll music that was spreading like wildfire over the land. It blocked out the horrible screaming (even though many would say it was, in itself, horrible screaming). Another escape was to leave the house and walk, usually to the Levittown Shopping Center but sometimes to my friend's home nearby. Brecht and I were best buddies throughout high school. We were as they say, "partners in crime," which was, in our case, literally true at times. His parents had a difficult marriage also, it seemed to me. Before I bought my own car, whenever Brecht and I went anywhere we walked, hitchhiked (often), or arranged a ride with some friends. I frequently hitchhiked alone, and after years of getting around like that I encountered a potentially dangerous situation only once. Fortunately, the would-be molester in the little black Volkswagen Beetle responded immediately when I insisted that he let me out, "right here, right now." He had driven me only three blocks, but his groping hand had invaded my space.

Longing to Get Away

As I moved into the higher grades of high school I continued to be troubled. My parents' wretched relationship upset me the most. I don't think I ever cried about this, nor did my brother, to my knowledge. But within each of us there was a seething, expanding repository of shame, embarrassment, resentment, deep anger, and even hate.

I hated my father because I considered him the main cause of my parents' fighting. While it was usually my mother who opened the fight with some angry words to my father, it was my father's strange ways that provoked my mother. He was "not like other men." I thought about killing him, but that idea didn't stay long in my mind because I knew I would be caught and that my life would never again be worth very much.

I thought more seriously about running away from home. I figured I could get away with this because, in my mind, I had the street savvy and life skills necessary to live on my own. I would just hitchhike to a nearby state and then ride the bus and/or train to some place out West. I'd get a job and start a new life. Eventually, the knowledge that I would go nowhere without a high school diploma, and the difficulty of getting that diploma while needing to work full-time, persuaded me to drop my plan to leave home. I thought often, however, of becoming a long-distance trucker when I got older. For the time I would stay, but always in my mind was the yearning to get away and live in peace and quiet. This yearning became, and continues to this day, a lifelong quest for peace and tranquility—both inner peace and peace in my home, surroundings, and relationships.

Tom's hatred for Dad was even more deep-seated than mine. One of his main reasons for despising Dad was that he greatly resented having to work so much, even though Dad paid him well. He was very embarrassed to be seen with Dad, even on the job. This was Tom's basic issue, I believe, not the amount or difficulty of the work itself.

Tom had been expelled from a Catholic high school in Philadelphia for not attending classes, had endured a school fire at the public school he transferred to, and had made it to his senior year at a third school. One day during the spring of his final year of high school, he marched into our home and threw his school books across the living room, intending for them to land on the polished wooden table in front of our picture window. But, because of his rage, he threw the books so hard that they glided right on into the window and shattered the glass. He then announced that he had just signed up for the U.S. Air Force, had quit high school, and was leaving for basic training. In a day or so, it seemed to me, he was gone. He very rarely came home after that. He just wanted to get as far away as he could. As I did.

High School Discipline

In the high school I attended, if students were caught being unruly (such as talking or joking around in class), the priests (and some nuns and lay-teachers) were quite adept at meting out punishment. This was usually corporal punishment in front of the other students.

Some of the punishments were mild and even comical for those of us "innocent" students in the class watching the unlucky guy (I never saw a girl being punished physically). One punishment was to have the boy go to a front corner of the classroom and kneel down, facing the corner, on a layer of hard kernels of corn. This was "horse corn" as we called it—the dry, rock-hard corn left over in a harvested field, baked for days or weeks by the scorching sun. The dried ears of corn were picked and then the kernels were scraped off. The student had to kneel motionless on these kernels while their bone-dry, sharp edges cut into the boy's kneecaps. While I never had to endure this punishment, I could (and still can) imagine the pain. The rest of us in the class were not to laugh or snicker, but get back to following the teacher's lesson plan. The boy stayed kneeling on the corn, trying hard not to wiggle.

Another form of discipline—this one I did experience—was to stand in a row with several other guys, each of us holding a very thick and heavy reference book. We each had to hold our book straight out, without bending or lowering our arms, and without moving our bodies. In just a few seconds the weight felt so great that our arms—due to the pain—started to sag, prompting the priest to strike us (not hard, but sharp) on our arms with his stick. We were to hold our books directly out, and each time we failed we were struck again. The pain finally became unbearable and, one by one, we each lowered or dropped our book. This ordeal was designed, as were all of the punishments, to remain in our memory when we were inclined to be disruptive in class.

Another punishment—rather mild—may have been designed for those who failed to do their homework and/or did not study for the latest test. I think it was also used for some who caused disturbances in class. While the other students were dismissed for lunch, the culprit was told to write 100 times on the chalkboard, "Stupidus Sum," the Latin expression for "I am stupid." The student was sometimes still writing when the others began returning to the classroom.

The most severe punishment—the one I can only describe as brutal— was when the priest smacked a boy's face with his hand (fortunately, it was with the palm only) over and over and over until the student's face became bright red. The redness may have been due partly to embarrassment (the whole class was watching), but I believe it was caused primarily by the re-peated and very strong blows to the face. Perhaps the capillaries under the skin broke from the repeated force of the blows. I suggest this because, in the two worst cases of this brutality that I witnessed, the priest struck the student anywhere from five to ten times (I am being conservative with these numbers).

I saw two priests abusing students this way on two separate occasions. In one of the instances the priest told the boy to kneel in the aisle next to his desk. He then said the boy's name triumphantly, paused briefly, and said angrily, "This is your life" (The name of a popular television show at the time). He then whacked the poor kid without mercy.

On another occasion we students watched as a priest had one of our comrades (one who sat near the middle of the row of desks) stand to receive his punishment. The priest then went to work in the customary manner. After each blow the boy stepped back, probably due both to the force of the hit and his involuntary reaction to escape the next strike. This went on until the priest had the student against the back wall of the classroom, after which the poor kid was allowed to return to his seat. We all knew that anyone who talked or laughed during these sessions would get the same treatment.

I even got a little taste of this type of discipline, but I don't think of it as abuse. I deserved it. Our religion teacher—a very tall priest who had the position of "disciplinarian" in the school—was speaking to some students off to the side of the classroom. I got behind him and was doing a silent imitation (mockery) of him (with my mouth contorted as his usually was) when he suddenly turned around and saw me. He had no doubt noticed that the eyes of the students to whom he was speaking were no longer fo-cused on him, but on something comical behind him. I quickly sat down in my desk at the very front of the room. He walked over to me and as I looked up sheepishly he slapped me so hard (one time) that the pencil in my right hand flew to the back of the class and hit the wall. (The classroom was similar in size to most of the others, holding 30–35 students in about six rows of desks.)

About 40 years after these incidents I spoke privately about them—on two separate occasions—to Brennan Manning, a non-practicing Franciscan priest of the Third Order Regular (TOR), the same order to which my high school priests belonged. He was a wonderful, godly man (now with his Lord in glory) who wrote numerous books and spoke very often, and intensely about the relentless love of God toward all people. He was at the time the most popular speaker at evangelical college campuses.

Brennan Manning knew most of the priests I mentioned and was about the same age. He expressed sadness at my accounts of school discipline, conversed with me about these and other issues, and let me know that the disciplinarian I mocked had died and the "This is your Life" priest was no longer in the priesthood. He also said to me, concerning the abusive priests, "They didn't know. . . ." I believe he intended to conclude with, "God's love."

With regard to these issues of school discipline I never, at the time, heard of any backlash or repercussions for the abusing priests—those who struck students repeatedly. No student ever cried or spoke disrespectfully to a priest. There may have been some complaints by parents to the school authorities if their children spoke of the classroom incidents. I have no knowledge of that, but the very fact that I and my fellow students simply accepted such discipline as part of school life, not as abuse (I never even thought of the idea at the time), suggests to me that students as well as parents submitted to these practices out of loyalty to the church. I suspect that most affected boys never even told their parents of the incidents. Things were very different in that era, and students who were punished in class were likely to receive more punishment (or at least scolding) at home, rather than sympathy, if they told their parents.

Laughing and Learning

The comedian in me emerged much more during my junior and senior years of high school, yet I rarely got in trouble with the priests, nuns, and laypersons teaching me. My most outrageous performances (which I often did with my good buddy, Joe) involved imitating the teachers. Joe and I were able to impersonate (usually without caricature or mockery) most of the faculty flawlessly. At first we did this covertly—in the hallways, in the classrooms (mostly before or after class), in the dining room, and elsewhere— wherever we had an audience of one or more. Some faculty got word of this, yet Joe and I never got scolded. We were not disrespectful. All we did was act and speak like the teachers, with their facial expressions, idiosyncrasies, and body language. They were so funny by themselves that we didn't need to add anything.

I remember a day when some in-school activity was cancelled and the other kids called for Joe and me to put on a show in the classroom. The bewildered priest finally gave in to the mob and Joe and I went full-steam ahead imitating not only that priest but just about every other teacher. The class was in an uproar and even took up a collection for us. This was my first (and only) time to be paid during my illustrious show-business career.

I loved to read and study just about everything, but especially math, the physical sciences, and psychology. Math was by far my favorite subject in high school, but for my off-school reading I bought numerous paper-backs ("Mentor" brand) on astronomy, physics, biology, and psychology. I even bought and read a big hardback containing all the major writings of Sigmund Freud. I never once remember either of my parents asking what I was reading or what I was doing in my room all those hours. There was, of course, no technology but a radio.

One of the best things my father ever did for me, educationally, was to forbid television in our home. I felt inferior about this, especially when I sat down at my school desk in the morning and the other kids were talking about the previous night's programs. A fellow student would sometimes turn to me and ask, "Did you see . . .?" and then stop and say, "Oh, that's right, you don't have television." I felt different and resented my father's prohibition.

I'm almost certain that his objection to television was due to the fact that watching it is such a passive experience. For a very short time at our home along the river we had a small, used, frosty, black-and-white set. I recall Tom and I sitting on the floor in front of the TV, glued to the screen, watching Hopalong Cassidy or some other such program, as well as the strings of commercials. Dad was not at all happy about it. When the set died soon after we got it he did not replace it. He wanted us to be active, especially outside. To this day I am grateful for Dad's firmness on the issue. In fact, except for bits and pieces on the sets of others, both Judy (the woman I married) and I lived without television until we were in our thirties.

As far back as I can remember, my father subscribed to a big-city daily newspaper and I looked at every headline—large or small—in all sections of the paper, and read many of the articles in full. When I do crossword puzzles now, I lean on my decades of newspaper reading to find many answers to the clues.

I say these things to illustrate the fact that I was always on a quest for knowledge, fun, adventure, challenge, and especially peace—peace most of all in my heart and mind, but also in my surroundings. I also was on a quest for grace—God's grace—although I didn't know what to call it at the time. I was becoming more and more concerned that I could not—and therefore would not—make it to heaven. I began to move away from thinking much about the church. I still went to mass every Sunday, however, to please Mom and to avoid committing another mortal sin.

During my final year of high school I began to think about college rather than religion. This was presented to us students not as an option, but as an expectation. I went to "college night" at the school and took home some brochures on several colleges, on aeronautical engineering, and other careers. I applied to three Catholic colleges in the Philadelphia area—La-Salle, Villanova, and St. Joseph's—and was accepted by all three.

When I mentioned to my parents that I would be going to college, my father objected that we could not afford that—it was only for the rich. Also, he had hoped that I would work with him and eventually take over the business. I remained firm and said that I would figure out some way to pay for the schooling.

Brecht and I worked for Dad that summer. With those earnings, a student loan, and a four-year, half-tuition scholarship from St. Joseph's College, I set my face toward a new phase in my quest. Dad said he would try to help with gas money and Mom said she would pack a bag lunch each day. St. Joe's, on the western edge of Philadelphia, was about a one-and-a-half hour's ride from home. I would live at home to avoid dormitory costs, and I had several fellow St. Joseph's students who wanted to ride with me and share transportation costs. September could not come too soon.

CHAPTER 4

Discovering God

Religious Upheaval

REGISTRATION DAY AT ST. Joseph's College (now University) was the first time I saw the campus. I parked my 1953 mint-green Ford on the big lot and went to stand in line at the registrar's station. It seems odd as I write this that I did not visit the school previously. In today's world, many parents travel with their college-bound son or daughter to visit not just one possible school, but sometimes two, three, or more. It did not seem odd to me then, however, since I had studied the college catalog, found the location on the map, knew of the school's high reputation and, most of all, this was the school that had given me a scholarship. I had been used to doing everything myself related to school matters since my early high-school years, so the lack of parental guidance or involvement at the time was something that did not even enter my mind. My mother and father, as helpful as they tried to be, had practically no awareness of my world. Neither one, during my time there, ever visited the college campus.

I enrolled as a pre-medical student, along with another 150 new pre-meds. In addition, I entered a program as a member of the US Air Force ROTC (Reserve Officer Training Corps). This was required of all the freshmen for their first semester (St. Joseph's was an all-men's college). I elected to take the second semester, receiving a military uniform, lots of marching practice, and instruction in some rather dull Air Science classes.

My freshman year was uneventful, except for one matter of enormous significance. Although I did not realize it at the time, it would change my life dramatically. My father, then fifty years old, became a believer in Jesus Christ. After a lifetime of searching for some kind of spiritual truth that answered the tough questions of life, he was pointed by a local pastor to the way of heartfelt repentance from sin and total trust in Christ alone for salvation—for now and eternity. He groaned from his heart a deep and sincere prayer of repentance and faith, and knew from that moment that he had been born again. If ever a man could be said to have been revolutionized, that could be said of my father.

As mentioned earlier, my father grew up in foster homes. His parents seem to have been lacking in any ability to parent. His mother—at least once—shoved his head into a toilet bowl for punishment. I heard that she lived some of her life in a home for the mentally ill and (I believe I heard) she died there. Her daughter (my father's sister) took her life years later after a career in nursing. I saw my father's father only once, very briefly, and never saw his mother.

During my freshman year in college, unknown to me, my father was becoming more and more troubled by the terrible evil in the world. Each day he would sit at the kitchen table after breakfast poring over the newspaper while drinking a pot of tea. This infuriated my mother, and almost always led to her yelling at him to get up and go to work "like other men." Almost always, a loud and angry fight ensued.

In the newspaper one day my father read of a particularly gruesome child-abuse case. This seemed to trigger something in Dad that was coming to a head. How could anyone do such a thing? What was the answer to such wickedness? How can such evil be stopped? Was there any hope for this world, and if so, what was it?

Frequently, while driving to and from jobs, my father went past a small independent Baptist church with a wooden sign prominently displayed in front: "Christ is the answer." The more Dad drove past this sign the more agitated he became. He felt frustrated because he didn't know what the words meant, yet he was desperately looking for answers.

Late one Saturday evening, while going home from work, Dad drove to the church with the sign out front. He knocked on the door of the parsonage next to the church building. Dad had heard that this pastor was a strong anti-Communist, and, since Dad was a loyal member of the John Birch Society (a staunchly conservative anti-Communist group) he felt that this pastor might be helpful in promoting some coming John Birch events.

The minister was very patient with Dad, even though Saturday evenings are often set apart by pastors for final sermon review or special times of relaxation, and trying to get a good night's sleep for the services the next day. The pastor listened to Dad's plans for fighting Communist influence in America, and then said to Dad: "This is all well and good, but what will you do if you succeed in stopping the spread of Communism and then die and go to hell?" This question led to a two-hour discussion on the gospel of Jesus Christ, after which Dad prayed to receive forgiveness and newness of life in

Christ. This was in March of 1962, in the middle of the second semester of my freshman year.

Because Dad's life was so revolutionized by his conversion he wanted the rest of us in the family, as well as anyone and everyone else he encountered, to experience the new birth as he had. Until the time of his death thirty-eight years later, his twofold passion in life was to study his Bible intensely and to witness to people about their need for the gospel. His previous energy for fighting Communism was now replaced by a zeal for the kingdom of God. He had found the answers to the biggest questions of life.

Since Tom was now in the Air Force, Mom, Rosemary, and I felt the full force of his excitement concerning his newfound discoveries about God, religion, and the world. He had started attending the small church whose pastor had led him to Christ, and more and more, as he matured in his knowledge of the Word, he saw what he thought were serious errors in the Catholic system.

Trying to help us see the light, with the best intentions in his heart, he denounced such cherished Catholic teachings as the authority and infallibility of the Pope, the exaltation of Mary the mother of Jesus, the rosary, indulgences, the mass, prayers to the saints and Mary, confession to the priest, purgatory, the necessity of baptism for salvation, and the legitimacy of the other sacraments in addition to baptism. Most basic of all to Dad, as he saw it, was the radical difference between the Catholic way of salvation by grace plus human works, and the biblical way of salvation by God's grace alone, through simple faith and repentance. Good works were to follow one's conversion, for sure, but they were not the cause of it.

In my opinion, Dad had swallowed some concoction of false religious ideas and now he was a man obsessed with convincing others of those ideas. I thought, "Who is this pagan—this one who knows nothing about God and the church, who never attended church except at times during childhood?" "Who is this unbeliever who comes marching into our home attempting to set all of us straight about God—we who are lifelong Catholics and loyal, well-instructed members of the "one true church"?"

I decided to ignore the many booklets and pamphlets he gave me to show how my Catholic doctrine was riddled with errors. I was always taught by the priests if a piece of literature or a book about religion did not have the church's "imprimatur" and (in designated cases) "nihil obstat" on the publisher's information page, we were not to read it. The only religious literature Catholics were permitted to read had these stamps of approval from the church. My stacks of Dad's "heretical" literature kept growing, but I did not read them.

Finally, when Dad saw that he was getting nowhere by giving me Protestant literature and by arguing our views back and forth, he asked me to do one thing: read my Bible. Since I had a Confraternity edition of the Catholic New Testament purchased along with my other required textbooks at the start of the school year, I easily agreed to that. The Pope even gave a special indulgence (time off in purgatory) to those who read the Bible. And since I had to read the book of Acts and Paul's epistles as part of my coursework in the religion classes (required of all Catholic students), I was already into the reading (and studying) of this new and exciting part of the Catholic Bible.

The Quest Intensifies

My major motivation for reading the New Testament had now shifted from academic requirements to proving that Dad was wrong and the Catholic Church right. We were both reading and studying the same biblical books that we both accepted as the infallible and authoritative Word of God, so it should not be difficult for me to show Dad the errors in his Protestant thinking.

But something else was happening. As I read, I paid special attention to a number of Bible verses that Dad had pointed out to me previously. These were verses that he was firmly convinced taught that the true way of salvation was by faith alone, and that the Catholic Church was in serious error with its doctrine of salvation through obedience to its teachings, rules, and requirements.

I continued to attend mass every Sunday with Mom and Rosemary, but instead of sitting and standing in my place, going through the motions, I read my Catholic New Testament and marked all of the verses that were leaping out at me. I actually felt a bit subversive, even though I was reading the sacred book accepted as one of the two great foundations for all Catholic doctrine (the other foundation was church tradition). I felt that I needed to hide—as much as I could—what I was really doing. Practically no one at mass brought any book with them. A very few might have a Catholic missal if they wished to follow the mass, but I never saw a Bible. In all of my Catholic schooling I never once, until college, had to read the Bible. Even though it was held as foundational, it was clearly not, in my religious education, presented as having any real importance.

My second year of college was much more interesting than the first. The 151 of us who started as aspiring doctors had been whittled down to 76. We were now seriously into the pre-med science courses, especially biology, physics, and chemistry. I loved them totally! We were told that if a student

gets through the pre-med course of studies at St. Joe's, he will almost certainly be accepted into a good medical school.

While I worked hard at my college courses, I also delved more and
more deeply into which version of Christianity was true—that of the Catholic Church or that which changed Dad so remarkably. Surprising myself, by
the beginning of my sophomore year, I, who set out to prove Dad wrong,
was now seriously considering the truth of Dad's views as well as the multiple errors of Catholic teaching.

I didn't tell Dad how my thoughts were changing. I didn't want him to
come at me like a bull in a china shop (his tendency) and push me to "get
saved." I was thinking very carefully about all of the issues and my quest
was by no means purely academic. Although I needed to understand the
intellectual arguments thoroughly before I made any personal commitment
of such magnitude, I needed to hear what God was speaking to my heart as
well as my head.

By October or November of my sophomore year, I was convinced that
the New Testament taught the way of salvation by grace through faith in
Christ alone, with no trust or hope in my own efforts. Eternal life was a
gift—pure and simple. Christ had done it all.

While I had been on a quest for God's truth, concerning the way to attain heaven and escape the eternal torments of hell, God was also on a quest
after me—specifically after my heart. While I now believed in my mind the
facts of the gospel, I was, however, experiencing tension within my heart,
soul, and will regarding the *implications* of those facts. Peter, Paul, Luke,
John, and other biblical writers clearly presented the gospel of Jesus Christ
as a mandate, not as an option. Yes, it was a gracious invitation, but it was
also a command. "You must be born again" to be received into the kingdom
of God, so that you "will not perish, but have everlasting life."

My growing tension soon led to a life and death struggle within me.
Now I was dealing with matters of my personal sin, repentance, forgiveness, and obedience to the will of God. Both my head *and my heart* needed
to be converted.

My struggle was threefold. First, what would my mother, Rosemary,
and extended family members on my mother's side think of me? Being
from an Italian family, they were (almost by definition) traditional Catholics. Since this was before the Second Vatican Council, the word "Catholic"
meant traditional Catholic. They would not only be surprised if I made a
personal decision to receive Christ in the manner of a conscious, born-again
experience, they might also be ashamed of me and possibly even oppose me.
Since my conversion to Jesus Christ as my all-sufficient Savior and Lord
would (of necessity, in my view) be accompanied by leaving the Catholic

Church, Mom would especially be confused and hurt. In addition, I liked Mom's family, and it was a troubling thought that I would be an embarrassment to them.

The second aspect of my hidden struggle concerned the Catholic Church itself. Without any question I would be excommunicated (expelled) from the church because of my mortal sin of apostasy (renouncing the "one true religion"). The church taught that, on the great judgment day, it will be far worse for someone who once knew the Catholic faith and then turned from it than it will be for the one who was never exposed to the Catholic religion.

The thought of being excommunicated was not what bothered me, since I now knew the true way to eternal life. What did concern me, however, was my standing at St. Joseph's. I knew that the administrative priests at the college would consider it a serious matter if I left the Catholic Church, and wondered if they would take away my scholarship or cause other problems for me.

My third concern—by far the most troublesome and serious—had to do with the matter of sin. No one had to convince me that I was a sinner. I knew I was living a life displeasing to God, but I also knew that God would forgive all my sins if I turned to God for salvation. However, I was determined not to receive Christ as a fire escape from hell.

I was convinced that the epistles of Saint Paul, the gospel of Saint John, and many other sections of the Bible taught that a person who follows God's command to turn to Christ in sincere faith and repentance would, at that moment, receive eternal life and forgiveness of all sins. I knew, according to the Word of God, that Christ's sacrificial and substitutionary death cleanses from all sin those who come to him with a broken and contrite heart. Through that born-again experience the sinner at once becomes a spiritual child of God and a citizen of heaven. If we die the next day, or the next month, or the next year, we will be welcomed into our heavenly home to be with God forever. Our salvation is by grace alone, not by living a certain quality of life. I was aware that God's plan of salvation through Christ may seem simplistic to some: a few minutes in sincere prayer secures our everlasting future with God in glory! The human tendency is to think that we must do good deeds and/or perform certain rituals to earn—to merit—God's favor.

While God does offer everyone a simple way of salvation—by grace through faith—it is by no means a simplistic plan. In my case, the only remaining roadblock to conversion was the matter of my own personal repentance, but this was no small thing. While I had not been living an outwardly wicked life, I knew God expected a total change in me. No one gave me a list of behaviors and thought patterns that I needed to delete from or add to my life, but from reading the epistles I saw clearly what new life in Christ and the way of Christian discipleship were all about. I knew I was being drawn toward what Paul calls the circumcision of the heart (Rom. 2:29), and that this involved a genuine turning of my whole self and future plans to Christ, who would be not only my Savior but also my Lord and Master. My twofold problem, however, was that I was unsure if I wanted to make this life-changing decision, and, even if I were willing, could I actually live the life to which I would be committing myself? I did not know what to call it at the time, but now I see that I was experiencing the age-old choice between sin and its partner unbelief on the one hand, and repentance and its partner faith on the other.

By early or mid-November, God had made it clear to me that the new birth involved turning from darkness to light, from sin to righteousness, and from self-will to God's will. However, even though the repentance question was now settled, as far as my will was concerned, I struggled with the matter of faith. I was not confused about eternal salvation being a gift of God's grace received by faith (faith meaning complete trust that God will do what he said he will do). But I was confused about faith for holy living. I was now looking beyond the initial experience of conversion to the life of discipleship until death. Here, faith took on a different aspect for me. I now needed to exercise faith (trust) that I could live the life of a Christ-follower.

I had never heard of the theological debate over receiving Christ as Savior as distinct from receiving Christ as Lord. It never occurred to me as I was struggling with this matter—what would be the most important decision of my life for all time and eternity—that Jesus as Savior and Jesus as Lord could be separated in the thinking of any true Christian. But could I live as a godly, faithful disciple of Christ?

Conversion

On the morning of Thanksgiving Day, 1962, I went to see my father's pastor—the one who led Dad to Christ late that Saturday evening in March. I cannot remember if I mentioned to my parents where I was going. As I look back now, I am amazed at my boldness (and spiritual hunger) to ask the pastor to see me on Thanksgiving morning. I had reached a crisis point over this eternal life-eternal death decision.

I sat down with the pastor in his office and asked some questions I had about salvation and the Bible. I don't remember what they were but his answers satisfied me. Then he asked me if I had been "saved." I knew what he meant even though the language was still new to me. I felt uncomfortable when he kept probing on the issue. I fumbled around for words while wanting desperately to get away. Eventually I told him I was saved, and that this took place a few weeks before. I don't think he believed me, but I thanked him for his time, excused myself, and left with a huge feeling of relief. I can feel the relief even now, decades later, as I write.

As I drove home, my mind and soul were working overtime. With little traffic to negotiate due to the holiday, I was literally weighing the matter of my eternal destiny. And the single issue holding me back was the question referred to above: "How can I know I will be able to live the life God expects of his children?" I was not interested in any "cheap grace," although I never heard this theological term until many years later.

Finally, I could fight this battle no longer. As I was driving along (I still remember the road and my intensity as if it happened yesterday) I knew the time had come. I began speaking to the Lord (with eyes wide open, of course), with words something like the following. "Lord, I don't know if I will be able to live the total Christian life as I long to do. I can't wait any longer to get assurance of that. But I will leave that matter to you. I can no longer live with this fear of hell—the destination of those who reject your invitation to repent and believe the good news of salvation through Christ's once-for-all offering of himself on the cross. I receive you now as my Savior and Lord, and I trust you to make me the person I desire to be."

Still driving along, I knew—without the least doubt in my heart—that I was now a born-again child of God. I was trusting Christ and Christ alone for my eternal destiny, with no reliance on myself. I knew—with total confidence in the Bible's teachings—that all of my sins were forgiven. This was truly salvation by faith alone—trusting completely in the Lord for the new earthly life before me and for life everlasting in glory.

Reaching home, I parked my car on the street and walked into the house. Because it was Thanksgiving Day and both Mom and Dad were home, I had no desire to add to the tension already in the air. I mumbled a few things to be sociable then went to my room. I can't remember for sure, but I think Mom cooked a delicious turkey meal since this was her Thanksgiving custom. Even though she probably did not sit with us at the table, the food was no doubt delightful and there was likely a sort of truce between my parents during the meal.

This was now Thursday, and Sunday was three days away. I knew I would soon tell Dad what happened. I also knew that I would be attending Dad's church from now on. And I knew that I needed to tell Mom what had just happened to me.

Dad, of course, was thrilled with my decision. As for Rosemary, I can't remember our conversation. But when I talked to Mom I surely broke her heart. This was not because I spoke about my decision to receive Christ. I don't think she understood what I was saying, but she listened to me respectfully. It was a different story, however, when I gently mentioned to Mom that I wouldn't be going with her to mass on Sunday and that from then on I would be going to church with Dad. This news—especially the piece about no longer attending mass—upset Mom terribly. She feared I would go to hell for leaving the "one true church."

I tried to explain to Mom that my decision was not about switching churches, and that I could continue going to mass if I wanted to. I was under no set of laws or obligations about where to attend church. My basic desire was not to leave some religion but to move toward some group of Christians where the Bible was being taught. Mom was hurt deeply, but for the next couple of days the issue did not come up again.

When Sunday came I went with Dad to the Baptist church. I attended Sunday school and the worship service. Some of the people were quite excited about me because I had come out of "Rome" and now had a personal relationship with Christ. Dad gave me a new Bible—*The Scofield Reference Bible*—with the text of the King James Version. I read it and benefited greatly from it and its copious notes and helps for years.

First Steps

I returned to classes after the Thanksgiving break and tried to explain my conversion to my best college friend—a Jewish guy named Danny. He preferred not to discuss the topic so I respectfully moved away from it. My conversion did not affect our friendship, however. We still went regularly to the fabulous Jewish restaurant across 54th Street where I had come to love hot pastrami on rye, with a Jewish pickle.

A few days into the week after Thanksgiving break, while I was having lunch in the college dining room with some friends, I heard my name called over the loud speaker. I was to report to the Dean's office. I promptly went to see the priest and he told me that my mother had phoned the college crying and grieving over my decision to leave the Catholic Church. The dean was rather stern and said I needed to return to the church.

I tried to explain to him, as I did with Mom, that I now had a personal, living relationship with Jesus Christ and that I now talked to God directly and received my guidance directly from the Bible. When I told him I knew that I would go to heaven if I should die that day, he lectured me about two very serious sins against hope: despair and presumption. Despair was the sin of Judas, the betrayer of Christ. He felt there was no forgiveness or hope for him, so he went and hanged himself. Presumption, the priest said, was what I was guilty of. Not even the Pope can have assurance of salvation, nor can he say that he knows he will spend eternity with God in heaven if he should die in the next moment. He can, however, hope so.

I met with the priest another time or two, asking him about numerous Bible verses that I had discovered in my eight-month quest after salvation. When he couldn't give me satisfactory answers, he said I would need to meet regularly with another priest, one especially trained in apologetics—that branch of Christian theology which explains and defends the faith in light of accusations and objections.

As I sat in the waiting room of the apologetics priest I was, literally, in fear and trembling. I was not terrified because of any hesitancy to face this man's arguments, but because of the fear of losing my scholarship or being expelled from school.

I met with him a few times, continually opening my Catholic New Testament to those cherished texts on which my assurance of salvation was based. When he realized I was unwavering in my views, he said (as closely as I can remember), "Your problem is that you are reading your Bible too much. I want you to promise me you'll lay off the Bible reading." As he said this I was still so afraid about my education funding that I lied to him by nodding yes: I would stop reading the Bible. He let me go, without having me return anymore.

I returned to classes, to the services at my new church, and to my Bible study. I heard that Mom had phoned (or gone to see) the parish priest at the local church. She desperately needed consolation about the lost condition of her son. The priest, apparently lacking even a touch of sensitivity, told Mom that I should be lined up against a wall and shot. After this, Mom was suffering even more deeply, but I didn't seem to be of any comfort to her by speaking of my discovery of grace.

As I finished the first semester and moved into the second, I loved both the science courses, and the study of the Scriptures. I benefited both from a small study group of fellow pre-med students and a Friday night Bible study group. I heard no more from the college authorities and life settled into a new normal. Several months after my conversion I was asked to preach at the old Fraser Mission (now gone) in the skid row section of Philadelphia. Like many inner-city rescue missions it had a neon-lit cross saying "Jesus saves." For my first-ever sermon I preached from Isaiah: "Come now and let us reason together, saith the Lord." I was excited about the whole experience, and to this day I still have a picture in my mind of the haggard faces of the 200 or so men fervently singing from memory such songs as "The

Old Rugged Cross" and "Haven of Rest," and looking up earnestly at me as I spoke.

I worked for Dad occasionally on Saturdays when my studies permitted. One incident in my new Christian life I will never forget because of the shock of the moment and its continuing effect on me to the present day. I had just finished my work in a high tree, removing dead branches and trimming others. I was "crotched in," with my climbing rope looped over a sturdy limb near the top of the tree. The lowest branches from the ground were about 12–15 feet high. I was coming down the tree trunk fairly fast on my rope, sitting in my climbing belt and working the knots in a rappelling manner, like a mountain climber coming down a cliff. I had done this many times. Suddenly, just as I passed the lowest branch of the tree, I literally "came to the end of my rope." As the last bit of rope slipped through my climbing knot I was in a free-fall. I fell the 12–15 feet to the ground and hit my head on a large rock with such force that I literally "saw stars" and flashing lights, because my eyes had closed from the impact. I don't think I went unconscious, at least not for very long. When I opened my eyes I saw Dad and another worker standing and looking at me, just as startled as I was. I told them I would be okay if I could just lie still for a while. As I prayed with my eyes closed all I could do was say "Help me, God" and rest in his care.

After some time on the ground I got up and tried to figure out what happened. I quickly realized that, because of the height of the tree, I should have re-crotched about halfway down the tree, so I would have had plenty of rope to descend safely to the ground. Because I never thought of doing this I ran out of rope and whacked my skull on the rock.

I never did go to the doctor for this incident. In our family we seldom went to doctors. If you could bounce back from whatever happened, you were assumed to be fine. As time went by, however, I began to have bad headaches, something I had never had before the fall. These have been a constant source of pain—often severe—to me for over 50 years now. A serious car crash a few years later gave me another concussion (if the tree fall actually gave me one) that I suspect has compounded the damage from the fall. The headaches have been the number one physical affliction throughout my life since I fell at the age of 19.

One Sunday morning as Dad and I pulled into the church parking lot we noticed something unusual. The pastor's car, which was always parked next to the church when services were being held, was instead parked at the parsonage a short distance from the church. After the services (someone other than the pastor preached), the church leaders asked all members to stay in the sanctuary for a special meeting. Not being a member, I waited outside for the news. It was tragic: the pastor had just been found guilty of a five-year adulterous affair. Not only that, he justified his conduct because (he said) his wife was cold toward him. He obviously felt that the fulfillment of his sexual desires superseded loyalty to his marriage vow, responsibility toward the other (single) woman, being a godly example to his congregation, and being a faithful disciple of Jesus Christ.

The news, as would be expected, rocked the church. Soon the pastor and his wife had moved away. As far as I know, he never acknowledged his sin nor asked the church for forgiveness. The other woman, I have since learned, repented of her sin, married, and moved on in her life to become a faithful servant of her Lord in vocational Christian ministry. One thing my father and I learned from this scandal was not to put our confidence in people, but in God. Men, and women, no matter how exemplary they may seem or how prominent their position may be as Christian leaders, will sometimes let us down. I was a believer for only three months, and Dad only eight months more, when this crisis came to our church. We learned a valuable lesson early in our Christian lives. By the grace of God, neither of us turned from our faith because of the pastor's hypocrisy, but instead we turned more intently to God and his infallible Word.

The Call

As I moved through the second semester of my sophomore year I began to experience a growing desire, and then a serious call, to study the Bible in depth. I was hungry to know the Scriptures more. Since I came to my new church I had been hearing remarks and stories about "Bible schools." These were institutes or colleges where the Bible was the center of the curriculum and where young (or older) people went to prepare for Christian service, either as a layperson or a vocational Christian worker such as a missionary or pastor.

The more I heard about such schools the more I wanted to go. But I felt conflicted, since I loved the pre-medical program and (at the end of my sophomore year) was ranked second out of the 76 pre-meds in our class. (They posted the students' rankings on the wall just outside the biology department office.) I had been excited about coming back for the critical junior year. Yet the call (from God, I believed and still believe) to attend Bible school in the fall was so persistent and strong that I knew I would be going. My thinking was that I could return to my program of studies at St. Joe's after some study at a Bible school if I thought that was the wiser route at the time.

Some friends in the church had attended a Bible school in Three Hills, Alberta, in Western Canada. It was named Prairie Bible Institute and was usually referred to as Prairie, but sometimes PBI. My friends spoke highly of their experience there, so I contacted Prairie and two other schools I was told about: Moody Bible Institute and Bob Jones University. After considering the three schools I felt strongly about attending Prairie. I applied, was accepted, and excitedly looked forward to September.

It didn't matter to me that Prairie had quite a reputation for the strict "social regulations" required of its students. The campus did not literally have "pink and blue sidewalks" as was jokingly said, but it was almost that way. Male students and female students were consistently kept apart. They attended the same classes, but the men sat on one side of the classroom and the women on the other. The same was true of the huge Prairie Tabernacle where services were held, and the dining room—except for the noon meal on school days when we had "mixed seating." This custom at noon was for students to learn how to behave in the presence of the opposite sex and to learn the proper etiquette of fine dining (as fine as it could be out on the barren, windswept prairie).

I learned all of these regulations and more, but none of this mattered to me. It was not that I didn't like girls; I liked them as much as the next guy (probably more). I was, however, released from keeping religious laws out of fear of hell. Voluntarily choosing a school with strict rules was consistent with, not contrary to, my newfound delight in living a life of true Christian discipleship in the light of God's grace. My fear of damnation had now been replaced by a freedom to love and serve God. I had moved from legalism to liberty: not a license to sin, but a liberty to enjoy and obey my Lord and Master.

There was sadness within me as I drove away from St. Joe's for the last time that year, knowing that it might be my last time ever. It had been a good experience in several ways, most notably because in the midst of my classes there I came to saving faith in Jesus Christ. And it was one of my required textbooks—the Catholic New Testament—that God used mightily to bring me to himself. While trying to prove my father wrong, I came to see—reluctantly at first—that his understanding of salvation by grace alone through faith, apart from works of the law, was the truly biblical teaching.

God's grace quest had brought me to an entirely new knowledge of the world, of myself, and of God. One huge chapter of my life had closed and a new one—one that would be directed by the Lord for the rest of my days—had begun to open. God, through his persistent grace, had been on a quest for my soul over the years, on the railroad tracks, and in the thousands of hours reading and studying in my room. I had also been on a quest—a quest for "salvation" (which I thought of solely as being saved from hell) and the peace of mind and heart that comes from the God of all grace. As I see it now, my heavenly Father had been moving first all through the years, and my "quest" had been merely a series of responses—some faulty and hesitant—to the prior persuasions of his almighty grace.

Instead of working for Dad that summer I took a home construction job offered to me through a friend at church. I worked on the dry-wall requirements of the houses and made good money. I learned—also through church connections—of a couple who would be driving their van to Prairie in September. They would be taking their daughter and several other students and they were kind enough to offer me a ride. It would be a trip of about 2,800 miles and, except for a very small amount of money I would contribute to help with gas, they would even pay for motels, meals, and tolls. I had never even imagined such generosity by anyone, anywhere, and to this day I am exceedingly grateful for them and for the grace of God through them.

I am happy to note that the hatred I used to have for Dad faded away once I started digging into the Bible, especially when I began to see that he might be right. After I became a believer and we were now brothers in Christ as well as father and son, we were even friends. The Holy Spirit gave us an inner unity and the church experiences brought us together. It also helped that I had worked little for Dad since I finished high school, working for other employers for the summers and mostly studying on Saturdays during school. The verbal fights that had sometimes erupted between Dad and me on the job were now a thing of the past.

Even though Dad was now a disciple of Christ, he and Mom still argued vigorously. Old habits die hard, and while Dad was probably doing his best to rely on the Spirit to keep him calm when tensions arose, he sometimes lost his temper with Mom. I never thought of the great toll those fights must have exacted from Rosemary. I was trying just to survive in that atmosphere and I'm sorry that I was not more helpful to my sister.

Because of the constant tension between my parents I was not sorry to leave home. I have no memory of saying goodbye to Mom, Dad, and Rosemary on the September day in 1963 when I began my long journey west. Actually, I was thrilled to be on the way. One of the reasons I chose to attend Prairie instead of one of the other schools was because it was so far away from home—much farther than any of the others. I did not want to be coming home for Thanksgiving, Christmas, Easter, or any other special days. I wanted to be gone.

The days of traveling took me through breathtakingly beautiful country, especially driving along the eastern and northern shores of Lake Ontario. In my life so far, this trip was the most exciting physical piece of my quest for adventure. At the beginning of each previous school year I used to cringe when the other kids would tell about their summer vacation trips with their parents. Some went to Niagara Falls, some to the Grand Canyon, and others to various exotic locations I could only read about. We were always too poor to travel anywhere, and I felt embarrassed when I had nothing special to say. It was the same feeling as when I had nothing to say each morning when the kids talked about the television programs from the night before or about their parents taking them to the new hamburger place in town.

But, on the adventure of my life, I sailed along with eyes wide open and heart and mind eager to embrace the fresh new way of life ahead. The only negative aspect of the trip was that the very generous couple providing the ride argued incessantly with each other. Whether it was which route to follow, which exit to take, or which motel to choose, they disagreed—often quite angrily. In fact, there was only one other couple I knew who fought more. But I was moving on and that was what mattered most.

PART TWO

Pursuing Spirituality

CHAPTER 5

Life on the Prairies

Greetings and Meetings

AFTER A WEEK OR so on the highways we climbed out of the van. The big green sign welcomed us: "Prairie Bible Institute." We had arrived at the campus bordering the northern edge of Three Hills, two hundred miles north of the United States-Canadian border. It felt good to stretch my legs and look around. The many other students who were arriving made the campus pleasantly busy.

In 1922 the school started with a handful of eager learners in a little farmhouse on the prairies. When I arrived in 1963, PBI had about 750–800 students in the Bible school and hundreds of other students in the grade school and high school. There were also hundreds of staff members (faculty and senior administrators were also known as staff, as were all spouses).

There was a healthy egalitarianism at the institute long before the word came into popular use. Each staff member was paid the same amount and had the same privileges. Thus, for example, in this large communal fellowship the founder and president, Mr. L. E. Maxwell, was paid the same as the laborer who shoveled manure in the barn. The only difference in remuneration had to do with the size of one's family. The larger one's family, the larger was one's monthly allowance. The president, whose children were grown and out of the house, would, as far as I could tell, actually have received a *smaller* paycheck than the farm worker who had children at home! I had heard and read about this very unusual place before I had decided to attend, and the simplicity of lifestyle appealed to me even then. Now, however, being in the midst of it, I was even more fascinated.

After registering, paying my bill, and getting unpacked in my assigned dormitory room, I started getting to know my fellow students. My roommate was from my home church so we knew each other quite well. Students came from all over the world to attend Prairie, although the largest percentage was from the Western Canadian provinces, the northwestern United States, and California. Being from the East Coast I was a bit out of place (especially with my strong Philadelphia accent), but felt comfortable at once. Our freshman class was about 300 students. These (and the student body overall) seemed divided about equally between men and women.

There were many spiritual growth opportunities, and almost all of them were required. Because I was pursuing spiritual things (and because there was nothing else to do in this vast oil and wheat country), I probably would have gone to them all anyway. There were Sunday school, Sunday morning, and Sunday evening worship services, chapel five days a week, and a Friday night missionary meeting. In addition, there were thirty-two student-led missionary prayer meetings every day from Monday to Friday. Attendance at one of these groups was strongly encouraged but not required. These were very important and meaningful to me during all four of my years at Prairie.

Student Work and Racism

Every Prairie student had to work 10½ hours a week on campus. This was called "gratis" because we were not paid for the work. We were giving our time and labor to PBI in order to keep down our tuition and room and board. And those costs were remarkably low—one of the reasons why I chose Prairie over the other schools.

Each student's gratis job was assigned to him or her. Some worked on one of the kitchen crews (breakfast, dinner, or supper), some on one of the farm crews (feeding and milking cows, collecting eggs, butchering chickens), some in the book store, some on the cleaning and painting crews and so on. There was also a print shop, an electrical shop, a barber shop, and a huge heating plant that kept the entire campus warm, including the high school and grade school buildings and their dormitories. The homes of the hundreds of staff members were also heated by the plant and its cobweb of tunnels. All sidewalks were free from snow and ice because the heat tunnels ran under them. Student workers served in each of these departments.

From that one small farmhouse, Prairie had expanded to a vast complex of structures (mostly wooden), roads, sidewalks, and underground pipes and wires. In almost all respects it was its own self-sustaining city. I was assigned to the school bakery which produced hundreds of loaves of bread each day for students and staff. Shortly after I began working there I was transferred to the milk pasteurizing plant next door to the bakery. Overseeing both the bakery and the milk plant was a man whose speech was a bit difficult to understand (for me, at least). He was a good man, but I had trouble with him for two reasons.

First, he reminded me of Dad in the days when Dad and I often quarreled on the job (when I despised Dad because of his fighting with Mom). I must have subconsciously transferred my hostility for Dad toward this baker, and I'm quite sure that the quarrels I had with him were instigated by me, not by him. I felt I knew better than he did, and he, just like my Dad, did not like that. So we argued.

Second, he was German, and I had a bad attitude within me toward German people. This racism did not come from my home, my relatives, my neighbors, or friends. In fact, the only possible source of this attitude came from my reading about the Nazis and their ghastly executions of the Jews in the Holocaust. Being a child growing up without television or a normal family life, I read voraciously—anything and everything I could get my hands on. Since we received a daily newspaper and this was in the 1950s and early 1960s, new finds—photos, records, diaries—were still being brought to light by Holocaust survivors and numerous investigators, especially Israelis.

The newspapers and magazines contained frequent accounts—often with gruesome pictures—of the horrors of the death camps, gas chambers, bunk beds, smokestacks, mass graves (before they were covered over), boxcars, and the detailed descriptions of how a group of people actually died after walking naked into the "showers." I think the hollow eyes of the living skeletons staring blankly into the cameras disturbed me as much as anything. I had not yet read Elie Wiesel's terrifying personal account, *Night*, but when I read it years later it did not shock me as much as the news reports did when I read them as a high-school student. Without any adult involvement in my hundreds of hours of reading, I grew to hate the Nazis and, by extension, the Germans—all Germans. I failed to make the distinction between Germans and Nazis, not realizing that only *some* of the Germans were Nazis. I was so blinded that I could not see that the vast majority of Germans, then and always, were high-quality people, just as can be said of any ethnic group on earth.

The baker at Prairie fit perfectly my stereotype of the typical Nazi commandant, including his first and last names. Even though I never would have considered myself to be such, I was a racist. I, who had worked well on jobs with Puerto Ricans, Cubans, and African-Americans, and who attended pre-medical classes with numerous Jewish friends, was a racist. I never asked the baker, but I'm fairly sure he moved me to the pasteurizing plant because of my propensity to argue with him.

I had a satisfactory relationship with the baker during the rest of the school year, although we didn't talk about anything except work, and that was very little. To this day I regret my attitude toward this faithful servant of Christ, and I am amazed that during the months I worked for him I never once thought of myself as a racist.

Summertime Issues

As the school year was coming to a close I had some major issues to resolve. I especially needed to know whether or not to return to Prairie for my sophomore year, and if so, whether to go back to Pennsylvania and get a job or to stay at Prairie as a "summer worker." I also needed to decide about resuming my studies at St. Joseph's, since I did not want to lose my pre-med knowledge by staying away from the sciences more than one year.

I prayed about these matters during the half-hour "devotions" each morning (before breakfast) and each evening (before lights out). While the "floor bosses" (now probably called resident assistants) could not make us pray and read our Bibles during these specified times, we were expected to do so. We were required to stay quietly in our rooms with the doors closed. I valued these occasions, especially evening devotions, and to this day I attribute very much of my lifetime spiritual growth to these times that were wisely set apart for our benefit. I loved the Bible reading, and underlined extensively in the Bible that Dad gave me. In my prayers, however, I struggled to stay on track, yet I knew God unscrambled my wandering thoughts and saw my intentions. Through prayer (much of it simply thinking and waiting on God), I was led to important decisions about the summer and fall of 1964.

I decided not to return to St. Joseph's and not to go back to Pennsylvania at all. Instead I would stay at Prairie and be a summer worker to earn my tuition and room and board for the sophomore year. These decisions were based on several factors. First, I realized how little I knew about the Bible and Christian truth, even after seven months of study (the school years were short because the many students from farms needed to be home by mid-April for sowing and able to stay on the farm until mid-September, to complete the reaping). I knew I had barely scratched the surface of all that I longed to know. My desire to study medicine had gradually been fading during my months at Prairie, while my spiritual quest had been intensifying. I had come to enjoy the atmosphere at Prairie greatly and wished to remain.

Another factor in my decision was that I had no desire to go back to the house on Ruby Lane that was associated in my mind with tension, fighting, and unhappiness between my parents. I saw it primarily as a house of gloom and I wanted to stay on the other side of the continent.

One more influence tugging at me to stay for the summer was a very attractive and intelligent redhead named Judy. I learned through the grapevine that she was staying for summer work, and this piece of information helped finalize my decision to stay. I had seen Judy around campus for months, but it was always across the aisle in classes, chapels, Sunday services, Friday night meetings, and in the dining room. The library study hall was divided by a floor-to-ceiling wall into men's and women's sections, so there were no social opportunities there. It was hard to do anything on campus but look, yet looks could accomplish a lot. When Judy started looking back (and smiling), I liked this place called Prairie even more. It wasn't hard to decide to stay for the summer.

For my summer work I was assigned to the landscaping crew. The large campus was beautifully kept with trees, shrubs, and flowers, and needed constant upkeep. This assignment suited me just fine due to years of experience with Dad. This very background, however, contributed to my downfall. The staff member in charge of landscaping was a German man who, again, fit closely with my stereotype of a Nazi officer and who must have (again) reminded me (subconsciously) of Dad. When he put me to work in a field where Prairie grew plants for future use, I disagreed rather strongly with him about how he was doing the job and trying to train me for the job. I, of course, thought I knew better than him how to work with plants, and after a day or two at that job I was transferred to the construction crew, which I thoroughly enjoyed for the rest of the summer.

As I look back at this memory—the second such experience in less than a year—I deeply regret my racism toward the German people, and I sincerely apologize to you of German lineage who are reading this. I prejudged you, especially men, before you were even born. I was guilty of racial prejudice, of course, but I was also guilty of the terribly evil and terribly harmful sin of racism itself. Once again, I'm certain that my know-it-all attitude and my racism led to the quarrels with the landscaper. He, like the baker, was a fine Christian. I went to school with the sons and daughters of these two godly men and they were solid believers, just like their fathers.

But that's not all. To complete the picture (and to my shame), I should mention two other experiences of racism toward German men. One was my home-room priest in high school, who also taught the German language. The other was my German teacher at St. Joseph's. In both cases my attitude was again the problem, and the difficulties I had had with these two men harmed my academic progress significantly.

There I stood, at the age of twenty, with four good men in my past to whom I showed considerable disrespect, only because they reminded me of the Nazis and of my father. I cannot explain in any scientific way how my years of intense Holocaust reading and living around Dad pulled my brain and mind toward racism, but I praise God abundantly that after my experience with the landscaper I have had no further incidents of (or conscious propensities toward) racism with respect to the delightful German people. After causing four sets of eerily similar experiences in four years, I rejoice in the God-given freedom—continually growing in me even now by the Holy Spirit of love—from my warped ways of thinking, feeling, and reacting. Only recently, after I started writing this book, did I look back over my life from ages 16 to 20 and realize my pattern of racism toward one special ethnic group. I thank God for his forgiveness of my sin.

The summer went by quickly. I enjoyed the work and the fellowship of other summer workers and staff, especially at the optional but welcome daily tea-time when we all sat together as equals in Christ, most of us being blue-collar types. I also enjoyed the leisure of the quiet evenings to read and teach myself the harmonica. Then, too, I appreciated the opportunities to preach at a local church at times, and to give my testimony at "street meetings" on Friday nights in the nearby towns and cities. In addition, I had the privilege of serving as a camp counselor (living in the cabin with about eight rambunctious boys) at two different camps—one in the majestic Canadian Rockies south of the tourist mecca of Banff. I spent profitable times with several good student friends, especially my close theologian friend Roy, and I very much benefited from the animated discussions with Roy on theological themes and the issues of life.

There was one further aspect of summer work that brought me great joy. During these months the social regulations were somewhat relaxed. The male students and the female students could mix together at some events, so Judy and I were able to get to know each other a little. One special occasion was a hayride where Judy and I sat next to each other and snugly jostled from side to side as the wagon rumbled along. This evening was the highlight of my summer. Also, as often as my work would allow, I tried to walk through the large kitchen. Judy's summer job was there, and if she could do so without being too obvious she slipped me a carrot or other treat being readied for the next meal. Such were the benefits of summer work.

Cultivating the Spiritual Life

The new school year began in mid-September. My gratis work for the sophomore year was grading English grammar assignments by freshmen. I loved the job because I loved the language. My inferiority complex from my high school years had been fading steadily since I became a Christian and began to learn who I was in Christ. It also helped to be far away from home.

The most important pursuit that occupied my mind and soul during my sophomore year—as it had during my freshman year—was my search for spirituality. But this year it became more intense. The apostle Paul wrote to those who were "spiritual" —or should have been— within the local churches, and requested that they help those in need (1 Cor 2:15; Gal 6:1. King James Version). He indicated that these believers were equipped by the Spirit to bring discernment, mature guidance, and whatever else might have been necessary to strengthen the household of God.

I longed to be one who was "spiritual" partly because the alternative was to be "worldly," "unspiritual," "non-spiritual," or even "against the faith." Paul used the concepts of spirituality, maturity, holiness, likeness to Christ, fullness of the Spirit, and similar terms in much the same way to indicate a faithful man or woman of God, and I wanted to be faithful. I wanted to do the whole will of God as a loyal, obedient servant. [1]

During these years I never once wondered whether, when I died, I would go to hell, heaven, or purgatory. I had not the slightest doubt about what happened that Thanksgiving morning while driving alone on Osborne Road in 1962. It was not as dramatic as the conversion of Saul the Pharisee recorded in the Acts of the Apostles, but it was just as real, life-changing, and convincing to me as his conversion was to him, and as Dad's was to him. At the most pivotal moment in my life (preceded by eight months of God's intense grace-quest) I received the "assurance of salvation." What the priest at St. Joseph's had called "the sin of presumption," I received as a blessing of soul-rest: deep, inner, spiritual confidence that "I am his, and he is mine." When reading the book of Romans I learned that God's Spirit is bearing witness with our (human) spirit that we are children of God (8:16). I often celebrated this remarkable and formerly elusive treasure that is sometimes called "The Witness of the Spirit." After my conversion I sang the great hymn, "Blessed Assurance," with a sense of particular delight. It was one of my father's favorites as well.

---

1. Since the mid-1960s, when I first began exploring the matter of spirituality, study of this vast realm of thought and life has expanded with such rapidity and intensity that it is a demanding task to try to stay aware of new developments in the field. One very important study of spirituality in the United States is by Linda A. Mercadante, *Belief without Borders: Inside the Minds of the Spiritual but not Religious* (New York, NY: Oxford University Press, 2014). Another highly valuable volume, giving the perspective of evangelical Christianity, from General Editor Glen G. Scorgie and nearly 200 contributors, is the hefty *Dictionary of Christian Spirituality* (Grand Rapids, MI: Zondervan, 2011).

But why did I long to live for God—to be a loyal, obedient servant of Christ living in close communion with God? If my eternal destiny in glory was now assured by grace through faith alone, why should I be so concerned about spirituality, holiness, and faithfulness? Yes, I read in the Bible about the "rewards" Christ will give when we stand before him after death, but since heaven was a place of perfect bliss for all who belonged to Christ, I couldn't make much practical sense of the idea of striving for rewards or "crowns." So I didn't embark on my quest for godliness because of rewards.

As a new believer I never thought about my motivation for wanting to live a serious Christian life. Whereas before, when my religious efforts were totally to escape hell (and, if possible, purgatory), my longings as a new Christian did not seem to originate in any formal thought process or pattern of instruction apart from reading the Bible and listening to sermons. In fact, as I related previously concerning God's bringing me to Christ for initial salvation, there was no great gulf between my coming to Christ for deliverance from hell and my coming to him for deliverance from sin. To me, these two notions of deliverance moved around in my mind as two sides of the same coin.

To long for deliverance from something negative, however, is quite different from the actual experience of that deliverance. Similarly, it is one thing to want to honor God wholly and another thing to actually please God in all of one's thoughts, words, actions, and demeanor. As a new Christian I lacked spiritual depth even as, by God's grace, I was developing a greater sensitivity toward sin. I came to view sin as an offense against God rather than against some official church body. This new perspective on sin was not due to any fear of God's judgment that might come to me in this life or the next. Because of the biblical teachings on God's saving grace I was gloriously free from all notions of condemnation.

However, I went somewhat overboard on grace in my daily living. I was, I regret to say, careless about sin. Because I no longer had to go through the bothersome and embarrassing ritual of confession to a priest in order to be forgiven, I took the grace of God too casually. I never, ever—even to this day—regarded the grace of God lightly when thinking of my great gift of eternal life in glory. But I did view God's ongoing grace as a kind of "automatic forgiveness" for any daily sins I may have committed. In addition, my conscience was not nearly as sensitive as I thought it was.

As I look back on those years, it is clear to me that, in some respects, I was not a very spiritual or godly Christian at all. I had the desire—the longing and "questing"—for holiness, nearness to God, and usefulness in his kingdom, but scarcely (if at all) aware of some sins of selfishness, sensuality, superiority, self-centeredness, and (perhaps ugliest of all) spiritual pride. Nevertheless, as I concluded my sophomore year, I was grateful for the way I was growing in my Bible knowledge and in my understanding of justification (being declared righteous and free from condemnation) and initial sanctification (being set apart and declared to be holy because of my new position in Christ). I also understood that, as part of my conversion experience, I received from God not only justification and sanctification but also regeneration (literally, being "born again"), and the baptism of the Holy Spirit. Through this spiritual baptism I had been joined to the worldwide body of Christ, his church, and had received the indwelling presence of the Spirit for godly wisdom, holy living, and the power for loving God, and loving my neighbor as myself.

After my second year at Prairie I returned to Ruby Lane to earn my junior year's tuition and housing, to pay off more of my student loan to St. Joseph's, and to get re-acquainted with my family and local church. Unlike most other students, I had been away from home for two school years, one summer, and two Christmas vacations. Because I had grown up largely alone, I had experienced no loneliness during my time away. I even turned down one or more invitations from fellow students to go home with them for Christmas. When I decided to go to back to Pennsylvania it was not because of homesickness, but because I needed to earn more money than I could by staying another summer on campus. I would again work for Dad in the tree and landscaping business and return to services and activities at the small Baptist church through which Dad and I came to know Jesus Christ.

It was good to see Rosemary, Dad, and Mom again. I can't recall if I saw Tom, since he was away most of the time in military service. It was also good to see the dear folks at church. I have few memories from the summer of 1965, however. Dad and I generally worked well together. Now that both of us were believers we argued much less than in our previous years. I cannot remember anything about the atmosphere in the home that summer, but I like to think that Dad and Mom had fewer fights, or less intense fights, because Dad was now a Bible-believing Christian. But I simply cannot recall.

Missions and the Crucified Life

I was excited to be back at Prairie for my junior year. I was delighted to see Judy again, and we returned to our subtle "romance" (if it could be called that) under the broad umbrella of the social regulations. Neither Judy nor I resented the strict rules. We went to PBI voluntarily with full awareness of the expectations of us. We did, however, long to be with each other regularly, and I tiptoed delicately around the social guidelines while trying to keep a clear conscience. I should add that the strict rules against talking with the opposite sex sometimes led to confusion and hurt feelings. A student could "like" another student but there was no "legal" way to discuss these feelings with the other person. I was called to the dean's office twice during my first two years at Prairie for talking to girls. The dean was a very gentle man, however, and even smiled slightly at me as he "scolded" me.

Because the deans had asked me to be a high-school counselor, I lived my junior and senior years in the Prairie High School boys' dormitory. The dorm had four floors and each floor had two counselors. This counted as my gratis work and I served as a counselor (especially for my end of the hall during the quiet evening study hours), friend, and policeman. I didn't have to do much policing. The boys (two to a room) were, understandably, quite rowdy at times, but overall were enjoyable to live with, talk with, and pray with. A good percentage of the boys had missionary parents who lived and ministered thousands of miles away. For these and for most other boys in the dorm, the counselors and deans stood in the place of parents.

The missionary atmosphere at Prairie was all-pervasive. Many missionaries and mission leaders from a large number of missionary-sending agencies and countries visited Prairie on a regular basis. Some were invited to speak in chapel or other meetings, some were on campus hoping to recruit prospective missionaries, and others came for refresher courses and/or sabbaticals for personal study, and spiritual refreshment. Along with the missionary prayer meetings these men and women enriched the spiritual life on campus and enlarged vastly a student's knowledge of the world and its people-groups. I liked them even though they were often boring speakers.

Continually before us as students was Prairie's goal of sending new Bible Institute graduates to "the mission field"—almost always assumed to be far away and across the ocean. An unfortunate side-effect of this emphasis was that there was very little mention of the high calling of pastoral ministry or of any other vocational service in North America, unless it was tied in some way to "home missions," such as mission agencies working with Indians, neglected children, or poor, humble churches away from the big cities. Rarely was there a visiting pastor speaking at chapel or a Sunday service, and the Friday evening gathering was (by definition) a missionary meeting.

Mentioned even less than pastoral ministry, and almost always referred to negatively when it was, was the high calling of Christian scholarship. A Prairie graduate choosing to "go on to further schooling" did so without, not because of, any active encouragement in that direction. Secular colleges and universities were viewed—for the most part—as godless, morally-bankrupt institutions that destroyed one's faith, and even "Christian" schools of higher learning were viewed with considerable suspicion. There

were no required textbooks for the Bible courses, nor for most of the theology courses. We were encouraged to study the Bible itself, without com-
mentaries or scholarly texts. Of course, the teachers' lectures in themselves
were textbooks of their own, compiled as they were from the research of
others. I know I would have benefited greatly if solid textbooks had been
required for the courses. And I would have had a much better education if
the biblical languages had been available. I would have eagerly studied both
the Hebrew and the Greek.

My final two years as a student at Prairie were occupied with classes,
life, and ministry with the high-school boys, planning the Junior-Senior
banquet, and helping as a script-writer on the yearbook. Judy, to my delight,
was the associate editor of the yearbook, and we just "happened" to arrive
early to committee meetings. In addition I continued attending the chapels,
Friday night meetings, prayer meetings, Sunday school, and the Sunday
morning and evening services, all of which were held in the Prairie Tabernacle, which was at the time the largest religious auditorium in Canada,
comfortably seating 4,300. (On special occasions 5,000 filled the Tab.)

The Sunday morning worship service in Prairie Tab was considered
the highlight of the week for PBI students, staff, many town residents, and
visitors. Mr. Maxwell spoke most Sunday mornings and the Tab was often
close to full. During my four years as a student at Prairie the majority of Mr.
Maxwell's sermons were based in Romans 6–8, or so it seemed. Also popular was Galatians 2:20, where the apostle Paul writes those classic words: "I
have been crucified with Christ." Mr. Maxwell's book, *Born Crucified*, had
sold many thousands of copies. It, and his additional books, *Crowded to
Christ, Abandoned to Christ*, and others, contained the essence of his views
on the spiritual victory available for every true believer. Mr. Maxwell also
taught the required courses on Luke (two courses), Romans, Hebrews, and
"Law and Grace," and his central message on the Christian's "death with
Christ" was as pervasive on campus as the missionary task of the church.
These were the two major emphases at Prairie: the great need of the world
for Christ, and the life of holiness, consecration, and full surrender of ourselves and our desires to the Master. Surely these were the two themes above
all else that God burned into me during my time at Prairie. I have been
extremely grateful all of my years for this dual focus guiding my steps.

But I had a problem. While I understood the missionary message and
even committed myself at an altar call to go to the mission field if God would
so lead, I did not really benefit much from the "born crucified" sermons
from Romans 6 and similar Scriptures. While I did come to understand
somewhat, in my head, Mr. Maxwell's essential ideas, in my heart and daily
life I did not apply—nor know how to apply—his preaching. He was a very

interesting, *very* lively speaker, however, so I never fell asleep. Furthermore, Mr. Maxwell always had powerful illustrations from real life, some of which have influenced me to this day.

In addition to the daily and weekly services, there were two special conferences each year. These were attended not only by all Bible school and high school students but by many visitors—both local folks and those from quite some distances. The "Keswick" (pronounced without the "w") confer- ence was a four-day "deeper life" series of meetings to which well-known speakers (usually from England, Scotland, or Wales) were invited to pro- claim the biblical truths about the life of holiness, surrender, and knowing God. We learned about dying to self and yielding our all to God, and there were sometimes altar calls for us to do business with God.

In the spring, after classes concluded, we had another conference. This one—the annual Missionary Conference—was eight days long and con- cluded with the Bible school graduation ceremony. As the name implies, this was a time of attending services (three a day, as with the Keswick confer- ence) and workshops devoted to reaching the world for Christ. The speakers were usually missionaries or mission executives and each one poured out his or her heart for the millions of lost souls who had never heard of Christ.

Behind the speaker, on a huge wooden sign, were the following stir- ring words (these were not just for the missions conference but were on the front wall of the tabernacle all of the time):

Is there a soul who died,

Who died because of me?

Forever shut away from Heaven

And from thee?

Because I tightly clutched my little earthly store,

Nor sent thy messengers to some distant shore?

While the more academically-minded students in our midst wondered about the theology of these words (as I still do), there is no doubt that they had an effect on all who saw them day after day, year after year.

These two annual conferences—the fall deeper-life conference and the spring missionary conference—correlated well with the two primary em- phases of Prairie life and teaching: the crucified life and the task of world missions.

Shortly before graduation the vice-principal, Mr. Will Jack, asked me to join the Bible school faculty in the fall. While I felt honored to be invited and would have enjoyed the teaching, I declined the offer. Without even a bachelor's degree and with no knowledge of the biblical languages, I knew God wanted me to obtain more training for preaching and teaching the Scriptures with excellence.

On my last day as a student at Prairie—on the final day of the spring conference—I rose excitedly. I would again spend time with Judy and her parents: farmers from northwestern Minnesota who had been on campus for several days listening to the messages, and looking forward to the graduation exercises for Judy and me. It was a Sunday afternoon and the Prairie Tabernacle was packed with all of the Bible school students, grateful parents, other loved ones and friends, and all manner of visitors and supporters of this great missionary-sending school.

Along with several other seniors I was invited to preach at the graduation ceremony. I spoke on the value and authority of the Scriptures. After we received our diplomas we were dismissed with a benediction. Judy and I, by pre-arrangement, went to a secluded spot on campus, where I put Judy's engagement ring on her "third finger, left hand," just as I had heard on a song years before. We were not allowed to be engaged while students at Prairie, but there was no law against buying a ring. It felt wonderful to be engaged to Judy!

The next day I left with some friends for Pennsylvania, and Judy left with her parents for Minnesota. Judy worked at home in preparation for our July 22 wedding. I worked for a huge car dealership where I had worked the previous summer, and earned enough to pay off the last of my student loan for St. Joseph's and still have some money to begin life together with Judy.

I also worked toward ordination. I knew we would be moving to Kansas City for further education and (I hoped) pastoral ministry. I therefore approached the leaders of the Baptist church through which I had come to Christ and inquired about ordination. They were receptive, so I diligently prepared my theological paper and other necessary materials. My examination committee consisted of about seven or eight area pastors and I felt good about the process. I was ordained on July 1, 1967. I have never cared to be addressed as "Reverend," but that title given me on that day has always signified a solemn and holy call upon my life and service for God.

About a week or so before the big day, with Rosemary along, I drove my blue and white 1957 Chevrolet to a little town in Minnesota named Gatzke. I had come to marry the farmer's daughter. I had a heart full of praise and anticipation, but I also had a tinge of apprehension: I was about to embark on an entirely new phase of my quest for adventure, purpose, love, knowledge, peace, and true spirituality.

CHAPTER 6

Marriage, Learning, Serving

Two Become One

THERE WAS JOY AT the wedding and reception, because this was God's doing, I was sure. Judy's parents, Bernard and Blanche Engevik, her six sisters and brother, and all of her cousins, other relatives, and friends were present and enjoyable. My mother had taken a train from Philadelphia, and it was nice to have Mom and Rosemary from my side of the family and two fellow classmates from Prairie as my groomsmen. With all of these family members and friends there were more cameras and flashbulbs popping than I had ever seen. Without a doubt I had never smiled so much in one day in my life, or in all of my life combined I imagine. We started with the formal photographs at the studio in the morning. By the end of the reception my face literally hurt from smiling. I dreaded when someone said, "Just one more."

The Engevik family pastor—the one who preached at the wedding— and his wife had graciously offered for our honeymoon their camper-truck situated on a pleasant wooded lot overlooking one of Minnesota's ten thousand lakes. It was rustic to be sure, but delightful.

Our one-week honeymoon was just what a honeymoon should be: Judy and I getting to know each other intimately in a quiet and beautiful setting (cell phones and computers had not yet been invented, and there was no television in the camper). We cooked our meals and did our dishes outside, and hung our laundry on the clothes line. Every morning after breakfast we each went a different direction into the woods to spend time alone with God and the written Word. Both Judy and I loved (and still love) the natural world, so we felt free and alive and very blessed to spend a week like this.

During my mornings in the woods I was burdened with one particular matter. It hit me quite forcefully that I was now responsible, financially and otherwise, not only for myself but also for Judy and any children we may have. In a moment, by saying "I do," I had doubled my obligations. Judy and I started our marriage with very little of this world's goods: a car stuffed with wedding gifts, our personal belongings from our single years, and a very small amount of cash. But we had no debt, hearts full of love, good health, and a very mighty and generous God.

At the tender ages of 23 and 22, with our marriage license, our Prairie diplomas, and my ordination certificate tucked away in our car, we walked in the woods with God. Early in the week I settled with God the matter of our future financial needs. To me it was largely a matter of spiritual logic. If I was trusting in God's promises in the Bible for my eternal destiny, I surely could trust God's promises in the same Bible for my daily provision and for Judy's as well. The inspired Scriptures, I reasoned, stood or fell together. There was to be no picking and choosing about which texts I would believe, or trust, or obey. "My God will meet all your needs according to the riches of his glory in Christ Jesus (Phil 4:19)," wrote the apostle Paul. This was God's promise to Judy and me as well as to the first century Philippian church. God would never fail to meet all of our needs according to his own wise manner and timetable.

Saturday, at the end of our honeymoon, we packed our goods and headed back to the Engevik home in Gatzke. On Sunday, I preached in their little church at the request of the pastor, and the next morning we said goodbye to Judy's family. We pointed the car south and set out for Kansas City, Missouri.

We entered Kansas City on a hot sticky summer evening in 1967. Little did we know that we were driving through one of the most racially-charged sections of the city. As we drove slowly along the boulevard, however, we noticed here and there the remains of fires, some with smoke still rising from the ashes. We found out later that the neighborhood had been a battle zone for the race riots during the preceding days. When we arrived at the home of a pastor friend and his wife we were both weary and thankful. A new adventure—a new part of my grace quest—had begun.

How did we decide on Kansas City? During our last year at Prairie, Judy and I (because we had an "understanding") were permitted to meet regularly alone to discuss and seek God about our futures. As Judy and I talked and prayed during these times we felt quite sure that God was leading us together for life, and we each desired to serve God wholeheartedly together after our wedding.

We were not sure how God was going to use us but our minds and hearts were open to mission work (in North America or elsewhere), pastoral ministry, educational ministry, or some other sphere of service. One thing we agreed on was that I should pursue further education. Because I had my two years at St. Joe's and four years at Prairie, Calvary Bible College of Kansas City welcomed me as a transferring senior. God willing, I would complete my bachelor's degree in one year and then enroll in the one-year Master of Arts program in biblical literature with a concentration in theological studies. I chose Calvary because I could obtain a bachelor's degree and a master's degree without a major move. As it was, we lived in four different places during our time in Kansas City, but all of these combined were not nearly as disruptive as would be moving to another part of the country after one year in Kansas City.

Adjusting

Our years in Kansas City began, understandably, with some significant adjustments. Judy and I grew in our mutual love and understanding and this was truly wonderful. Because I felt that I knew her well even before our wedding our transition into married life seemed natural and easy to me. Judy was then and is to this day very easy and delightful to live with.

Even though we adjusted well to each other, and I adapted right away to our new surroundings, Judy was a bit bewildered by life in the big city. Except for one summer doing child care in Minneapolis as a teenager, Judy had never lived in a city. Even so, she adjusted quickly, although she missed the farm life and especially her family. I was not as sensitive as I could have been to her loneliness for her loved ones, since there was nothing in my background to compare to her closeness with her family.

Our first home was a pleasant second-floor apartment for which we paid $75 a month to the woman who lived downstairs. We were about four blocks from the college and just across the parking lot from a large grocery store, a drug store, and a laundromat. We were also on a bus line. Judy got an office job in center city and I got a part-time job in a large music store. We walked, car pooled, or took the bus as much as we could and used our car only when necessary. Even though gasoline was very inexpensive compared to today's prices, we had to conserve our dimes in every way possible.

We did, however, give ten percent of all our income to God's work, not because we thought this was a strict law of God mandated for all Christians by the clear teachings of the Bible, but for other reasons.

First, we learned early in our Christian lives that consistent, proportionate giving—taken out before any other spending—was a source of deep joy and blessing to us. Second, we read much in the New Testament about the importance of giving liberally to God's work so that the gospel could be spread widely over the earth. Third, we knew that in the Old Testament the minimum expectation of the Lord was for his people to give a tithe of all they received. Surely we could give at least that much. Fourth, we looked upon our money—whether little or much—as all belonging to God, and faithful stewardship required an intentional, God-centered approach to all of our resources. Fifth, from our Prairie days we knew of the great poverty and affliction of people all around the world, and we wanted to help feed the poor, care for the sick, and provide out of our abundance for their sustenance—both materially and spiritually.

One of the first items on our agenda in our new city was to find a church where the Word of God was preached in a balanced and robust manner and God was worshipped in spirit and in truth. We heard about Central Bible Church, where the well-known Dr. Walter L. Wilson had been the long-time pastor, and we started attending there. It was a good place for us, and we helped in the children's church.

The church had a ministry to prisoners, so one weekend (I think it was a Sunday afternoon) I went with a group of men to St. Joseph, Missouri. As we parked next to an old two-story building one of the men told me that the jail was on the second level, and on the first level was where the first bank robbed by the notorious Jesse James was located. We used an outside metal stairway to get to the jail so I did not see what was inside downstairs.

We did not hold a service and the men were not released from their cells, but we were permitted to walk freely in the hallways by the cells. We could talk to the men through the bars. There were no barriers between visitors and prisoners other than the metal bars, spaced about four or five inches apart.

I remember talking with one prisoner as he and I sat on our haunches on opposite sides of the bars. After introducing myself I asked him why he was in jail. He said he came home one day and found his wife in bed with some man. He flew into a rage, killed the man, and was now facing years in prison for murder. He then said something I have never forgotten: "Sex rules the world." He meant that the sexual impulse is so powerful in people that it often exerts a practically irresistible control (a rulership) over their minds and actions, blocking out whatever twinges of conscience and common sense may be trying to break through in the heat of passion. Because some people, including some in high places, are so obsessed with sex, it comes to rule their lives and therefore, at times, rule large numbers of people, even nations. I listened to him, tried to understand him, commiserated with him, opened to some Scripture verses with him, prayed with him, and said goodbye. I felt very sad as I walked down the hallway, on display for the other men to gaze at while I passed their cells.

The same grace quest by which God had drawn me toward the cross was at work in these men, not because they were especially bad and needed to repent and believe the gospel more than most people, but because they were mere mortals—ordinary human beings needing a Savior and a hope-giver. Possibly some of them, as had been with me, were searching for a genuine salvation, and possibly some of them, as with me, were searching for a genuine spirituality—a way of living meaningfully in the realms of both the material and the non-material.

Classroom, Church and Family

After two years at St. Joe's and four years at Prairie, I entered a culminating one-year program of studies at Calvary, which led to a Bachelor of Science degree the following May. My dual major was Bible and Missions—the same as at Prairie. The studies were profitable and enjoyable, with the highlight being the study of the Greek language used in the writing of the New Testament and other early Christian literature.

I was absolutely in my glory reading and translating directly from the epistles of John, the gospel of John, and other Bible books. In a very real sense, this desire to work from the Scriptures in their original languages (which was one of the main reasons I chose Calvary) was one expression of my quest for a truly biblical spirituality. I had felt somewhat hindered without the language tools to dig more deeply into the written Word.

At my ordination examination, one of the examining pastors had asked what I intended to do in the coming months and years. I said that I would be continuing my schooling for Christian ministry and I hoped to serve in a local church as a youth pastor or a senior pastor. Now, after a few months at school and working at the music store, I was offered a position as assistant pastor of a small (45–50 in attendance) mission church in Kansas City North. My responsibilities were primarily to lead the youth activities and shepherd the young people, but also to preach and assist the pastor in other ways as needed. I spent a year in this ministry, after which the pastor, due to his intensifying medical studies, stepped down and I became the head pastor.

I enjoyed both the youth work and the tasks of the senior pastor, especially preaching, and visitation. Looking back now I realize that my sermons in those years were probably a bit too academic, even though no one ever said that to me. Between my very exciting (and demanding) studies in Greek and Hebrew, my ministry at the church, and my life with Judy, I felt very rich and very blessed.

I started my master's program one year after we had arrived in Kansas City. As I said above I loved the studies, especially in the Scriptures. The theology courses, however, did little to advance my knowledge of such topics as the trinity, the person of Christ, the Holy Spirit, human sin, God's work of salvation, and the end times. Some students complained to the administration that these courses were not being taught at a graduate level. The students were correct. We longed to study theology more deeply and widely and wanted to be exposed to other perspectives on these topics by having to read and discuss vigorously other theologies and their systems. Instead, we were taught an approach called "dispensationalism," which is a way of looking at the overall plan of God throughout human history and was then (and is now) a popular framework to help one see the big picture from Genesis to Revelation. While it is a respected and orthodox system of theology it does not go "outside of itself" very much to delve into other Christian approaches (such as Lutheranism, Wesleyanism, Pentecostalism, and Eastern Orthodoxy). The original *Scofield Reference Bible* and the *New Scofield Reference Bible*, which have helped many people, including me, are prime examples of dispensationalism.

From dispensationalism I came to accept (with some discomfort) such doctrines as the sharp distinction between Old Testament "law" and New Testament "grace;" the cessation, by the end of the first century, of the more controversial gifts of the Holy Spirit (such as miracles, healing, and tongues); and certain ideas about the future coming of Christ. For me, the theological milieu at Calvary was too restrictive as a way of expressing the worldwide plan of God for the ages.

In the spring of 1969, while Judy and I were nearing the completion of our second year of marriage, our first child was born. Joan Marie entered this world at the University of Kansas Medical Center. I had been given permission to be present at the delivery, but because there were complications with Joni's birth I was not allowed in the birth room. Disappointed, I sat through much of the night in the waiting room reading Sanday and Headlam's exegetical Greek commentary on the book of Romans. There would be a major test on this material in just a few days.

A Well-timed Ending and a Surprise Letter

In November of 1969, after nearly two years at the church, I concluded my pastoral ministry at Harmony Baptist. Among other factors the serious financial situation of the church was major. I had been the first "full-time" pastor of this church plant. The leader of the congregation, just before my resignation, had said to me that the financial position of the church could not sustain my present salary much longer. I believe that God used this circumstance, among others, to give both him and me peace about the conclusion of my service at the church.

With my pastoral responsibilities concluded, Judy and I began to think about my completing the master's degree in just one more full-time semester instead of the three part-time semesters we would have needed if I had continued pastoring. In praise to God I was able to schedule and complete all of my remaining courses, including my thesis, in one final semester at Calvary. I received my Master of Arts degree in Biblical Literature in June of 1970.

During my final semester at Calvary Judy and I had been thinking, praying, and gathering information about possible ministries for our future. We were willing to go anywhere in the world and do whatever God called us to do, and we saw ourselves as a team—Judy, Joni, and I—with each of us equally important to God in this major decision. We would have no debt when I graduated but neither would we have any money.

During my graduate studies I had served as a TA (teaching assistant) for the academic dean. My responsibility was to help him with the teaching of his course on how to study the Bible. He gave the lecture and I led students in the outworking of the materials through class projects. This was my first teaching adventure and I was grateful for the opportunity.

One of my teachers strongly advised me to pursue doctoral studies at Dallas Seminary, while another wanted me to consider staying in Kansas City to work on a doctorate at the University of Missouri, so that I could teach at the college. We also corresponded with missionary agencies concerning teaching national leaders, especially in Africa and Europe, but experienced no freedom to pursue this option. One reason for this was that the mission societies wanted me to have a doctorate. Even though I felt that my spiritual gift was teaching and though I hoped someday to obtain a PhD, this did not seem to be the right time for more schooling. I had been a student for nine straight years after high school and, while I don't think I could ever tire of high-quality education, Judy and I felt that she should be home with Joni. I desired to serve God as a full-time teacher of ministerial students, but no doors were opening in that direction.

About two or three months before graduation I received a letter from the Vice Principal of Prairie Bible Institute, Mr. Jack, inviting me to join the faculty. This came as a total surprise. As I mentioned previously, during my senior year at Prairie three years before this, he had also asked me to join the faculty. But because I did not have a bachelor's degree (and knew how much I didn't know) nor did I have teaching experience, I declined his offer.

Now, with what was probably only a short time left in Kansas City, Prairie was once again inviting me to become part of the Bible Institute faculty. This time I considered the request much more seriously. Since nothing else was opening and since Judy and I were quite familiar with the campus, the staff, and the way of life on the Canadian prairies, we felt this may be God's way for us. After prayer and further discussion we agreed that I should contact the Vice Principal and accept his offer, which I promptly did.

At the end of June we rented a moving truck, sold our beloved Chevy, packed our earthly goods, said our goodbyes, and headed north to Canada. Judy, Joni, and I fit like three peas in a pod in the cab of the truck. Actually, our second daughter, Laurie, made the trip with us as well, although I had no idea that Judy was expecting another child. We did know, however, that God would go before us and travel with us.

I was beginning a new phase of my grace quest. At the time, as I look back now, my quest for a fuller spirituality was prompted far more from God's heart and persistent grace than from within myself. I was basking in the sunshine of God's favor and enjoyable circumstances, while he was drawing me gently yet firmly into a deeper and purer knowledge of himself.

Return to the Prairies

We pulled into the Prairie campus in early July. It was just about seven years since Judy and I, unknown to each other, had first arrived as students. Then, with the great unknowns of life before us, we each were shown our dormitory room with its bunk beds, rustic furniture made in the carpenter shop, metal basin for washing, and a pitcher for drinking water. Now, as a staff family, we were shown our new home—a two-bedroom basement apartment about one block south of the campus and across the street from the Three Hills swimming pool. The fourplex in which we lived was painted a pleasant mint-green color and Judy soon made the apartment a home.

I needed to return our rented truck to Great Falls, Montana, according to the contract. The truck company had centers only in the United States. When we left Kansas City the rental agency had installed a governor spring to control the gas pedal, and this was not to be tampered with or removed. Because of this I could drive no more than about 55 miles per hour. While this speed was tolerable on the trip north with my family in the cab, it seemed painfully slow driving alone over the empty grasslands of southern Alberta and Montana.

After turning in the truck I went to the bus depot and bought a ticket for the morning. I then rented a cheap hotel room for $5.00, just across from the bus station. It was a hot night and the room had no air conditioning or fan. There was a neighborhood alley cat whose occasional screeches wafted into my room through the open window, yet I fell asleep weary, nearly broke, and very content. The next day the bus carried me home.

While I was setting up my office in the faculty building and preparing for classes, Judy was busy getting used to life as a staff member. Since we had spent four years as students at Prairie and had worked on the summer crews (two summers for Judy and one for me), we knew our way around the campus quite well and knew many of the staff as friends.

There were still things to learn, however. Much of our learning, as in Kansas City, had to do with ways to live economically on our very small monthly remuneration. Judy and I had no complaints about this because we had joined staff willingly, each with a strong desire to serve the Lord joyfully in this very strategic hub of world missions. We knew God's promises of provision by head, by heart, and by experience—most recently during our three years in Kansas City. Judy and I had always lived with little (she much more so than me), yet even though our needs were considerable our wants were few.

We agreed with the financial policies of Prairie's founders and leaders, especially their overall guideline of not going into debt. If there was a need (and there were many, all the time) everyone trusted God together to provide. Staff meeting was every Saturday morning, and all staff (spouses also, if possible) were required to attend. Here we prayed together and had an exhortation from the Bible. If the farmers needed a new tractor, the printers needed a new press, or the cooks needed a new oven, the financial managers ordered these as money came in. Everything possible was made or done by Prairie's staff. Even building new dormitories, offices, or staff homes was done by dedicated and highly skilled staff members instead of outside contractors.

Prairie's overriding policy was to keep student tuition low in the grade school, high school, Bible school, and correspondence school while staying free from debt. Donors knew that every dollar given to Prairie Bible Institute (the umbrella name for all four schools, the Prairie Tabernacle, and several related ministries) was being used to move God's work forward instead of paying off debt and interest.

Prairie was a city unto itself. When, for example, student and staff hunters gave us choice cuts of deer, elk, and moose meat, we stored them in the spacious butcher shop. Each staff family had their own meat locker and could use the butchering table and tools as needed, as long as one did not mind the odor of bloody, moist sawdust on the floor. Once we were given a quarter of moose and a good staff friend taught us how to butcher it. It tasted as good as the best beef I ever had. There was also a used clothing store and a staff grocery store where prices were kept as low as possible.

The weather, as Judy and I had learned from earlier years, was—except in the summer—usually very cold. The only month free of frost was July. In winter the temperature was often so far below zero that only when the temperature was -20° Fahrenheit or below did the Prairie kindergarten cancel classes. The principal felt that walking in that kind of weather was a bit too much for the little ones. Most everyone walked everywhere on campus since cars—for those who could afford them—were too expensive to operate. The Prairie garage graciously allowed staff to rent a car for five cents a mile when we needed to drive to Calgary, Red Deer, or even to the States.

We entertained guests, usually students, every weekend, sometimes both Friday and Saturday evenings. Judy always managed to put great meals together. The students loved to get out of their dorms and come over to play games (sometimes getting very raucous) and experience normal "home life." Of course the students could come only in groups of men or women, but they—and we—always had very enjoyable times.

In March of our first winter on staff Laureen Dawn joined our family. Because Judy was having complications in the Three Hills Hospital, our local doctor drove us in his own car on a (literally) wild 60-mile ride to the Red Deer Hospital. Once again, as with Joni's birth, even though I had obtained permission to be with Judy in the delivery room, I was asked to wait outside during the birth. Fortunately, the anticipated C-section was not needed, and Laurie was delivered within 15 minutes of our arrival at the hospital. She was a delightful addition to our family, and Judy and I now felt doubly blessed!

Life was good for the four of us in our little basement apartment. I got a used sled and built a sturdy rectangular open box on top of it so that Judy or I could pull the children around the campus and around the town over the ever-present snow and ice.

After one year of attending the Prairie Tabernacle for the weekly services, as almost all staff members did (and were, I think, expected to do), we moved to the Bethel Evangelical Church in town. Even though our move raised eyebrows among some staff (Were we disloyal, or even rebellious?) it turned out to be a very good church experience for us. The huge Tabernacle, with its focus on students, missions, and the crucified life, had been a good place for Judy and me as students, but we now desired the smaller local church life that revolved around the entire family. Bethel Church was a wonderful body of spiritually-minded believers where the four of us were very much at home.

CHAPTER 7

New Directions

In the Classroom

I WAS 26 YEARS old when I started my teaching career. I was assigned to teach courses in Bible Study Methods (later called Introduction to Exegesis), first year Homiletics (preaching), and English Grammar. All of these were required courses for freshmen and I loved each one. The students were enjoyable and very respectful, and I felt right in place. I had a student worker to help with grading and other responsibilities, and, although quite busy, I did not feel overwhelmed by my teaching duties.

As time passed, I became involved in activities beyond my teaching. I published some popular-level magazine articles and wrote a biweekly newspaper column called "The Question Box" for the Red Deer Advocate, central Alberta's main newspaper. People sent in questions (or I made them up) about the Bible and religion, and I answered them in about 350 words. There were, in addition, Sunday preaching opportunities throughout the province and even a five-week preaching tour, with a men's quartet, to Ontario and Michigan to promote Prairie and help recruit students.

In all of these activities I continued my quest to know God more and to experience more the spirituality that I knew about in my head, but not in my daily activities to the extent I knew was possible. Because things in my life were proceeding smoothly, I did not, in my seeking after God, have the sense of deep need and urgency that I would experience in the not-too-distant future. Yet God continued his grace quest after me and in me, to form me more fully in the image of his Son.

Those years in the early 1970s were some of the best years of our family life, and of my life ever. Judy was able to be at home with Joni and Laurie, the Christian fellowship both on campus and in our local church was very good, and my teaching was fulfilling. After my first year on the faculty I was asked to teach, in addition to preaching and exegesis, General Biblical Introduction (how we got the Bible, as well as its trustworthiness), the epistle of James, and (what came to be) a very large adult Sunday School elective on the gifts of the Holy Spirit for the Prairie Tabernacle congregation.

I was also doing a lot of reading and studying in areas that were not related to my teaching, and I was deepening my knowledge of topics that I previously knew little about. My personal study during these years had a profound impact on the rest of my life and teaching, and in some categories of thought I changed my views significantly.

The Return of the Lord

One area in which I spent considerable time was in the doctrine of eschatology (study of the end times), focusing on the relation of Christ's return to a future time of extreme tribulation and distress mentioned frequently in the Bible.

Up until this time I had believed (somewhat hesitantly) that Christ would return both before the time of the great trouble as well as after it. The first time, I was taught, was for Jesus to remove all of his true followers from the earth, so they would not have to endure the severe trials to come upon humankind, and the persecution and martyrdom that would befall other Christian believers—supposedly those who received Christ after the others had been taken up. Christ's coming at the end of the tribulation time was to bring back to the earth the previously removed group of believers so that, after Christ defeated all his enemies, they would reign over the earth with him for a thousand years.

I began to doubt that I would have thought of the idea of these two comings of Christ if I had not been taught it in books, classes, and the original *Scofield Reference Bible*. In fact, it wasn't until the 1800s that the pre-tribulation return of Jesus was introduced to Christian theology.

The more I read the New Testament on its own, without looking for the doctrine of a pre-tribulation coming of Christ, the more I began to realize that such a doctrine isn't there. I could clearly see the Second Coming of Christ as a glorious event following a time of severe distress, tribulation and persecution on the earth (Mark 13; 1 Thess 4:13–5:11; 2 Thess 1:3–2:12). But I could not see in the Bible, with my admittedly fallible reasoning, the idea of a prior coming of Christ.

What convinced me that Christ's coming for which we should all be looking will not occur *before* the time of great trouble on the earth but *after* it, was that this is the natural reading of Jesus' Olivet Discourse in Matthew

24 and 25, Mark 13 and Luke 21. While this discourse of Jesus is, without doubt, difficult to interpret with the precision we would like, it seemed obvious to me (and still does) that there is no indication of two comings of the Lord in this most extensive section of his teachings about his return.

I knew that this was not only a debate among scholars. The most important practical issue, in my view, had to do with the matter of endurance and alertness in times of trouble—something that all of us need, and will need, as long as we live. I considered the truth that Jesus never promised his followers a life of comfort and freedom from trials and opposition. In fact, he promised just the opposite (Matt 10; John 12:23–27; 15:18–27; 16:33; 17:11–19). He said, "No servant is greater than his master. If they persecuted me, they will persecute you also." Jesus also said, "My prayer is not that you take them out of the world but that you protect them from the evil one."

I once read that some Western missionaries to the Chinese people before the Communist takeover in the middle of the twentieth century had taught the pre-tribulation coming of Jesus, with its understanding that true believers will be removed from the earth before the time of great tribulation and persecution that is to come. But when the new, ruthless, Communist rulers brought harsh living and working conditions to the people, and severe persecution and even martyrdom to the Christians who refused to deny Christ, the believers were very confused and unprepared for this era of distress.

The terrible events that had come seemed to them to be the great time of trouble predicted in the Bible. Yet they had been told that Christ would come and take them from the earth so that they would not have to endure the tribulation events, including the persecution and martyrdom they were experiencing. The missionaries, of course, were expelled from the country by the Communist rulers and the Christians had to learn, from their own direct Bible study, how to live and stand strong in this new, hostile, anti-Christian environment.

Large numbers of Chinese Christians stayed true to God, even though they had to go underground to practice their faith together. From that time onward many of the churches abandoned the idea of a pre-tribulational escape from the earth and adopted the more natural way of reading the Olivet Discourse of Jesus in Matthew 24 and elsewhere, in which Jesus says he will return *after* the terrible time of distress to come over the whole earth. Large numbers of Chinese believers, from that time to the present, have lived courageously for Christ through awful trials of many kinds, including severe persecution. And many Chinese Christians no longer believe that they will be lifted from the earth to escape whatever tribulations are yet to come.

From my rethinking of this issue I saw how important and relevant the matter is. With many of today's churchgoers lulled to sleep in their comfortable homes and splendid houses of worship, they experience very little if any opposition from unbelievers as long as they keep their Christian convictions (if they have any) to themselves. They and their children appear to be totally unprepared for major times of tribulation and persecution to come on earth.

While I had always loved the classic passage on Christ's return to call us—living and dead—to meet him in the air (1 Thess 4:13–18), I noticed that the text does not reveal *when* this event will occur. I came to the conclusion that, if the pre-tribulational view is correct, I have nothing to worry about. I won't be here during the horrific events to come. I even hope that such a view is the biblically correct one. I hope my interpretation is wrong. But if the post-tribulational view is the actual doctrine taught in the Bible, as I have come to believe, then at least my family and I will be, I trust, ready and faithful for whatever comes, even martyrdom.[1]

What is taught in our churches on these matters is not merely academic. Instead, it has much to do with our understanding of the way of the cross to which we are called—the way of suffering and self-denial. It also has much to do with our readiness to stand unflinchingly for Christ no matter what opposition we must face.

Journey to the Holy Land

As I continued reading, studying, teaching, and preaching I had a growing desire to travel to the Bible lands, especially Israel. My spirit of quest—in this case after travel, adventure, and spirituality—was acting up again. I came across a magazine ad inviting pastors and Christian leaders to organize and lead a trip to the Bible lands. I obtained the information, discussed it with Judy, and we set the departure date for July 23, 1973, leaving from Montreal. It would be a 15-day tour. According to the travel company, I needed to recruit four paying travelers to receive my trip at no financial cost.

---

1. Two books that were highly influential to me in my move away from the pre-tribulation rapture view are *The Church and the Tribulation,* by Robert H. Gundry (Grand Rapids, MI: Zondervan, 1973), and *The Blessed Hope,* by George E. Ladd (Grand Rapids, MI: Eerdmans, 1956).

If I recruited eight people Judy could also come at no cost. Recruiting additional passengers would help pay for our round-trip airfare between Calgary and Montreal and for child care (Judy's sisters) and spending money.

I worked on recruiting tour members and served as the liaison between them and the travel company. I also studied our itinerary and prepared my talks—both educational and devotional—to use at special historic sites and on the bus as we travelled from site to site. Fortunately, there would be local guides in each country who spoke the language and took our group to the precise places of interest.

Nineteen pilgrims signed up and, along with Judy and me, were a very excited group who met in Montreal. We flew to Paris and then to Greece, where we spent time in Athens and Corinth. After Greece, we toured Lebanon, Egypt and Cyprus, and then spent a week in the "Holy Land"—Israel.

In every country we traveled we concentrated on the ancient historic sites known for their associations with biblical persons and events, especially those that scholars had established as genuine or probably genuine. There was no doubt about certain places, such as the judgment seat at Corinth, the ruins of ancient Tyre, the major bodies of water (such as the Nile and Jordan rivers and the Sea of Galilee), Jacob's Well, and the Garden of Gethsemane. Even those places that were not identified with certainty (such as the Mount of Transfiguration and the dungeon where Jesus was possibly kept overnight between his capture and his trial) held great interest for everyone in our group, because we could still visualize the remarkable events that took place, if not at these very spots then likely close by, in settings similar to the ones known to tourists.

One result I did not expect from walking in the steps of Jesus was a troubling sense of uncertainty and doubt about the reality of my Christian faith. My problem was not that I doubted the historical basis for Christ's life and ministry in the Holy Land, but just the opposite. After a couple of days in Israel, thinking of this man from Galilee walking about, eating, drinking, sleeping, gathering firewood, and doing his laundry, I was so struck by the total humanity and earthiness of Jesus that I wondered how someone like this could be the Savior of the world and, even more, God in human form.

How could one particular man who lived in this particular place at one particular time in history be the eternal Creator and Ruler of the world, and my personal Savior? He surely seemed like a remarkable person, but how could the infinite be one with the finite? To me, the truly awesome, omnipotent, and omnipresent God, a being so "other" and so mysterious who exists eternally in a blazing cloud of holiness, could not be localized in a human body with all of its limitations. Or could he?

Fortunately, this jarring stream of thought lasted only a few hours and did not hinder my leadership of the tour group. I dealt with the matter within my own mind, reviewing the biblical teaching that Jesus, while fully human, was also fully God. Yes, the mystery of the incarnation was just that—a mystery (1 Tim 3:16). But a mystery is not a contradiction, even though we are not capable of fully understanding it or explaining it.

Because I believed firmly in the factual, historical basis for the earthly Jesus—his righteous life, his stunning other-worldly teachings, his miracles, his lamb-like slaughter on the cross for all humanity, and his resurrection and glorious ascension (Phil 2:5–11)—I knew that the truth of the gospel and the factual basis for the teachings of Jesus stood or fell together. If the historical details of the gospels are accurate, as numerous scholars of ancient history have demonstrated, then Jesus truly was claiming to be God in the flesh. When he said "I and the Father are one" (John 10:30) and "Before Abraham was born, I am" (John 8:58), he was declaring what he believed was eternal, infallible truth.

I reminded myself that if Jesus was making these claims so boldly and backing them up with miracles (John 8–10) then he was indeed the perfect One of God. It seemed to me that the only other serious options one has to choose from are that Jesus was a liar or that he was a crazy man. In either case he was neither the eternal Son of God nor the Savior of the world. In either case the Christian faith must be rejected because it is based on lies or the rantings of a delusional, self-appointed wild man. My crisis of faith, if it could be called that, faded away to nothing.

Stirrings of the Mind—and the Spirit

As I returned to teaching in the fall I recognized within me a resurfacing of my earlier quest—upon completion of my master's degree—for deeper knowledge and further proficiency in my fields of study. I had been learning much through my teaching and my personal research, but I was also discovering how much I did not know and how many questions I needed to ask, and attempt to answer. I grew hungry for more. This was not a desire to pack additional information into my brain, but a longing to enter the world of Christian scholarship more fully in order to serve God at a different academic level than was possible in my present position. I believed that God was calling me to pursue further studies so that I might be qualified to teach and write with the depth (and, I hoped, the clarity) that was increasingly needed in the worldwide educational task of the church of Jesus Christ.

My experience at Prairie, both as a student and as a teacher, had been quite pleasant, and I had no urge to move on. I believed strongly in both the missionary emphasis of the school and its focus on holy living. But the longer I was at Prairie the more I felt God prompting me to search for schooling opportunities to further my education—to move toward a PhD degree.

I had heard of the Evangelical Theological Society (ETS) and knew it was the major evangelical scholarly organization in North America for the advancement of biblical and theological studies, and related fields.[2] Many of the leading scholars in these fields—most of them faculty members in college and seminaries—were members of the ETS. I was excited to learn that in December of 1973 there would be an ETS conference at Wheaton College. This was to be the 25th annual meeting of the society and the emphasis would be on recent advances in New Testament Studies. There would be many papers presented on this discipline as well as in related disciplines by top scholars from North America and around the world. Non-members were permitted to attend.

I went to the Principal of Prairie, T.S. Rendall, and asked him for permission to attend this conference and to receive financial help for air travel, lodging, and meals. He gladly granted my request with the proviso that I would give a report of the conference at one of our faculty meetings. I eagerly agreed.

I was one of the first to arrive at the Wheaton campus, and as I stood in the dimly lit foyer with my suitcase I saw three men standing nearby. I walked over to them and asked if they knew where the registration desk was. They weren't quite sure, but one of them suggested that we leave our luggage there and first get something to eat. They welcomed me very warmly and invited me to join them.

I was in awe. When they introduced themselves to me I instantly knew their names from their scholarly writings and reputations. Here they were—luminaries in their respective fields—and I was eating with them!

The days of the conference were packed with so many concurrent presentations (mostly the reading of scholarly papers) that I could attend only those that interested me most. In addition, there were plenary sessions during which there were no other presentations. In these, since the focus was on New Testament studies, major scholars such as F. F. Bruce and I. Howard Marshall delivered keynote addresses. After one of these sessions I shared donut holes and coffee with Dr. Bruce—the leading evangelical

2. By "evangelical" I refer to a set of Christian beliefs that includes the necessity of a "new birth" experience—not necessarily dramatic or able to be pinpointed—and the urgency of spreading the saving gospel of Jesus Christ throughout the earth; evangelicals also have a high view of biblical inspiration, trustworthiness, and authority.

biblical scholar in the English-speaking world. Even though I continued to be in awe of this truly outstanding scholar, I felt perfectly at ease talking with him, even briefly. He was very down-to-earth and friendly, as were the other scholars I had the privilege of meeting and mixing with.

This conference was the most significant event in my professional life since I began studying in Kansas City six years earlier, and it would continue to be such for many years to come. When I gave my report to the faculty at Prairie I not only summarized a number of key papers, noting especially their distinctive points and the ensuing discussion, but I also expressed how the camaraderie and mutual respect of these scholars for one another was a delight to see. It was not that they had no disagreements among themselves. In the pursuit of truth they did, at times, dispute the weight of evidence and the logic of arguments. But such disputation took place without rancor or personal animosity, as far as I could discern.

I knew that this level of specialization was not for everyone, but I also knew it was extremely important for some to devote their lives to such scholarship to guard Christ's church from error, to keep the central message of the Scriptures pure and prominent, and to pursue answers to the large number of biblical, theological, ethical, and historical questions that cried out for better resolutions than the ones often offered.

There was much work to be done in these areas of study, and I knew God was calling me to join these serious men and women in their pursuit of truth. In my never-ending quest for a fuller spirituality, I knew that my scholarly growth was to have a prominent role. I promptly joined the ETS. I was welcomed as an associate member because I did not have an advanced-enough degree to be a full member. I was truly honored, however, to belong to such an association.

CHAPTER 8

Which Way to Go

A Difficult Quest

AFTER THE ETS CONFERENCE I entered diligently into the task of searching for schools with doctoral programs where I might study. At this time I was considering a PhD in either Old Testament or New Testament. I communicated with schools and scholars, and discussed the situation and prayed about it with Judy. She and I were in agreement about the new direction before us, and we felt a great need for God to lead us according to what would be best for each member of our family. Our children were just as important to God as we were.

Two large barriers stood before us, however, distinct yet closely related. The first was where to study and the second was how to finance our move, tuition, and living expenses for the next several years, during which I hoped to study full-time. Judy offered to work outside the home, yet the children would only be six and four when I planned to begin study. How would we manage that?

As the months passed I began to suspect that, to my great disappointment, I was not likely to be admitted into a high-quality doctoral program with only my MA from a school that lacked regional accreditation. Even though my grades at St. Joseph's, Prairie, and Calvary were high and my recommendations strong, the schools (Prairie and Calvary) where I did my biblical and theological studies were not (as far as I could surmise) considered to have a high enough academic quality for admission into the doctoral programs I preferred. (No prospective school said these things to me, however.) In addition, the best schools wanted applicants to have a Master of Divinity degree (which would take two or three more years to earn) or at least two years of full-time graduate study. My MA was technically a one-year program.

Since I did not think I should spend money to earn another master's degree nor pursue a doctorate at a school lacking the academic rigor, superior faculty, and scholarly reputation I sought, I settled on a less-than-ideal option: I would study as a special student at Princeton Theological Seminary, concentrating on New Testament Studies. I had applied for but was not accepted into the doctoral program at Princeton, but was told that I would be welcome as a special student or as a student in one of their master's degree programs. I did not apply to any other schools.

Princeton had an excellent New Testament department, especially with the world-class Dr. Bruce Metzger (who, to me, lived in the same rarified atmosphere as Dr. F. F. Bruce), but I did not wish to spend additional time before entering doctoral studies. Yet this seemed to be my best course of action: studying for one or two years to show that I could do the work well at this high level and then (I hoped) be accepted into the PhD program in New Testament at Princeton. Even though the school accepted a very small percentage of applicants into its doctoral programs (four out of 40 applicants to the New Testament PhD program in the year I applied), I thought that I should at least try.

Since there were no grants or scholarships available for special students, Judy and I would need to find other ways to support our family of four and pay for my tuition, textbooks, and fees. However, there were very few ways to earn extra money while at Prairie. I sold World Book Encyclopedias for a time, but I could not devote the time necessary to earn much. I could keep honorariums for preaching in area churches if the invitations came to me apart from the Prairie church relationships office, but there were not many of those.

An idea came to me, however. Since my 1973 tour to the Bible lands had been quite successful, I would offer another tour in the summer of 1975, just after concluding my service at Prairie. This time Judy would stay home with the children and I could potentially earn a good part of the money I would need for school tuition and living expenses. So I planned another 15-day tour, with a different travel company that allowed me to customize the tour as I desired. Of course we would spend a week in Israel, but we would also visit some countries new to me: Italy, Turkey, and Jordan. I was very excited about this coming opportunity.

Breaking Away

I remember the day I went to see the principal of Prairie. I think it was in the fall of 1974. I informed Mr. Rendall that I would be resigning from the faculty, to be effective June of 1975. I mentioned that there were three reasons for this decision, but the latter two were not of major importance, and would not, of themselves, lead to my decision.

I told him that my chief reason for leaving was that God was calling me to pursue studies toward a doctorate and there were no adequate options in western Canada. I said my decision was a matter of obedience to God's leading. I then mentioned my two additional reasons. One was that there was an atmosphere at Prairie that fostered a looking-down on the task of serious biblical and theological scholarship. This was not, as far as I could tell, a deliberately negative attitude. However, with Mr. Maxwell and many faculty having no more than a Bible school education themselves, there was little awareness of or appreciation for the world of evangelical scholarship and scholars. These scholars, I was learning, were diligently working from the Scriptures to address the serious issues of the day and the best ways to teach the Bible to their students to equip them to preach and teach on these issues. I mentioned to Mr. Rendall that this atmosphere was not encouraging for me or for students I knew who longed to develop their intellectual gifts as well as their Christian character and missionary zeal.

My final reason was that I found it extremely difficult to support my family on the small monthly allowance we were given. I emphasized that this would never, by itself, cause us to leave Prairie, because we knew that Prairie kept tuition costs extremely low only by the sacrificial living of the staff. God had always provided for us, and if we were called to stay at Prairie he would continue to provide. The principal, a naturally reserved man, probably offered a few words, but I cannot remember what they were.

To travel from Prairie to the eastern coast of the United States we would drive a small to medium-sized work truck with a large box built on the back and over the cab for storage. We would also be pulling a small two-wheeled trailer. I noted that the box was made from very heavy plywood and did not have dual rear wheels. The truck had 140,000 miles on it, and with our belongings (including all of my books—"dead weight" as they say) and the four of us on board, I wondered if the truck was overloaded.

I asked some friends at the Prairie garage who were auto mechanics about the load and they, after looking over the tires and the heavy load, said the weight should not be a problem. We would drive to Pennsylvania, unload, and stay briefly at my parents' house in Levittown until we found a place to rent near Princeton—not far across the Delaware River in New Jersey. As a favor to the owner of the truck who wanted to get it back East, we would drive it for him. In return we would have no moving expenses except gas for the truck. Or so we thought.

Ten Days on the Road

After nine very enjoyable years at Prairie—four as students and five as staff—and after saying our many goodbyes to dear friends, we rolled out onto the highway, and headed south. Just as when, after our marriage, we left Minnesota for Kansas City, and when we left Kansas City for Prairie, we were once again leaving with no debt but with little money. Our wallets were thin but our hearts were full with emotions: anticipation, gratitude, and a certain amount of apprehension on my part.

The whole process of preparing for further study, and with it our leaving a secure place we loved where our children could receive a free Christian education, and where I could have probably taught for the rest of my life, had been much on my mind over the past couple of years. It was on my mind as I drove along with the three most important people in the world sitting next to me. This was a major new phase of my grace quest and I was truly thankful that it was, above all else, *God's* grace quest, and that God was always seeking the best for his children.

Our trip, to put it mildly, was a major ordeal. As we covered the 2,400 miles we had four breakdowns and two near-breakdowns. We were overloaded—way overloaded. The weight and heat combined to blow a tire three different times, two of these on our first day of travel. Even after we unloaded about 1,000 pounds at a relative's home in Minnesota, we had a wheel bearing come apart, a bent axle, another blown tire, and troublesome radiator hoses.

It was in northern Illinois when we had the problem with the wheel bearing and the axle. The garage man told us that it would probably be a day and a half before the necessary parts would arrive from Michigan. Our family held hands in a back corner of the garage and asked God to help us. We had no money for a motel. A worker saw us and called a local church deacon who, with his fine Christian family, put us up for the night, washed our clothes, and fed us all very well. We were very thankful to God and to this family. Our two darling girls took it all in stride, and after ten days on the road (instead of the six we had planned) we pulled up to the curb on Ruby Lane.

It was good to see Mom, Dad, Rosemary, and Joe (Rosemary's husband). After we unloaded the truck and stacked our possessions in Mom and Dad's garage, I flew to Montreal to meet the tour group. Unfortunately there were only eight of us this time. While the sightseeing in the Bible lands was truly fascinating, as on the previous trip, I did not earn anything toward our coming tuition and living expenses. Actually, I lost money on the tour. A large part of our projected income, therefore, would not be realized. This, along with the unexpected truck repair bills during our drive from Alberta to Pennsylvania, left us with even thinner wallets than when we left Prairie.

A Beginning—and an Ending

The following six months—from July to December—were the most difficult time of my life since I had become a Christian thirteen years earlier. These months were stressful for me professionally, but also for the life of our family, each of us in a different way. There we were, living in my parents' home and trying to scrape enough together to pay one month's rent whenever we found a place to live. Our children, being only six and four, were grating on my dad's nerves with their playful antics (especially in the evenings) and very lively personalities. We knew we needed to move right away.

Because housing was too expensive in the Princeton area we rented the upstairs of a beaten-down house in Morrisville, Pennsylvania, just across the Delaware River from New Jersey, and not far from Princeton. We were adjacent to a small trailer park and had a bar next to us. The red neon light flashed "BAR" on and off until midnight or later. Our girls became friends with an affectionate mutt who roamed about the gravelly area. He had been hit (more than once, I think) by a car or cars and was blind in one eye, had a leg missing and had other problems as well. His name was Lucky! Judy and I did not think of ourselves as lucky or unlucky. Rather than luck, providence is the word that best describes God's individual care for his children. We knew God would always guide us and provide for us according to his infinite wisdom and grace.

We had brought no furniture with us, but Rosemary and Joe helped us get a few used items. Our bed was set up in the living room and the girls slept on foam pads in a bedroom. In the kitchen we had a Goodwill table and four chairs. We had little but we had one another. Even better, God had us.

Judy got an office job at a business near Princeton and I cared for the girls at home until we enrolled them in suitable schools. I began classes at Princeton Seminary after a consultation with my advisor, Dr. Metzger. He did not keep an office at the seminary, but worked out of his home close by. I met with him at the seminary. He was as pleasant and kind as Dr. Bruce, and I felt very privileged to sit in his classes and those of the other New Testament professors. I knew no one on my first day, but met a young man named Jim, a new PhD student in New Testament, and we quickly became good friends.

As the days went by, however, I found it more and more difficult to study, primarily because of money matters. Our financial situation, as well as difficulties with our youngest child's schooling, weighed heavily on my mind, so heavily that I knew our family circumstances had to change—very soon! I remember sitting in the seminary library at a small desk next to the window. I gazed outside at nothing in particular. My books were open but my thoughts were far from academic matters. I was thinking and praying with sadness filling my heart.

After Judy and I discussed and prayed much about our situation, I withdrew from school about one week after the start of classes. While this was extremely painful I knew it was the right course of action. If I withdrew early in the semester I would receive back most of the student loan money I had paid when I registered. I had hoped we would not need to borrow for tuition because we would have the income from the Bible lands tour. But God, who could have brought together a larger tour group, allowed a different set of circumstances.

Another major consideration was that I had no certainty of being accepted into the highly selective doctoral program even if I did very well during my time as a special student. For the current year my friend Jim was one of the four accepted and I was one of the 36 who was not. Next year there would probably be another 40 highly-qualified applicants. As I considered all of our circumstances together I concluded that God had led us across the continent for some reason other than to study at Princeton. We felt that we had been obedient in moving, but we needed to discern what we should do now. And we knew that each of us in the family was equally important to God.

Bleak Days

The days and weeks that followed my withdrawal from classes at Princeton were the bleakest I had ever experienced. To bring in some income, I worked part-time for Dad and part-time at a convenience store two or three nights a week, from 11:00 pm until 7:30 am. We had bought an old car that, to our chagrin, was costing us a lot of money in repairs, yet it was our only transportation. As soon as I arrived home from the night shift Judy would take the car and drive to her job. Because Laurie's preschool was costing more than we could afford we had to take her out of it. Judy and I traded off between our jobs, child care, and sleep.

At least we ate well. Since we qualified for food stamps and I often did the shopping, I had my eyes opened in a surprising way. The government gave us such an abundant supply of food stamps that I deliberately selected some items that we could never have afforded otherwise, just to use up our stamps. What we didn't use, we would lose. I still remember the glare in some customers' eyes as I went through the checkout line displaying our canned crab meat and frozen lobster as well as our food stamps. I was very uncomfortable and left the store as quickly as I could. I felt daggers in my back as I hustled out.

These were strange and difficult times and there were some days I was very low. There I was: a former pre-med student, a recipient of bachelor's and master's degrees, an ordained minister, a former pastor, a fledgling writer, a former Bible professor, and a leader of two Bible lands tours. But at the present time I was a husband and father on food stamps, living with my family in a fire trap (there was a fire in the lower level of the house while we lived there), and working the graveyard shift at the convenience store. And we were considerably in debt.

Without a doubt, the biggest question in my mind was not "Do you still love us God?" or "Why have you forsaken us?" but "Why, dear Lord, have you brought us all this way?" I had no doubts about God's goodness and mercy following me all the days of my life, but I was baffled about what to do next. I considered (briefly) quitting my work at the store and taking a full-time job—outdoors or indoors—wherever I could find decent pay. But I felt quite sure this was not the way to go.

I then did what I clearly did not want to do. I phoned the vice-principal at Prairie, Mr. Jack, explained our situation, and asked if he wanted me back on the faculty. After a short while I heard back from him and the answer was yes. He suggested, however, that we wait until the following summer to move because the courses had all been assigned for the present school year. I thanked him for his very supportive attitude and assured him that Judy and I would let him know our decision after we had discussed and prayed about the matter, and had the confidence that our returning to Prairie would not be taking the easy way out. We were grateful to have this option before us, even though we would still need to support the family until next summer.

Not the Way We Planned

In the midst of these bewildering days I renewed contact with one of my Bible professors, Dr. Glenn Goss, from Kansas City, one under whom I had served as a teaching assistant. He was now teaching at Philadelphia College of Bible and told me of a church in Flemington, New Jersey, that was look-ing for a pastor. Their previous pastor—a much-loved man—had been with this church for over 30 years until he retired. They now had been without a pastor for nine months. I contacted the church leadership and, due to Dr.

Goss's recommendation, I was invited to preach at the morning and evening services. The church was named Calvary Baptist Church and it was about 15 miles west of Princeton. They already had two or three others whom they were considering for the pastoral position.

Over the following weeks I preached several times at the Flemington church and then met with the pulpit committee, after which the committee voted to recommend me to the congregation as a candidate for pastor. Judy and I prayed that if God be pleased we would get a 90 percent vote of the congregation on the first ballot. On December 30 the church members invited us to come with a 90 percent vote. We accepted the call at the church's New Year's Eve service. In the midst of all these happenings, Rosemary and Joe had their first child—a handsome baby boy named Scott.

There was much to do. I first contacted Prairie and explained that we would not be coming next year. Judy and I then resigned from our jobs. We said goodbye to Lucky the dog. The church folks welcomed us warmly and graciously helped us move into the parsonage next door to the church. We enrolled Joni in her new school. Because the church leaders offered me a generous salary package, Judy would be able to be at home and give more attention to Joni (6 ½) and Laurie (4 1/2).

The four of us, especially Judy and I, were quite run down from the events of the past six months, but we praised God together for leading us to this new home, new church, new community, and new ministry. As just mentioned, the parishioners helped us move the 30 minutes from our Pennsylvania apartment to Flemington, across the Delaware River over the area where George Washington crossed the Delaware on Christmas Day. They were amazed at how little furniture we had, and generously helped us furnish the parsonage. I was 32 and a pastor once again, this time with no classes to study for, while, by God's grace, I shepherded the flock of God. This new direction was not the way we had planned, but we believed it was God's way for our family at this time.

This grace quest—God's and mine—underlay the turbulent events of the past year. This I firmly believed. But I just as firmly believed (by experience as well as head knowledge) that, even though the way of discipleship involved many bumps, twists, reversals, and conundrums, God's way was always the best way.

CHAPTER 9

A Pastor Once Again

Settling In

AFTER THE WHIRLWIND OF the previous year, our family was grateful to be settled again. I would never have thought, however, one year earlier while teaching in western Canada, that twelve months later I would find myself sitting at a pastor's desk on the east coast of the United States. It took some time for this fact to register in my mind and heart.

Flemington was a small, pleasant borough in north-central New Jersey, known mainly for two things: it was the county seat and it was a popular tourist destination—especially on weekends. There were cut glass and pottery industries, Flemington Furs, historic buildings, and many interesting shops. Calvary Baptist Church was situated on the south side of town, so we were not in the center of the flow of visitors.

Even though I still felt stunned by the events of the past year I desired to give every ounce of myself and my energy to the ministry of the church, after the needs of our family, and my own relationship with God. Fortunately, I enjoyed most aspects of pastoral ministry, and looked forward to walking from the parsonage to the church building each morning.

In a typical week I gave most of my time to the preparation of sermons (I preached both morning and evening on Sundays) and lessons (at times I taught an adult Sunday school class) and to the care of the people. By the latter I refer to such activities as visitation (in homes, hospitals, nursing homes, and sometimes at places of work), counseling (with individuals, engaged couples, and married couples), and discipleship with those who desired to be more effective in their service for Christ.

During my years as pastor the attendance was consistently good and the offerings were consistently very good. I did not wish to know, however, who gave what. All I saw on my desk, at the beginning of each new week, was one sheet of paper showing the amount given for the Missionary Fund, the amount given for the General Fund, and the sum of these two at the bottom of the page. The people were generous and cheerful givers.

My approach to preaching—including both substance and style—was to use the expository method. By this I refer to the preacher taking a passage of the Bible—perhaps two or three verses or maybe as much as 15–20 verses. The length is irrelevant, but the key factor is that the preacher looks at the text and the surrounding context as a whole, and then "exposes" the truth or truths in these verses in such a way that the treasures of the text emerge as a unified and practical word from the Lord.

I would try to construct my sermon around one central point from the Scripture text that would hold the listeners' concentrated attention as the sermon unfolded. Early in my ministry training I was taught to give my sermon like a rifle shot rather than a shotgun blast. A sermon scattered in many directions will not have the impact of a bullet striking the target: the mind, heart, and will of the person.

Because I had always believed in the value of preaching expositorily through whole books of the Bible—this being the best way to feed the sheep with a balanced diet of the Word—I began a Sunday morning series of sermons on the book of Genesis. I did not labor over every verse, but neither did I skim over any important part of the narrative.

Before the sermon, from the pulpit, I read the whole Scripture portion for the day, and skipped no verse or passage, even those that might cause some to feel uncomfortable. I even read publicly and preached from chapters 19, 34, and 38 (terrible chapters indeed) and I never received a single complaint from anyone in the congregation (or in other congregations where I later preached through Genesis).

I also preached through the books of 1 Corinthians (one-and-a-half years) and James (17 weeks). I enjoyed equally the preparation and the preaching. The highlight of my preaching career, as far as enjoying the preparation is concerned, was the two-year period during which I worked through the truly remarkable book of Genesis.

I look back at my high-school experience of reading Genesis, which I did just because I had read that all well-educated people were knowledgeable about the Bible as literature. At the age of 15 I pushed myself painfully to complete the book of Genesis. In my mid-thirties I reveled in reading and studying each section for the coming Sunday's sermon.

Tensions and Compromises

As in any church congregation there were tensions that rose to the surface from time to time. The most difficult one for me during my years as pastor in Flemington had to do with the Sunday morning worship service. After a year or so at the church I tried to change one aspect of the service that seemed to me to hinder the total worship experience. After I tried several times to communicate to those involved what I felt needed to be improved, I realized that I was getting nowhere, and that to push the matter further would lead to a serious break in the unity of the church.

I had not been asking for a major change in the service. It was a minor matter on the surface, but to me it had a major effect on the worship atmosphere. I was disappointed but believed that God was asking me to set aside my opinion for the sake of church unity. I continued, therefore, to come to church on Sunday mornings with the joy of the Lord as my strength. I refused to allow the problem to make me sour and discouraged as I worshipped God and preached the Word of the Lord.

Another area of tension had to do with changing the church constitution. I brought this up because I had been bothered by a certain inconsistency in the church covenant which had practical ramifications in the life of the church. It was not a major concern to me, as the previous issue was, but it did trouble me—not primarily because the covenant was inconsistent but because a certain requirement was not biblically mandated. I wanted to either change the wording or drop the phrase completely, but this received even more resistance than the previous issue. Again, I let go of the matter to keep the unity of the church.

In both of the problem areas just mentioned I felt then (and feel now) that God led me in the way of restraint. God's holding me back from insisting on my own way was, I believe, his producing in me the ninth fruit of the Spirit—self-control (Gal 5:23). I was grateful, for I never again wanted a "C" on my report card for this character trait.

If I did the right thing in these two matters, as I think I did, it was due to God's control of my emotions. I certainly felt anger rising within me concerning these issues, and I thank God even now for holding me back from expressing that anger, and for putting the matters at rest within me for the remainder of my years at the church.

Did I compromise on those issues? Of course I did. I followed a saying I heard many years ago: "Compromise is not [necessarily] a dirty word." In my early years as a Christian, whenever I heard the word "compromise" there was a negative connotation to it. To compromise was to be weak when one should be strong, and involved backing down on some clear biblical teaching regarding matters of doctrine or morality.

It is true, regrettably, that many individuals and organizations calling themselves "Christian" do compromise clear and essential teachings of the Scriptures. Such has been the case for centuries, even though Jesus and the New Testament writers repeatedly warned of this danger. But many compromises are good and necessary in moving forward with the program of God.

Sometimes it is difficult to know how, and even if, we should compromise on a given matter, but we may always be confident that God loves to hear and answer the prayers of a local assembly and its pastor for spiritual discernment.

Being young, idealistic, and full of energy I had other ideas for the overall improvement of our church along New Testament lines. I was especially concerned that I not be thought of as the all-purpose leader of the church, wearing simultaneously the hats of preacher, teacher, administrator, counselor, visitation pastor, and innovator/director of new initiatives.

My understanding of spiritual gifts was that these special abilities were given by God to his people for the good of the whole church, and that no one person—senior pastor or otherwise—could possibly have them all. It frustrated me, and at times exhausted me, to try and wear numerous different hats that some of the people expected their pastor to wear all at the same time.

Because of my concern regarding this matter I preached on spiritual gifts and tried to explain to the church board members why I needed their partnership—as co-elders with me—in doing the work of the ministry. I also introduced to the board other aspects of the "body life" concept of the local church that I felt were more in line with the teachings and practices of the early church than the traditional model of one full-time paid pastor trying to do everything.

My ideas resonated with some of the leaders but not with all. Reluctantly, and with considerable disappointment, I let these matters drop in the interest of church unity, and after one-and-a-half years as pastor I had reached the peak of my frustration. I cannot put the blame on "obstinate" church leaders, however, because I don't think I did a very good job of leadership. I did not have training in this aspect of pastoral life: how to work with lay church leaders and effect change in a collaborative way to become more effective and fruitful shepherds of the flock.

The Saving Decision

By this time in my pastorate at Calvary Baptist I faced a decision. I could continue to bang my head against the wall (figuratively) and try to influence the church leaders to change in ways that I believed were necessary, and likely face resistance and opposition that increased my frustration, or I could choose a very different course. Few—if any—in the church would be aware of any difference, no matter which decision I made. But I would know in a big way—in my heart and soul.

After much prayer and thought I chose a course concerning which I said nothing to anyone in the church. I decided to continue giving myself fully in ministry to this fine congregation and community, but without trying to change anything through formal, official means. Certain church leaders had their entrenched ways of doing things, so I gave up any expectations of bringing about structural change. These leaders were consistent Christians who seemed to love God as I did, but we did not see things in the same way.

My decision, however, was much more than a negative stance toward structural change. Actually, it was a positive, life-giving approach to my ministry that I believed (and still believe) was for the health of the church body at that time, and my personal health and joy.

In brief, I would concentrate my ministry in those areas where I felt best equipped by God, and therefore able to serve the people joyfully as I worked within the organizational structure of the church as best I could.

Was this an unwise compromise? In my view, not at all. I was convinced that no one should serve as a pastor without deep joy in the Lord. A joyful, contented, and consistent shepherd will have a flock that is contented, healthy, secure, and eager for new pastures. This was the kind of shepherd I desired to be, but I knew it would only be possible by the every-moment grace of God and not by my knowledge, cleverness, or human effort, no matter how determined I might be.

Something happened within me after I set this new course for my pastoral ministry in Flemington. My previous (self-imposed) burden to change the church in external ways had now been lifted. The heavy weight of wearing so many hats was lighter, because I now focused primarily on preaching, visitation, and counseling/discipleship with individuals, and marriages. Since I no longer felt responsible to be the agent of formal change, the burden of administration became much lighter. I felt a new freedom and enjoyment in my life and service for God.

Good Times

The church was very good to me and our family. Here we were, Judy and I in our mid-thirties, for the first time in our marriage having money for "discretionary spending." Among several benefits, the people gave us a 30-day paid vacation every year. One summer our family of four enjoyed a transcontinental camping trip from New Jersey to California and back, driving a southerly route going west, and a northerly route returning east. We were able to visit with family and friends along the way, with the highlight being a week spent in the very small but delightful home of Judy's parents and siblings in the mountains northeast of San Diego (they had moved there from Minnesota eight years earlier).

We drove a blue station wagon with a back seat that folded down, exposing a good-sized carpeted area on which Joni and Laurie played as we drove along (there were no seatbelt laws in those days, and I don't think our station wagon was even equipped with seat belts). Our tent, sleeping bags, camp stove, and everything needed for each overnight was bundled in a tarp on top of the station wagon.

I had been planning this trip for a year and my childhood longing for adventure—especially travel to far-away places and experiences—was still a very big part of me. Our journey was highly enjoyable and beneficial for each of us, and we rejoiced and praised God when we rolled into our driveway a month later. It was quite a contrast between, on the one hand, thinking back over our sightseeing at such places as Carlsbad Caverns and Yellowstone National Park and, on the other hand, remembering the first few days at the beginning of each elementary school year when I had no special summer activities to report on in class.

I will never forget this trip, and I look back upon it as a gracious gift from the Lord who made it possible at that time in my life to function as a vital link in his grace quest. He used this journey to bring me closer to himself and to the life of true spirituality that he desired and I desired. There was no one spiritual high-point for me on the trip but rather a daily sense of gratitude throughout the whole adventure. And gratitude, I have learned over the course of my life, is a transforming virtue.

I returned to my pastoral responsibilities with enthusiasm and, as mentioned earlier, with a new outlook on my part in the life of the church. I was free to concentrate on the twofold advice that I gave to students beginning their first pastorates: "Preach the Word and love the people."

I was always encouraged by the responses to my sermons. Some of the folks, probably out of obligation or custom, shook my hand and said nice things (such as "thank you" or "good talk") on the way out of the church, but others had obviously been affected for good and wanted to tell me about it.

In my years at Calvary Baptist I received only a couple of complaints about my preaching, and these were in the form of requests to be a little less academic in my sermons. One person, for example, early in my pastorate, asked if I would stop using the overhead projector in Sunday morning sermons. I thought it was a helpful teaching tool, but for some it was a distraction. I stopped using it but felt irritated at the request.

Now, many years later, I agree with the thought behind the appeal. I now believe, as this parishioner indicated, that much can happen during a sermon when the people can see the preacher's face clearly and without distraction. The sincerity, intensity, compassion, and seriousness on the preacher's face (and his or her body language generally) may communicate as much as the words themselves. Almost all of my preaching since this incident has been deliberately without technology.

The highlights for me as a pastor were when men, women, boys, and girls received Jesus Christ as Lord and Savior, when people (these recent converts and others) were baptized, and when believers grew cognitively and volitionally in their lives of discipleship. Nothing can compare (at least for me) with the deep joy and satisfaction of seeing people moving steadily and seriously toward the fulfilling of the Great Commission ("Go into all the world . . . .") in the spirit of the Great Commandment ("Love the Lord your God with all your heart and with all your soul and with all your mind and with all your strength, [and] love your neighbor as yourself").

Living in north central New Jersey had certain advantages. Our family enjoyed New York City, especially lower and midtown Manhattan. We went to the Jersey shore for swimming and boardwalk games. We attended the free "Plays in the Park" productions in northern New Jersey, just across the river from Manhattan, where Broadway actors and others donated their time and talents to put on some excellent plays on beautiful summer evenings under the stars. And we took sightseeing trips to Philadelphia, Washington DC, Boston, and Niagara Falls, and spent several summer vacations in Maine, close to the ocean, due to the kindness of one of the dear church families.

CHAPTER 10

Pastoral and Personal Concerns

Stirrings

THE UNCEASING QUEST OF God as he taught and led me daily aroused in me, regularly, my own quest. And, even though life in Flemington was good and the church was healthy, I could not forget the reason we had made such a major decision as that of leaving our home in Canada. I continued to hear God's call within me to pursue a doctorate in order to return to teaching at the college or seminary level.

I felt blocked, however, by the same set of issues at work in my involvement with Princeton Seminary. And I must admit to some times of great discouragement while shepherding the flock in Flemington because of this major concern in my heart and mind. Even now as I write, over 35 years later, I recall vividly how low in spirit I was at times. I also recall, however, God's remarkable, sustaining grace during this time. He gave me his joy, and the joy of the Lord truly was my strength.

I trust that my lowness of spirit in some of my personal times did not hinder my effectiveness in my pastoral ministry. I am very grateful that, though I sometimes felt cast down, I sensed at these very times God's grace giving me buoyancy and the will to serve the people well. In fact, I even came to the point of saying to God that I was willing to serve this congregation for the rest of my life if he so desired.

I had become involved in some activities outside of church and home. For example, I was active in the Evangelical Theological Society and read papers at some of the meetings, and spent a day in research and contemplation at the Princeton Seminary library several times a year. As to my burden regarding how best to use my gifts to serve in the coming years, I handed this over to God repeatedly.

Mental Gymnastics

I have written enthusiastically that the preaching of God's Word gave me great satisfaction. However, toward the end of my second year as pastor, there was a crisis coming—another crisis—and I knew I had to face it soon.

As I stood at the pulpit preaching I was always aware of the possibility that some in attendance might not be true followers of Jesus Christ. In light of this I always—at some time during the sermon—explained in brief the message of the Bible that everyone is sinful and needs to respond to God's invitation to come to him through the cross of Jesus Christ, to be saved for time and eternity. I always—not necessarily at the end of the service—included a plea to those present who had never received Christ in true repentance and faith to "receive him now—today!"

But I had a problem, and it was growing worse every Sunday. Basically, it had to do with my telling the truth. When I urged people to "come to Christ today," whether they were regular attenders or visitors, I would also emphasize that God was reaching out to them and to all people to bring them by his grace into his spiritual family. God longs for everyone to be saved, I said.

My difficulty was that I was becoming more and more aware of a contradiction in my mind between this open invitation to come to Christ and the idea that everyone—before his or her birth—has been predestined to go either to heaven or hell, and nothing can change God's sovereign decree.

The latter view, which has come to be known as the Calvinistic or Reformed view of salvation, is in contrast with the Arminian or Wesleyan view that I was preaching. My issue was that I regarded myself as a Calvinist, because I felt that Calvinism was what the Bible taught, yet I was preaching as an Arminian. The tension within me was becoming unbearable. I knew I needed to present the truth of the Bible consistently, no matter what the consequences would be. Yet, what was the truth?

When I came to the church as a pastor I did not have this problem. I was a Calvinist, but a reluctant one, because the "horrible decree" (John Calvin's own words) of unconditional predestination was extremely difficult to accept, both in my mind and in my heart. Yet I was determined to be faithful to God's Word. God's ways were just and good, and his wisdom was past finding out.

When I offered an invitation on Sunday mornings before my conversion from Calvinism to Arminianism, I would qualify my words enough so that they did not contradict my Reformed theology. "I urge you, if you sense God working in your heart right now, drawing you to himself, then come to him in repentance and faith to receive his gift of salvation. God will not turn away anyone who comes to him." Of course, in my mind, I assured myself that my words were true and biblical because the only ones who would come to God were those who had been predestined to do so. They and they alone are given true repentance and saving faith. So my words in themselves were true, but I felt insincere by leaving out the huge Calvinistic qualifications.

As time progressed I felt I could no longer perform these mental gymnastics on Sunday mornings. I began to study in a fresh, new way the biblical teachings on how people come to Christ. I studied the major Scriptures that seemed to support Calvinism and the major Scriptures that seemed to support Arminianism. Gradually I was returning to the Arminian view that I had held for my first several years as a new Christian. And I was becoming more and more excited about this renewed theology that was fitting together harmoniously and biblically. I no longer felt discomfort while I was inviting people to come to Christ.[1]

Even though the church congregation had no idea of these struggles, I felt a freshness and a freedom as I preached, counseled, served, and lived daily. While I had then and have now numerous Calvinistic friends—ones I have deeply respected for many years—I knew that I must preach the Scriptures as they unfolded to me.

God does not expect us—whether Calvinists or Arminians—to devise a flawless theological system with no loose ends, no questions unanswered, and no elements of mystery. But he does ask us to study his Word with diligence, attention to both the grand narrative and the details, open-minded attention to other views, honesty, humility, and eagerness to believe and obey what we are finding. He also asks us to love and respect all people, including those with whom we disagree on predestination and the universal salvific will of God.

---

1. One work that confirmed me greatly in my return to Arminianism is *Grace Unlimited*, edited by Clark H. Pinnock (Minneapolis, MN: Bethany, 1975). The chapters by Pinnock, Jack Cottrell, I. Howard Marshall, and James D. Strauss helped me most.

Heartache

My father and mother separated and sold their house on Ruby Lane soon after our move back to the States. Mom moved into an apartment in Penndel and Dad, in time, moved to Chambersburg, Pennsylvania, and then to Tucson, Arizona. They never divorced, but as far as I know never saw each other again after their separation.

Because we lived only about 30 minutes from Mom, Rosemary, Joe, and their children, we were able to visit with them from time to time. From this point on, however, especially after Dad moved to Chambersburg, we saw Dad only occasionally for the rest of his life, and it was only when we made the trip to visit him. He spent the last 14 years of his life in Tucson.

One of the greatest heartaches of my life had to do with my relationship to Dad after he and Mom separated. My heartache had nothing to do with their breakup, however, but grew out of the phone conversations Dad and I had regularly, usually about every other Saturday morning.

I would call and ask him about his everyday life, and before long he would bring up the Bible and his beliefs, as well as the "rotten" condition of the world and local churches. I mostly listened to his thoughts because he (almost always) had to be the one speaking. Few people were willing to listen to him for long, especially since his way of "discussing" was basically *telling* others what he believed—in a very forceful manner. He did this with me also, but he was my father and I was used to his way of speaking.

I listened to his statements and at times made a brief comment of affirmation or asked a question. This worked fine for my earlier period in the pastorate at Flemington, but as time went by Dad started asking me if I agreed with him on this or that point. Where I could agree I said yes, and often supported him with a Scripture verse or two that reinforced his idea. Where I could only partially agree I tried to emphasize the truths on which we thought the same and tried to soften my disagreements with him on the other matters, often saying (because I believed it) that he might be right and my ideas may be wrong. I tried to follow what the book of Proverbs suggests: "a gentle answer turns away wrath (Prov 15:1)."

There were some issues, however, on which I simply could not agree with Dad, and with these I tried to evade giving a straight answer. As time went by I felt more and more uncomfortable stepping around the elephant in the living room, trying to pretend it was not there.

The biggest elephant that stood in the midst of every conversation—the one that seemed to be getting bigger and more restless each time—was the topic of unconditional predestination. In Dad's Calvinistic view the Bible clearly teaches that, before the creation of the world, God chose every person who ever lived or will ever live to experience either eternal blessedness in heaven or eternal damnation in hell. God was completely sovereign in this selection process, and there was not the slightest element of foreseen good or evil in the predestined individual. Some were selected (elected) for unending happiness and some were selected (reprobated) for unending suffering. This eternal decree encompassed every man, woman, and child, including unborn babies and mentally disabled infants and adults.

This divine plan, Dad believed, was clearly taught in the Bible. The idea of a person "choosing" by "free will" to receive Christ's gift of salvation was, in Dad's view, a false teaching, because it gives the glory to man instead of to God. Dad held that salvation cannot be freely given by God (that is, it cannot truly be by grace) if a person has any choice in the matter. Such "choice" would then be a human work, and the Bible teaches that we are saved by grace alone, not by works. The "free-will disease" had poisoned the church of Jesus Christ horribly, and Dad hated it.

I finally came out and told Dad I no longer believed in his idea of absolute predestination. He exploded (roared) over the phone with alarm at the deception I had come to believe. I had no doubt that Dad sincerely believed that his doctrine was plainly taught in the Bible, and that the free-will position was not. (As written earlier, I also had sincerely believed in a similar way.) But as I listened to Dad carefully when he spoke (always forcefully and without compromise), I noticed two other factors that were subtly at work, apart from what he thought was straightforward Bible teaching.

First, because he saw himself—especially before his conversion—as such a "filthy sinner" he believed strongly that he had absolutely nothing to do with his salvation. He felt that it would be boasting to attribute his rebirth to himself in any way. He was a very, very grateful man, and when he sang "Amazing Grace" ("that saved a wretch like me") he sang so loudly and sincerely that he appeared to be already transported to eternal glory.

The other matter I noticed (subjectively, I acknowledge) was that he reveled in the amazing fact that God chose *him*. God wanted *him*. God had a personal interest in *him*. This choice by the God of the universe contrasted sharply with his childhood experience in which neither his mother nor father seemed to want him—at least not enough for him to live with them. I believe he so badly wanted to be wanted, to be chosen, that he interpreted the Scriptures on predestination the way he did. He did not realize, however, the contradiction in his thinking. In his mind he believed that God elected preborn individuals completely apart from any foreseen good or bad in the person. In other words, God was completely arbitrary in his choice. Yet in his heart (as he told me one time) he felt that God must have "seen something" in him to choose him. This would allow Dad to take some credit for being elected—an idea Dad would strongly reject. I never pointed out this contradiction to him, even though it seriously undermined his whole theology of salvation.

As time went by and Dad regularly expressed his astonishment and disappointment in me for not agreeing with him on this matter, I knew that I had to make a very difficult choice. What to him was a healthy argument over the issues was to me a deeply upsetting experience, because he never learned how to debate an issue calmly and with respect for the opposing view.

Because he became so loud and dominant when I phoned, and this reminded me very painfully of his former arguing style with Mom and sometimes with me, I told Dad that I would no longer enter into discussion with him on the predestination issue. I think I also said the same thing concerning any issue we disagreed strongly on. I would have been glad to discuss any topic at all with him, but I would not let myself be exposed regularly to his strongly argumentative tone and volume.

Dad was never unkind, but his passion for certain topics was so overwhelming to me that I felt battered and bludgeoned after every phone call unless I agreed totally with him. Our last discussion of a vigorous nature took place about 1978, and for the next 22 years—until Dad died in 2000—I had mostly shallow conversations with him. The subject matter that excited both Dad and me more than any other in the world—the character of God and his amazing revelation in the Bible—was no longer a significant part of our conversations.

This was my decision, not his. He would have argued about any issue in the Bible every day of his life if he had someone to argue with. But for my psychological health I made the decision I did. It was his forcefulness (which often came across to me as anger), not the issue under discussion, that troubled me so deeply. I had tried to bring up a variety of topics in the Scriptures that I felt we could talk about in a mutually encouraging manner, but his way of seeing the Scriptures on the subject always had to prevail. So I stayed away from, or lightly touched on, or stopped talking about many issues that were very important to each of us personally.

For the last quarter of his life on earth Dad and I discussed very little that really mattered. This has been one of the greatest heartaches of my life, but I look forward to many delightful conversations with Dad in glory, when we both shall be like Christ.

Some Awkward Experiences

I continued serving God by preaching the Word and loving the people. However, I did not do everything right. After I had been pastor for a year or so a young couple came to me and said that they would no longer be serving as (volunteer) youth leaders. When I asked why, they answered that I never seemed to show any interest in them or the youth program. I had never asked how the youth group was doing, nor had I ever taken part in any of the youth activities.

They were, sad to say, correct. Because I had never heard any complaints about them or the youth program I simply assumed all was well. I apologized to them and thanked them sincerely for their service. I have shaken my head sadly over the years, wondering how I could have been so negligent and unappreciative. They were fine Christian people.

I can remember only one time when someone disagreed with a specific point in one of my sermons, although there surely were other instances unknown to me. I was preaching expositorily through Paul's first epistle to the Corinthians, paying close attention to every section of Paul's letter. When I came to chapter seven, verses 10–16, I preached on marriage, separation, and divorce. After carefully studying the topic in depth for years I had come to the conclusion that, while God's design for marriage was a lifelong union, there were cases (as with repeated adultery, desertion, or serious abuse of a partner or children) when divorce was the right step to take, and the one divorcing the offending partner was not guilty of sin for doing so.

A certain couple (not church members, but uninvolved folks who always sat as close to the back door as possible) strongly disagreed, although I did not know it at the time. They stopped attending church after that Sunday. When I contacted them after several weeks the man told me he could not possibly sit under the preaching of a pastor who believed that divorce could ever be a right decision. I suppose (I hope) he would have allowed legal separation in extreme cases, even if not legal divorce. I told him I was sorry that he would no longer be coming to our church, and I wished him and his wife well. I had no hard feelings toward them and no feelings of regret about my position on this topic.

Overall, the church folks were very understanding and supportive, and we had a lot of good times together. One Sunday morning during a time of baptisms I was standing in the water-filled baptistery next to a young man who had recently received Jesus Christ. I had come to know him well, and just before I lowered him (head and body) into the water I said, "It's been good knowing you, Hugh." The congregation erupted into laughter and it took me a second or two to understand why. When the time of mirth passed I immersed him and all was well. He emerged alive.

I remember one Sunday morning service above all others. While I was preaching I noticed an unfamiliar face in the congregation. A man was sitting by the center aisle next to a woman whom I assumed (rightly, I learned) was his wife. The man's face stood out to me, partly because it seemed somehow larger and brighter than the faces around him and partly because he smiled a lot, actually beaming, looking straight at me.

After the service as I was mingling with the people, I saw this couple and started to shake the man's hand. As I looked closely at him, he had a big grin on his face. To my astonishment he was the former pastor of the small independent church through which Dad and I came to Christ—the man I had gone to visit on Thanksgiving morning years before. He and his wife had driven by a while ago and saw my name on the church sign, with times of Sunday services.

While we were glad to see one another after some 15 or 16 years, there was a certain awkwardness because of his affair. It was on my mind and I suppose it was on his mind also. He and his wife and I chatted a bit in the church foyer and then they were gone. I had wished to bring some closure to our relationship. I especially wanted to know if he had repented of his sin and asked the congregation for forgiveness, but he was gone before I could raise those issues. I have never heard from him after that Sunday meeting.

One day Judy and I felt we should drive to New York City to visit a relative, one with a very troubled life. We had no phone number for him but we did have an address. We drove through the Holland Tunnel onto the island of Manhattan, parking our car on the street in front of his apartment building. I was hesitant to park there because this was the Lower East Side— the roughest, most drug-infested, poorest, and most crime-ridden section of the city.

Judy and I climbed the narrow wooden stairs (about ten flights) and located his room. The door was wide open and every light in the apartment—at least those we could see—was on, all with bare bulbs. It was daytime. We knocked and called his name several times, but there was no answer. We asked someone in the hallway if they had seen our relative and were told that he had been there just a short while before. We stepped inside the apartment and called his name again. We saw no one, but the bathtub was filled with grey, dirty water, and a squashed cockroach was stuck to the kitchen wall. Every burner on the gas range was flaming.

We lingered a while and wrote a note to him saying that we had visited. We then left with sadness in our hearts. Some years later we heard that he had been found dead on the grounds of a hospital for the mentally ill in southern California. We had wanted to talk with him about Jesus Christ the Savior and Good Shepherd, but we did not have that opportunity. Our confidence, however, was in the mighty truth of Genesis 18:25: "Will not the Judge of all the earth do right?"

The Door Opens at Last

Ever since my crisis experience a year-and-a-half into the pastorate, I had been praying about and investigating options for a PhD program. I still could not get away from the call of God to pursue a doctorate so that I could teach in a college or seminary where both academic rigor and hearty spirituality were emphasized. I felt that my gifting from God was much better suited to the classroom than to the local church.

During my years as pastor I kept meeting those who were students at or recent graduates of nearby Drew University. Thirty-seven miles north of Flemington, Drew was a private institution sponsored by the United Methodist Church, consisting of the College of Liberal Arts, the Theological Seminary, and the Graduate School, that offered a variety of masters and doctoral degrees. Because my academic interests had been shifting from biblical studies to theology and ethics, I was most interested in the PhD program in Theological and Religious Studies. After hearing a steady stream of positive remarks about the Drew Graduate School, and knowing of its solid academic reputation, I applied to the program in Theological and Religious Studies in the fall of 1979, to begin doctoral work in the fall of 1980.

Because of my experience with Princeton—the only other doctoral program to which I had applied—I had considerable apprehension and doubt concerning the likelihood that I would be accepted. The same issues that stood in the way of my entrance into Princeton would be evident to Drew's graduate admissions officers as well. The only optimism within me regarding acceptance came from my deep assurance that God is supremely powerful and wise, and does only what is good and right for his children who desire his will alone. In my better moments I knew God would do what is best, not only for me but for Judy, Joni, and Laurie.

Finally, in February of 1980, I received a letter of acceptance into Drew's PhD program in Theological and Religious Studies. I was elated and very, very thankful to God. This had been a major yet elusive part of my quest for spirituality, and now God had opened the door. I re-read the acceptance letter several times.

Soon after receiving the letter I informed the leadership at Calvary Baptist that I would be resigning the pastorate as of August 31. I said that we would continue living in the Flemington area because to rent in Madison, where Drew was located, would be a lot more expensive.

In addition, I told them that our family would become involved with a different church after I concluded my service as pastor. They were surprised to hear this and asked me why. I replied that, according to the guidelines I had always been told, pastors should make a clean break with churches from which they resign. This keeps the church people from looking to the former pastor instead of to the new one for guidance, weddings, funeral services, and the operation of the church. It would also keep the former pastor from the temptation to comment about the new pastor's sermons or leadership style. Overall, the former pastor's presence in church services and activities would surely be a hindrance to the health of the church, and possibly to the new pastor.

The church leaders did not agree with such a policy. They saw no reason why I should not stay and worship at Calvary Baptist, since we would continue to be in Flemington. In fact, they said the church people would be offended if our family left the church. After considering these matters, Judy and I felt we should stay at Calvary. We loved the people, our children loved the people, and I would be so engrossed in my studies that I would have no time (nor interest) for meddling in church affairs.

The congregation had a delightful celebration for us as we all reviewed the past five years and looked to the future. I started classes in September and Judy continued her (now full-time) job as office manager of a local business, where she had been working part-time for the past two years. The church trustees graciously allowed us to live rent-free in the parsonage until the new pastor and his family moved it. This turned out to be about six months after I concluded my pastoral ministry, at which time we moved to a pleasant two-bedroom apartment at the north end of town.

During the five years I worked on my doctorate neither I nor the church people had any difficulties with my presence and involvement in their midst, at least there were none that I knew of. The church had been, and continued to be, a good place for our family, and we all enjoyed the vibrant fellowship.

Perhaps because I was now a full-time student who grew a full beard (it was the fashion among male doctoral students), and our family sat toward the rear of the church at services, I blended right in with the congregation. We continued our giving to Calvary, supported the new pastor and his family, and participated in the Tuesday evening prayer meeting as often as we could. We attended congregational meetings (since we were members) and I preached from time to time when the pastor asked me.

CHAPTER 11

Doctoral Studies and So Much More

Digging In

IN THE FALL OF 1980, at the age of 36, I began my doctoral studies, and in the spring of 1985 I received my Doctor of Philosophy degree. These years were, as I had expected, the most rigorous time of study I had ever experienced. The difficulties had to do not only with the quantity of work (reading, research, writing papers, preparing for intense class interactions) but also (and especially) the quality. After the first week of classes I knew that I had taken a significant leap into the brave new world of advanced synthesis and analysis. I loved the studies, even though the work-load seemed at times overwhelming.

Because I had passed the required exams in reading theological German and theological French before the start of classes, and because I was attending classes full-time, I was able to complete the course work in two years. I concentrated my studies in historical theology and historical ethics and, even though Drew was by no means a conservative university, I had very good—actually enjoyable—relationships with the faculty members under whom I studied.

I felt blessed to have some strong Christian classmates in my courses and even some professors who desired to be faithful disciples of Jesus Christ. Not once did I feel pressure to compromise my evangelical convictions. I reveled and prospered in the atmosphere of open inquiry, the mutual respect between students and faculty, and the camaraderie among students.

After completing the course work I spent eight weeks preparing for the comprehensive (qualifying) exams. These exams were offered in August and January. Some students took a whole year to study for them, but I knew I should sit for the exams as soon as I could, in August, while I was in a full-study mode and much of the material was fresh in my mind.

Students in my area of study were to select their examination topics from four categories—one topic from each category. We needed to choose one historical period, such as Medieval, Reformation, or Enlightenment and Modern. I chose the Patristic era and was expected to know everything (major figures, background, literature, and especially theological developments) from the second to the eighth centuries. Next we were to choose one theological/philosophical topic and the major thinkers and ideas in this subject from pre-Christian times to the present. I chose the problem of suffering and evil, covering such topics as how evil came to be, why a perfectly good and powerful deity would allow evil and suffering, and whether the existence of horrifying evil and suffering throughout human history disproves the existence of God. The above two exams were eight hours long, and consisted of about five or six questions each. They were written exams, not orals.

The other two exams (four hours each, also with five or six questions per exam) had to do with two major historical figures who wrote significantly and sufficiently in theological and religious matters to provide a body of material to master. The only stipulations were that neither figure could be from the historical period I chose, nor could the two figures be from the same period. I chose John Calvin and John Wesley primarily because of the way their writings had affected me personally, rather than the fact that they were highly influential in Christian thought and history.

Two months after I took the comprehensive exams my mother died from cancer. She was almost 72. Rosemary cared for her very lovingly and unselfishly during the years preceding her departure from this life, especially as the disease worsened and our mother moved into a nearby nursing home. Rosemary deserved a gold medal.

Something remarkable happened about a month before Mom died: the cleaning woman for Mom's room in the nursing home led my mother to a personal relationship with Jesus Christ. After a lifetime of trusting in the rules and rituals of her church she came to know and trust her Lord and Savior personally. She then understood—both in her head and in her heart—the simplicity of the Gospel that Dad, Rosemary, and I had received from the gracious and merciful hand of God. Mom had always been a kind, honest, and troubled person, and now she was at peace.

Grace and John Wesley

The only remaining requirement for the PhD was to write an original dissertation and to defend it in an oral exam before the three faculty members who served as my dissertation committee. The other graduate school faculty and students were also invited to attend my defense and to question me as well. Researching and writing the dissertation occupied two-and-a-half years—longer than all of the other requirements combined. I gave much of that time, however, to other concerns: interim pastoral ministries, writing for publications, working as an auditor of school board and county accounts, serving as one of the teaching assistants for the Drew Seminary Dean, Dr. Thomas W. Ogletree, and searching for a teaching position after graduation.

My dissertation was titled "The Concept of Grace in the Ethics of John Wesley." Preparing it was an arduous task, but I would choose the same topic again without hesitation if I had the same requirement before me now. My dissertation director, a highly-regarded ethicist named Dr. Edward L. Long Jr., was helpful and pleasant to work under.

Why did I choose this topic? First, Wesley's life and teachings had affected me more than those of anyone throughout history other than Jesus of Nazareth. I loved his clear, Scripture-infused mind as well as his bold, disciplined, and unselfish manner of living and ministering. I longed to research more.

Second, my personal intellectual pilgrimage had been steadily advancing in the direction of Christian ethics—historical as well as contemporary. I had travelled from biblical studies to theology and now to ethics, holding closely to the first two as I explored the third. Since ethics has to do with one's everyday life and experiences in the real world, and everything about Wesley was decidedly pragmatic, my interests in both Wesley and ethics could come together nicely in answering some real-world concerns (I focused on the natural order and the political order).

Third, since "The Ethics of John Wesley" was still far too broad for a dissertation subject, I narrowed my focus to the one concept in Wesley's thought that affected me the most: the grace of God.

For all of my Christian life until I discovered Wesley I had only a partial understanding of grace. From what I had been taught and gleaned from numerous readings and sermons, I considered grace to be the unmerited favor of God expressed toward people, based on the all-sufficient and finished work of Jesus Christ on the cross.

The key thought to me was that God's favor is totally unmerited. Absolutely nothing we are in ourselves or can do on our own can earn God's favor. He loves us freely and gives us eternal salvation apart from any works.

As the apostle Paul writes, "For it is by grace you have been saved, through faith—and this is not from yourselves, it is the gift of God—not by works, so that no one can boast" (Eph 2:8–9).

I understood that truth and reveled in it. It had dramatically and eternally changed my life at the age of 19. But I increasingly sensed that there was more to grace than God's favor and mercy leading us to glory. When I started studying Wesley's sermons, letters, and essays, I saw a major facet of grace in the New Testament that I had been missing. Grace is not only God's unmerited favor toward his people, but also his actual strength, energy, and power flowing from him to us and in us, accomplishing his will in our lives and through our lives.

We are not only redeemed by grace through faith; we live and serve God and our earthly brothers and sisters by grace through faith. I saw this clearly in 2 Corinthians 12:9, where God speaks: "My grace is sufficient for you, for my power is made perfect in weakness." Here, "grace" and "power" seem to be equated. The writer of the book of Hebrews conceives of grace in a similar way: "Let us then approach God's throne of grace with confidence, so that we may receive mercy and find grace to help us in our time of need" (Heb 4:16). Here, from the throne of grace, flows both mercy (loving-kindness and favor) and grace (God's energy at work to help us). In the words of John Wesley:

> As soon as ever the grace of God (in the former sense, his pardoning love) is manifested to our soul, the grace of God (in the latter sense, the power of his Spirit) takes place therein. And now we can perform, through God, what to man was impossible.[1]

In this quotation I saw another great truth that added to my growing excitement about grace: the grace of God, especially as divine power, is in John Wesley's writings so closely linked with the workings of the Holy Spirit in a person's life that the power *of* God's Spirit sometimes becomes virtually indistinguishable from the power *which is* God's Spirit.[2]

The discovery of these truths about grace as the personal Holy Spirit indwelling me, and indwelling all of God's people, filled me with a deep sense of truth and hope concerning my struggles to live the victorious "higher life" I had heard about years before as a new believer sitting with the other students in the Prairie Tabernacle.

---

1. "The Witness of Our Own Spirit," Sermon 12 in *The Works of John Wesley, Volume 1, SERMONS I, 1–33*), edited by Albert C. Outler (Nashville, TN: Abingdon, 1984), 309.

2. Robert Vincent Rakestraw, "The Concept of Grace in the Ethics of John Wesley." PhD dissertation (Madison, NJ: Drew University, 1985), 138–43.

My discovery, in time, also gave me clarity and some optimism concerning the state of the world and the ways God's Spirit may work to bring about desperately needed reformation of the social order, the political order, and the natural order, and to bring about especially real and lasting spiritual revival.

The Quest and the Blessed Crisis

The highlight of doctoral work for me was not the course work, nor the comprehensive exams, nor the dissertation, but a very personal experience related to my never-ending quest for spirituality. I had never been seeking spirituality for its own sake, as a "thing" to possess or be possessed by, but so that I would be a useful servant of God, "full of the Holy Spirit" as Stephen (Acts 7:55). "Being spiritual" seemed to be synonymous with being holy, godly, mature in Christ, filled with the fruit of the Spirit (Gal 5:22–23; 1 Cor 2:15; 3:1), and united with the Lord so as to become "one with him in Spirit" (1 Cor 6:17).

I had been struck again by Galatians 6:1, which speaks of "you who are spiritual." These were the ones who, in God's eyes (and Paul's), should gently restore the Christian who had fallen into sin. I longed to be one who is spiritual because this was God's will for every one of his children. It was not optional. It seemed to me that all those who called themselves "Christians" needed to seek true biblical spirituality in order to worship God "in spirit and in truth" (John 4:23–24) and to be of genuine help to those in need. I deeply desired God to produce in me "the mind controlled by the Spirit," of which Paul said "is life and peace" (Rom 8:6).

For my first 20 years as a follower of Jesus Christ I experienced some times of spiritual success and some times of spiritual defeat. Fortunately, the latter did not dominate but they did trouble my mind and soul.

From the time God revealed to me his way to salvation by grace through faith, in 1962, I was searching for the highly elusive (to me) truth about the way to live the remarkable life of godliness described and prescribed in the Bible. I was especially struck by certain statements in the epistles of Paul, but also by the words from the Torah and from Jesus: "Love the Lord your God with all your heart and with all your soul, and with all your mind and with all your strength . . ., [and] your neighbor as yourself (Mark 12:30–31)."

During these years I grew steadily (but sometimes shakily) in my Christian life through the reading of the whole Bible (about 12–15) times, reading good Christian literature, hearing and preaching numerous sermons and Bible lessons, serving as pastor in two churches, earning BS and

MA degrees in Biblical studies, missions, and theology, teaching Bible and preaching courses to college students, and studying the church fathers, ethics, and more in two years of PhD coursework.

Over these years, however, I was hungering for a more consistently victorious Christian life. I had some areas of my life (attitudes, actions, words, thoughts, omissions) in which sin was sometimes the victor instead of the vanquished. I didn't know how to take the "next step" (if there was one) to live a life more pleasing to God—a life of true holiness.

For the first half of this period of searching I was (as I related earlier) under the influence of Keswick teaching on (what was variously called) the deeper life, higher life, crucified life, surrendered life, and other such labels. Most of the key points of Keswick teaching are found in Romans 6–8, especially chapter six. I learned that even though I had been crucified with Christ, in order to have victory over sin I had to continually "reckon" (count, consider) myself dead to sin and alive to God (Rom 6:11, KJV), and surrender my will, hopes, ambitions, and all of my "self" to God. I also had to present my body and the parts of my body to God, not sin. Victory over sin was available to those who did these things and who "let go and let God." Human effort and struggle were not emphasized in Keswick theology. In fact, to some Keswick-oriented teachers, they were part of the problem rather than part of the solution to the "self-life."

While I knew that most of these teachings were biblical, I felt there was something more I was not seeing, or not being taught. I longed for holiness and true spirituality more and more, but sin was still a bothersome presence.

During my years under Keswick theology I was also reading many books in the Reformed or Calvinistic tradition. While a good number of these works helped me significantly in increasing my thirst for God, I was not able to find the way to positive spiritual living.

Reformed theology emphasizes the inbred nature of sin in every person, even born-again Christians who have the indwelling Holy Spirit. There is a way of living righteously to some extent, by reading the Bible and being faithful in prayer and refusing the lures of the tempter.

While both Keswick and Reformed teachings are based in the Bible and overlap in essential points, they both left me with a negative view of the extent of godliness possible in this life. And the Reformed approach stressed our inbred sinfulness so much that it failed to present a robust picture—attainable in this life—of the joyful, holy, Spirit-filled person we may become.

One Reformed theologian friend of mine told me he believes there is an element of sin in everything he does, even when he is worshipping God or helping others. Sin is ever-present in the life of every Christian, he believes, and taints all that we do and are. We must continue to struggle upward, even though we will regularly slip back down the hillside.

After 20 years into my Christian life I was more frustrated than ever. I confessed every sin that I was aware of, and I knew that God forgave me, but I did not really expect to live as a consistent conqueror in Christ. Perhaps Romans 7 ("What I want to do I do not do, but what I hate I do (vs 15)") was the best any Christian can hope for in this life. Yet I did not believe that such a view was biblical, and I determined that I was not going to settle for that!

One evening in March of 1982, in our small two-bedroom apartment in Flemington, a major breakthrough came as I was reading one of John Wesley's sermons, "The Scripture Way of Salvation." For the previous year or so I had been reading Wesley's numerous writings: his letters, journals, essays, sermons, and edited works by others that he highly valued. I had come to appreciate Wesley greatly, and now I was reading some of his sermons for a course on Wesley I was taking from Dr. Thomas Oden, a formerly liberal theologian who had moved wholeheartedly to a healthy biblical conservatism. Concerning "The Scripture Way of Salvation," Albert Outler, one of the premier Wesley scholars of the last century, said, "If the Wesleyan Theology had to be judged by a single essay, this one would do as well as any and better than most."[3]

Wesley's sermon is based—very appropriately for him—on "You are saved through faith." By the words "saved" and "salvation" he includes not only our initial coming to Christ for forgiveness and pardon (justification) but also our being set apart to be conformed to the image of Christ (sanctification). Both are accomplished by God's free grace (his favor and power) as we receive them by faith (God's work of opening our eyes and enlightening us to the truth, and giving us the trust, belief, conviction, and assurance that he will do what he has promised in his Word as we call upon him like little children).

John Wesley thought much and wrote much about the issue of sin in those who are justified. He said that even though new followers of Christ are regenerated and inwardly renewed by the power of God, they come, before long, to realize that not all sin is gone from their lives. They now feel two principles in themselves, plainly contrary to each other: "the flesh lusting against the Spirit"—nature opposing the grace of God. If they are true Christians, however, they seek to overcome sin in their lives by worshipping God in spirit and in truth, taking up their cross daily, and denying

---

3. Albert C. Outler, ed. *John Wesley* (New York, NY: Oxford University Press, 1964), 271.

themselves every pleasure that does not lead them to God. Wesley's following remarks are pivotal:

> It is thus that we wait for entire sanctification, for a full salvation from all our sins, from pride, self-will, anger, unbelief, or, as the Apostle expresses it, "Go on to perfection [Heb. 6:1, KJV]." But what is perfection? The word has various senses: here it means perfect love. It is love excluding sin; love filling the heart, taking up the whole capacity of the soul. It is love "rejoicing evermore, praying without ceasing, in everything giving thanks."[4]

John Wesley never used the words "sinless perfection." He did use "Christian perfection," but also such terms as full salvation, entire sanctification, and—his favorite—perfect love. While God's people wait for full salvation by serving him with works of piety and works of mercy, they also need to receive from him "a conviction of our helplessness, of our utter inability to think one good thought, or to form one good desire; and much more to speak one word aright, or to perform one good action but through his free almighty grace, first preventing [preceding] us, and then accompanying us every moment."[5] Wesley then explains the faith that is necessary for receiving the gift of perfect love:

> It is a divine evidence and conviction, first, that God hath promised it in the Holy Scripture. Till we are thoroughly satisfied of this, there is no moving one step farther. . . . [I]t is a divine evidence and conviction, secondly, that what God hath promised he is *able* to perform. . . . It is, thirdly, a divine evidence and conviction that he is able and willing to do it *now*. And why not? . . . He cannot want more time to accomplish whatever is his will.

Wesley continues:

> To this confidence . . . there needs to be added one more thing, a divine evidence and conviction that *he doth it*. In that hour it is done. God says to the inmost soul, "According to thy faith be it unto thee!" Then the soul is pure from every spot of sin; it is clean "from all unrighteousness." The believer then experiences the deep meaning of those solemn words, "If we walk in the light, as he is in the light, we have fellowship with one another, and the blood of Jesus Christ his Son cleanseth us from all sin."

---

4. John Wesley, "The Scripture Way of Salvation," Sermon 43 in *The Works of John Wesley, Volume 2, SERMONS II, 34–70*, edited by Albert C. Outler (Nashville, TN: Abingdon, 1985), 160.

5. Ibid., 166.

Wesley then urges his listeners and his readers to ask God for this gift:

> You . . . shall not be disappointed of your hope: it will come, and will not tarry. Look for it then every day, every hour, every moment. Why not this hour, this moment? . . . If you seek it by faith, you may expect it *as you are*: and if as you are, then expect it *now*. It is of importance to observe that there is an in- separable connection between these three points—expect it *by faith*, expect it *as you are*, and expect it *now*! . . . Stay [hold back] for nothing. Why should you? Christ is ready. And he is all you want. He is waiting for you. He is at the door![6]

As I read these words, I realized that this was the truth I had been missing for my twenty years as a child of God. I knew God commanded his children to be filled with his perfect love,[7] but I had never heard that this full salvation was actually possible in my life right then, by faith, apart from religious works. In fact, I had been taught (directly and indirectly) that these Scriptures referred to an ideal toward which we should strive but never expect to live successfully. This teaching discouraged me, and even, at times, gave me license to sin. I wondered: why would God command us to live a certain way yet not enable us to live that way?

As I pondered these solemn yet exciting and liberating words of John Wesley, I knew I was at a crisis point in my life, as I was when I was born into God's family years earlier. God was stirring me deeply, and I then re- ceived Wesley's words as though God were speaking them to me. I knew that the time had come. I cried out to God silently and asked him for the full salvation I had come to see as God's will for his children in this life. I came poor and needy, thirsty and desperate, expecting his blessing by faith (trust) alone, just as I was, and at that moment.

With the same confidence I had when God brought me to initial salva- tion, I believed at that moment that the work had been done. I felt no tin- gling, heard neither bells nor angels singing, but simply rested and rejoiced with gratitude and astonishment that God had begun a new work in me. I knew I had much to learn (and still do) about this new understanding of the spiritual life. But I also knew that God had graciously worked in me—in my head and in my heart.

I did not start to live a sinless life after that special evening, nor have I ever thought of myself as sinless. I sometimes violated God's Word, and when I did I repented by confessing the sin to God and anyone I may have

---

6. Ibid., 167–69.

7. In such Scriptures as Matthew 5:48; 22:37–40; 1 Corinthians 10:13; 2 Corinthi- ans 7:1; 1 Thessalonians 3:12–13; 5:16–24; 1 John 3:3–6; 4:16–18; 5:18.

hurt. God graciously forgave me and I moved on, trusting God's perfect love to flow through me again. I knew that Wesley never taught that a believer who has an experience (or crisis) of entire sanctification (or "second blessing") is thereafter guaranteed never to sin. Furthermore, any sin in such a believer of which he or she is unaware (since no one in this life is perfected in love in an absolute sense) is continually being washed away by the blood of Christ (1 John 1:5–2:6). Wesley's references to sin in the believer, in the context of "Christian perfection" and "perfect love," refer to *conscious* sin in the believer, not the sins concerning which one has no knowledge.

I have not been the same since that experience. I came to start the day with (among other important thoughts) the very encouraging awareness that, unless I am convicted otherwise, I *am* living for the glory of God. I also rejoiced greatly in the truth that living in victory was not only *possible* but *promised* by God to all of his children who walk by the Spirit and live the glorious crucified life (Gal 5:16; Rom 6:1–14). Holiness and happiness are blended closely together as I "pray without ceasing" throughout the day, and as I look to (and expect) God's Spirit to produce his delightful fruit in and through me (Gal 5:22–23). The very real *expectation* of continuously being filled with God's perfect love, as I walked closely with him, was the key to this new life from God.

My purpose in relating this very private experience is not to advocate for Wesley's views or anyone else's views. I am simply telling my story. God's moving in me, after the long years of my quest, from the gloom of Romans chapter seven to the gladness of Romans chapter eight, has brought me into a new space—a wide open space—of freedom, joy, and peace in my personal life and in my service to those in need, both materially and spiritually. My story is one among millions of stories that could be told by God's people, many of them probably quite different from mine. One common denominator (I hope) in all of them, however, is that one's growth in holiness and spirituality is an ongoing experience—a lifelong process. If there are crisis experiences after the new birth for some Christians, they are never once-for-all. Every child of God must continue, until the day we see Christ, living closely to God and making progress continually in love for our God and our neighbors.

Inquiring After the Next Assignment

In the summer of 1985, after receiving my PhD degree and after living nearly ten years in New Jersey, we moved to Dallas, Texas. I had accepted a position as Professor of Theology at the Criswell Center for Biblical Studies.

This was a fully-accredited Bible college offering masters as well as bachelors degrees. Not long after I joined the faculty the school's name was changed to The Criswell College.

During the two years before the move Judy and I had invested a good deal of time, energy, prayer, and discussion into a search for the college or seminary that would be a good fit for me and for each of our daughters. In all, Judy and I sent 160 personalized letters (I phoned each school to get the correct name and title of the right person to contact) to about 130 schools in the United States and Canada where I thought I might do well on the faculty. I sent my personal data with each letter: degrees earned, positions held, references, items published, family information, and other relevant materials.

I was surprised how very few full-time positions were available, but then I recalled the very serious words of the Drew Graduate School dean when our entering class commenced our program of studies. Do not, he stressed, begin doctoral work in theological studies with the expectation of finding a faculty position in the field. The jobs are not out there; the market is saturated. Only if you love the scholarship for its own sake, and you long to search deeply into the primary sources of your area of specialization, should you go forward on this venture!

In addition to the paucity of positions available was the fact that many schools had a doctrinal statement that faculty had to agree with. Some schools required, for example, belief in a pre-tribulational rapture of the church or a Calvinist understanding of predestination, neither of which I could, in good conscience, say that I agreed with. Among the 130 or so schools I contacted for a possible position, I did not include any school with a doctrinal statement I could not sign.

Nevertheless, amid the unfavorable atmosphere, I was gratified to hear back from over half of the schools I had contacted. Most of the academic deans thanked me for sending my materials, expressed interest in them, and said they would keep them on file in the event that a position might be coming open. Only a few deans said they had, or might have, a position opening in the near future.

With these few deans I spent hours on the phone and even interviewed at three of the schools, one of which was only in the planning stage. I was accepted for a one-year position at Trinity Evangelical Divinity School near Chicago, after which my position would be considered for renewal. Judy and I did not think that we should move our family under such tenuous circumstances. The Criswell College, however, offered me an unrestricted position, and Judy and I considered this to be God's next place of ministry for us.

As we were packing for our move to Dallas, I noticed an appeal for blood donations. Our local blood bank was depleted. Since I had done this several times before, I went to the local hospital and lay down on the cot. The technician drew my blood but, unlike the previous times, I did not recover well. In fact, I became white, my blood pressure dropped dramatically, and I began to lose consciousness (I think I did for a time, but I can't be sure).

When I was becoming more alert, I was aware of several white-coated medical personnel surrounding my cot and speaking with such a sense of urgency and concern that I knew I was in trouble. Eventually, after the medical team worked on me for a while, I could sit on the edge of the cot and then stand. After being convinced that I was able to leave, the doctor told me very solemnly to never give blood again, and when I arrived in Dallas to be seen by a cardiologist as soon as possible. I had no idea then, at the age of 41, that this seemingly minor incident would introduce a new, major, difficult dimension of life to me for the remainder of my years on earth.

CHAPTER 12

Dallas Days and Dallas Nights

Being Southern Baptist

IN THE SUMMER OF 1985 we moved to Dallas and, for the first time in our lives and with a loan from a good friend, we bought a house. We were located just a few blocks from Interstate 30 and could easily get on the freeway to downtown Dallas where The Criswell College was located.

Judy found employment in the Evangelism Department of the Baptist General Convention of Texas, just across the street from the college. Joni and Laurie attended high school at First Baptist Academy, also very near to the college.

The largest and most prominent structure in the midst of the prime commercial property was the First Baptist Church of Dallas. The senior pastor of First Baptist at the time was the renowned Dr. W.A. Criswell, after whom the college was named. Dr. Criswell was highly esteemed not only within the Southern Baptist Convention (the SBC—his own denomination) but within many other conservative Christian denominations and groups. He was best known for his emphasis on expository preaching and his vigorous defense of the inerrancy of the Bible.

First Baptist at that time was the largest church within the SBC (some said it had about 28,000 members) and had a huge budget. The church contributed heavily to the worldwide missionary program of the SBC, and provided the facilities, rent-free, where the college made its home just across the street from the church.

We became members of the First Baptist Church where all Criswell College faculty were required to join, give their tithes, and attend all services—Sunday School, Sunday morning, Sunday evening, and Wednesday evening—unless we were preaching or otherwise ministering elsewhere. I was informed, as time went by, that these indicators of loyalty were monitored by the college leadership. During the school year all college faculty, as well as all students, were required to attend daily chapel. The faculty members were to sit together in a certain section at the front of the historic First Baptist sanctuary, where chapel was held, so that our attendance (or lack of it) could be easily noted.

My primary responsibility was to teach the Systematic Theology courses, which task I gladly shared with Professor David Dockery. David was a warm brother in Christ as well as a top scholar and highly esteemed teacher. In fact, all of the faculty and administrators (all men, except one woman who taught English) were easy to be around, and each had a heart for God and the truth of the gospel. The President was Dr. Paige Patterson and the Vice President for Academic Affairs was Dr. Richard Land.

It was also my responsibility to teach Christian ethics, not only the basic course required of all students but electives (which were my choice) in biomedical ethics, the ethics of war and peace, and other vital topics. As time went by I was asked to teach additional courses such as Introduction to Philosophy, Basic Apologetics, Advanced Apologetics, and Baptist History and Distinctives.

I loved the subject matter of each course I taught. Everything interested me. But I had a problem—a serious problem. Except for one section of theology that I had taught at The King's College in New York during my doctoral student days, I had taught none of these courses! Some of them, such as Baptist History and Distinctives, I had never even studied. In addition, every course lasted eight weeks, and classes were held for every course four days a week: Tuesday through Friday. Monday was to be a day of rest and recovery after the preaching and other ministries of the Lord's Day, in which many students and faculty were involved.

Exhaustion

My serious problem was exhaustion, which is the one word, more than any other, that immediately comes to mind when I think of my three years in Dallas. No other word comes even close. Having to prepare new material (new courses were regularly and unexpectedly being added to my schedule) for several classes, four days in a row, left me utterly exhausted almost all of the time. I remember, as if it were yesterday, preparing for the next day's classes until two, three, or four o'clock in the morning, and then rising about five or six o'clock in order to be on time to drive the four of us to downtown Dallas for our work and studies.

My perfectionist nature was not compelling me in my class preparation, as it might have been under other circumstances. I was simply trying to put together a decent class session for the next day—a session that would be valuable for each student and would give them their money's worth. I refused to slack off in my preparation, but I know that at times some class sessions were not at the highest level of excellence I expected of myself.

One day after class a tall young man walked to the lectern as I was gathering my books and teaching materials. I stopped and gave him my attention. He said he was bothered by the way I started my class sessions—or didn't start them. He said that I took valuable class time to talk about this, that, or some other thing before I began teaching. He wanted to get into the course material right away. Then he looked into my eyes and said something I will never forget: "I know what you are doing."

I was smitten with shame and sadness because I knew he was right. I mumbled something to him, apologized, and thanked him for speaking to me about the matter. He was right because—I regret to say—there were times in that course when I simply did not have enough material prepared. I simply had no time or energy left to prepare another ten or twelve minutes of material, and I deliberately chatted with the students at the start of class about whatever was in the news or on their minds. It would have been better for me to start class right on time—my custom—with the material I had and then, if I needed to, dismiss the class a bit early. Not many students will complain about a course whose classes end early once in a while.

This is my most embarrassing anecdote in the book, and I very much wanted to leave it out. I reluctantly decided to include it to illustrate how desperate I was in trying to make it through each day. And my reason for wanting to illustrate this is to encourage some poor soul reading this who feels a sense of desperation about their present, seemingly inescapable, work load. Perhaps they may be helped by knowing that they are not alone, and that someone else understands, at least in part. Never before in a course I was teaching, and never since that polite but firm rebuke from the student, have I done such a thing. To the best of my recollection, this is the only negative comment I received or learned of concerning my teaching in Dallas—from student, faculty, or administration. There were no class evaluation forms, however, that students were expected to fill out at the end of each course, just as there were none at Prairie Bible Institute.

Another way I attempted to survive, after I had been teaching at the college for a year or two, was to cancel Friday classes about every other week. I did not put such a policy in the syllabus because it was not really a "policy." It was, above all, an escape mechanism in my mind. It gave me some hope, some light at the end of the tunnel, that I could look forward to during the long nights of study and preparation.

Rather than establish a fixed practice, I simply announced to the students on a Tuesday or Wednesday that we would not be meeting that Friday. Occasionally I varied the routine, but most of the time we met seven out of every eight class days. I never asked permission to do this, because the administration would have had to make a decision about the matter, and I was quite sure the answer would be "no." I basically followed a "don't ask, don't tell" policy.

Why did I not approach the leadership about the struggle I was having? Part of the reason was that I felt—especially as a new faculty member—that I just needed to buckle down and do the job expected of me, without complaint. In addition, I thought that the teaching load would become progressively easier after I taught each course at least once. First-time preparation is always the most difficult and time-consuming.

Instead of the pressure decreasing, however, it increased. As I mentioned above, new courses were regularly being added to my teaching schedule, sometimes with very short advance notice. And these were frequently courses I had never taught. There were times, I am glad to say, when I was consulted about which courses I would be teaching during the coming quarter or quarters. Overall, however, I did not feel free to ask for an arrangement of courses different from the one I was assigned.

Even with the stress of preparation I loved the students (very warm and respectful) and the subject matter of every course and every class session I taught. My strong interest in and excitement about the material kept me going, and so did the powerful grace of God that not only held me up but also moved me forward. I knew, however, after a year and a half or so at the college, that in order to preserve my health I needed to find another school in which to teach. I once again began to ask, seek, and knock, and Judy was in full agreement in her prayers and thoughts.

As time went by I learned that Bethel Theological Seminary in St. Paul, Minnesota, would need a person to teach theology and ethics starting in the fall of 1988. They might even need two such new faculty members at that time, depending on possible changes within the faculty. The Dean of Bethel Seminary was the well-known and highly-respected theologian Dr. Millard Erickson, whose very popular three-volume work on systematic theology was the chief textbook I used in my theology classes at Criswell. Dr. Erickson invited me to come, with Judy, to Bethel for an interview with the search committee. I was also to teach.

The visit to Minnesota went well, and after two further visits, with more interviews and classes to teach, the faculty voted to call me to serve with them as Associate Professor of Theology. We would move in the summer of 1988. I was delighted and honored to be invited to serve with such a highly-regarded faculty, and I was equally grateful to know that we would be moving to a situation that seemed to be much better for me.

I made an appointment to meet with the president of The Criswell College, Dr. Patterson. He received me warmly, for he was a friendly and warm-hearted man. I explained to him that I would be resigning from the faculty, and when and where I would be moving. It was not so easy explaining why I was leaving, and my mind is fuzzy as I try to recall just what I said. No doubt I mentioned the great difficulty I had been experiencing with the scheduling of courses. Paige was very sorry to receive my resignation. He made some very appreciative remarks and urged me to stay, but he saw that I was quite sure about my decision. We talked a bit more and he graciously wished me God's best.

I continued to teach the fine students (almost all of them men) in both the undergraduate and graduate divisions, but I had a lightness in my step that had been missing for quite some time. I went to see a cardiologist once a year, as I was instructed after my blood-donation incident while packing to move to Dallas, and I was told to continue this practice after we moved to Minnesota.

Abortion

In the spring of 1988 I was watching the local evening news. A woman was standing in front of several microphones speaking eloquently about protecting a woman's right to choose. She was the director of the largest abortion clinic in the Dallas area at the time: the Routh Street Women's Clinic on the main highway going north out of Dallas. She spoke persuasively and without rancor.

Within the next day or two I phoned the clinic, introduced myself, and stated where I taught ethics, and asked if I might be able to schedule an appointment with the clinic director. I explained that I did not intend to argue but to interview her, so that when I taught on abortion in my classes I would clearly be presenting both sides of the hot-button issue. This was my teaching policy on all controversial matters, as much as class time would allow. On the following day, I believe, the receptionist phoned and set up an appointment for me with the director.

During my nearly three years in Dallas I had driven past the clinic several times. I knew what that gray, nondescript building was—set back and low on the east side of the highway—and I had looked at it each time with sorrow and revulsion. I had watched a film ("Eclipse of Reason") of an actual second-term abortion (20 weeks) produced by a doctor who had performed or presided over some 75,000 abortions at the largest abortion clinic in the world in New York City. He even admitted that he had aborted one of his own children and persuaded the expectant mother of another of his children to have an abortion. This doctor, Bernard Nathanson, had become horrified at what he was doing, quit performing abortions, and was now speaking out, writing, and producing films against what he considered a terrible evil in our society. He even spoke of "the satanic world of abortion."[1]

During the abortion film no faces are shown, but each step of the procedure is very clearly shown in color, including the cart next to the patient on which were placed, in order, the parts of the baby's body as they were removed from the womb. The body parts had to be set out like this so that, when the procedure was over, it would be evident that every arm, leg, organ, hip, and every other body part could be accounted for. Nothing should be left inside the woman or girl to cause infection.

I knew that in the fourth month the baby is eight to ten inches long, and by the fifth month the mother feels the baby's movements. I also knew that any abortion during these months would necessitate a forceps to grasp the parts of the baby. Because the developed child already has calcified bones, the parts must be twisted and torn away, leading to profuse bleeding. The head usually needs to be crushed before it may be removed. This type of abortion—the kind used in "Eclipse of Reason"—is known as a D and E (dilation and evacuation).

I arrived at the clinic early for my appointment and drove behind the building and parked. After I shut off the engine I looked to my right and there, close to my car, was a very large metal dumpster, with the cover closed and locked with a heavy padlock. No one had to tell me what was in the dumpster, and I shuddered as I looked at it—right next to my car. I think I was expected to park out front.[2]

1. Julia Duin, "Bernard Nathanson's Conversion," in *Crisis* (June 1996), at www. ewtn.com/library/prolife/bernconv.txt (accessed March 16, 2014).

2. I had recently read and reviewed a truly sad, gripping, and revolting book by S. Rickly Christian, *The Woodland Hills Tragedy* (Westchester, IL: Crossway, 1985). The book tells the true story, in great detail, of a large shipping container found in 1982 on the home property of Malvin R. Weisberg in Woodland Hills, California. Weisberg owned and operated a medical laboratory in Santa Monica. Inside the container were 16,433 aborted human fetuses. They were large enough to be counted individually. Some had been in storage since 1979, according to tags. When I drove into the Routh

As I stepped to the front of the clinic I was surprised to see vertical steel bars over the door and window. I pressed the doorbell and was greeted by a very pleasant woman. I introduced myself and she invited me in. The office was very bright and attractive, and two young-looking women were sitting at a desk to the left. They smiled at me so radiantly that I was disarmed momentarily.

I was not sitting long when a woman—also very pleasant—invited me into an inner, somewhat darkened room and said the clinic director would be with me soon. I was surprised that I was seated in this room, on the same row of metal folding chairs where two girls—or very young women—were sitting dejectedly, one or two chairs between them, most likely waiting for their turn. What especially surprised me was that I was staring right at the nurses' station—about twelve feet in front of me—with a pair of swinging doors to my left. I felt sure that the doors led to the rooms where the abortions were performed.

My hunch was confirmed when I saw someone come through the doors and go to the nurses' station. While I watched this person talking to one of the nurses or staff, I was baffled concerning whether this employee was a man or a woman. He or she wore a full-length, forest green apron or overcoat (the type used by surgeons in hospitals) that was spattered and even soaked in large areas with blood. I knew it was blood.

The most striking aspect of this person's appearance was his or her head—especially the face. The person scarcely looked human, with a large flat face that was totally devoid of expression. Adding to this strange sight was a very full head of dark, disheveled hair. After a short talk with the woman at the desk and a lingering glance at me, the person went back through the swinging doors. I never did decide whether this was a man or a woman, but I had no doubt about what this person did behind those doors.

Soon after this incident the clinic director came and introduced herself, shook my hand, offered a brief apology about where I was asked to wait, and led me to her nicely arranged well-lit office. She even offered me a coke. We talked seriously for about 30 or 40 minutes, following a list of questions that I had prepared. She answered politely but with a bit of irritation at times, probably because she had been asked these questions so many times.

Toward the close of our session she pointed to the free literature on an end-table that, she said, contained the answers to all the questions I had asked, and even some I hadn't asked. During the meeting I had respectfully interacted with some of her answers and even introduced my testimony of

Street clinic and parked next to the large, locked dumpster, I could only think of the Woodland Hills tragedy.

Christ, but she seemed to have little interest in my remarks. After a while we parted company with a handshake. I thanked her for her time and help.

Within a few months after arriving in Minnesota I contacted this director and invited her to co-author a Two Views book with me. It would be arranged as a series of letters, with one from her presenting some thoughts and arguments for the pro-choice position, then one from me answering her and offering my perspective from a pro-life position. She would then respond to my letter and so on. She replied politely but declined my offer. Years later I saw her name mentioned in some national magazine or newspaper, with the comment that she had left the abortion industry. I felt a great sense of gratitude to God.

The Move

When we placed our house on the market we were informed that, at that time, there were about 40,000 homes for sale just in Dallas County where we lived. Because of major setbacks in the oil industry few homes were being bought. Judy and I had a very good real estate professional, a friend whom we knew would work hard to sell our house. She helped us with everything, including a sale price that would be attractive in the distressed economy.

As the time for our move approached, we were glad to have a potential buyer. He was a single man who signed a purchase agreement with us, but he could not close the sale before our moving day. Given these circumstances we entrusted the transaction to God and to our realtor friend and moved to the Twin Cities, where we rented a house in Shoreview, not far from Bethel College and Seminary.

Our oldest daughter Joni, after graduation from First Baptist Academy, had a year earlier moved back East—to Flemington—to work for a while before considering college. Our daughter Laurie, with one year of high school to complete, moved to Shoreview with us. Our plan was to rent until the house in Dallas sold, and then buy a house near Bethel with enough room for the four of us if and when Joni desired to return to Minnesota. We settled into our new home, kept in regular touch with Joni, and prayed for the soon sale of our home.

As I looked back on our move to Dallas I asked, "Did God make a mistake in opening the door for us to move to Dallas, since our three years there had not been pleasant for any of us? Did Judy and I not listen properly to God's direction?" I thought a little on these issues, but not much. We had asked God for guidance according to the invitation in the book of James:

> If any of you lacks wisdom, you should ask God, who gives gen-
> erously to all without finding fault, and it will be given to you.
> But when you ask, you must believe and not doubt, because the
> one who doubts is like a wave of the sea, blown and tossed by the
> wind. That person should not expect to receive anything from
> the Lord. Such a person is double-minded and unstable in all
> they do (Jas 1:5–8).

When we prayed, we had no doubt that God would guide us. Judy
and I have found over the years that we may sometimes have doubts about
which course of action to take, right up to the time of decision or even after,
but we entertain no doubts about whether or not God will guide us rightly,
or has guided us rightly when we prayed together about some issue—great
or small. In other words, our confidence is always in God, not in our imagined keen minds or clever arranging of circumstances.

Yes, I have sometimes wondered about certain choices in life concerning whether I made a proper decision or not, but I quickly move on to the
promise of Romans 8:28, that God will work, either by permitting or ordain-
ing, all things together for good to those who love him. My responsibility is
to trust and to obey what he shows me, as I attempt to discern that.

Being on a pursuit for God and the spiritual character he longs to form
in me and in each of his children is not like coasting on a wagon down
a long, smooth, gently-sloped hill with fields of flowers on the sides. It is,
rather, like climbing a rough and steep mountain with our hands and feet,
sometimes in the midst of wind and pounding rain, looking expectantly for
the next ledge or cave where we might rest a while before climbing again.
The quest to the mountain top is very different from the glide to the valley
floor, but the quest to the glorious heights with God is directed wisely and
lovingly by the One whose grace is always sufficient for each stage of the
climb. "The Sovereign LORD is my strength; he makes my feet like the feet
of a deer, he enables me to tread on the heights (Hab 3:19)."

CHAPTER 13

Liking Minnesota

Bethel and Bethany

JUDY AND I—THIS TIME with Laurie—had now returned to Minnesota. Twenty-one years earlier my new bride and I were walking and praying in the beautiful Minnesota north woods. Now we had returned, not to the woods but to the growing, lively metropolis of Minneapolis and Saint Paul: the Twin Cities. An information packet at one of the downtown Minneapolis hotels said: "Welcome to the coldest city on earth."

When we said goodbye to Minnesota years before, I never had the slightest thought of moving here someday. It never occurred to me that the yet-unknown winding course of our married life would bring us back to the state of Judy's birth and childhood and into a wilderness where I would be guided, tested, and sustained by God in ways about which I knew very little.

From the start I felt comfortable with living in Minnesota. I learned that "Minnesota Nice" is not an empty slogan. The people were quite friendly and helpful as I began to make my way around.

I learned that a big part of winter life in our new state revolved around events on the ice, such as hockey, curling, car crashes, and ice fishing. With ice fishing men and women walk (or drive, if the ice is thick enough) out on a frozen lake, drill a hole through the ice, drop their line and wait for a bite. This has become quite a science and adventure for many who live in "the land of 10,000 lakes." (I've heard it is more like 15,000.)

After we settled in our home I set up my office at the seminary. Bethel College and Bethel Seminary are located on the same beautiful grounds in Arden Hills, separated by only a short walk along Lake Valentine. There is a hill between the two main buildings so either side can refer to the other as "over the hill."

The official name, Bethel College and Seminary, was later changed to Bethel University. The institution was affiliated with and under the governance of the Baptist General Conference (BGC), a denomination situated in the theological center of the rapidly growing evangelical movement. It had pietistic roots and was known for its "irenic spirit." I found Bethel to have a pleasant, healthy atmosphere, and found the President, Dr. George Brushaber, and the Seminary Dean, Dr. Millard Erickson, to be congenial and wise leaders under whom to serve.

The seminary courses were arranged in an academic year of three quarters, and I was very glad to have my whole year of teaching laid out before me months ahead of the beginning of classes. I was expected to give my input concerning the course schedule and even, at times, the hours I preferred to teach. All of my teaching was in the areas of my specializations: theology and ethics. Bethel faculty members were held in high regard by the administration as well as by staff and students.

Our family was adjusting to the new normal. Laurie enrolled in her senior year of high school and worked in the Bethel dining room as well; Joni was living and working on the East Coast; and Judy had accepted a position as office manager in one of the local churches, Bethany Baptist Church of Roseville. The senior pastor at Bethany, Rev. (later Dr.) Bruce Petersen, was a Vietnam War vet, a former high school English teacher, and a Bethel Seminary graduate. He was a wise, faithful preacher of the Scriptures and very generous with his time, abilities, and means. The church was doing well under his care.

Judy and I joined the church, although this was not a requirement for her employment. Judy saw her position as a ministry primarily, not as a "job," in the same way that I had always considered my teaching to be, first of all, a ministry. From day one of our marriage we viewed ourselves as partners in God's kingdom work and servants to those with whom and for whom we labored.

Bethany Baptist was a BGC church (this affiliation of churches and ministries is now named Converge Worldwide), so there was an affinity between our church and Bethel. The largest church bodies in Minnesota were Catholic and Lutheran, while evangelical Christians were found among BGC, Evangelical Covenant, Evangelical Free, Assemblies of God, and similar conservative churches.

Housing Crisis

One difficult aspect of our early months in Minnesota had to do with our former home in Dallas. It had not yet sold. The man who had signed a purchase agreement with us to buy the house, to our chagrin, backed out of the deal. Our real estate agent and personal friend in Dallas worked diligently to sell the house, but with 40,000 other homes in the depressed market in Dallas County, nothing was happening. Each month we were paying rent to live in Shoreview and making mortgage payments on our home in Texas.

Because we were unable to continue this arrangement, we lowered our asking price for the house as much as we reasonably could, but this did not help. We contacted the company that held our mortgage and tried to work out a plan with them, but they were adamant that we needed to make the full payments as agreed upon. We asked if we could pay half the amount, or just the interest, until the house sold, but they would not agree. I told them about the mortgage insurance policy we had, but learned that because we chose to move from Dallas for another job rather than having been laid off from my place of employment, our mortgage insurance did not apply.

After considerable thought and prayer, Judy and I agreed to discontinue payments on our home in Texas. We simply did not have the money to continue as we were, and we believed that we should not borrow to make the payments. After several months of missed payments and several sternly-worded letters from the mortgage company, the unfortunate situation came to an end. We lost the house and our investment in it (fortunately not large) to a foreclosure.

Even though this was a legal way to escape our difficulty, Judy and I still felt sad that we were not able to sell the house. We were definitely not, however, sorry that we had moved from Texas to Minnesota.

To our great surprise and delight, one year after moving to Minnesota we were able to buy a house just eight miles north of Bethel and ten miles north of our church. We had understood that the foreclosure would do major harm to our credit and prevent us from purchasing a home for at least several years. However, God arranged matters differently.

Some very fine people (God always seems to use people!) blessed us with personal loans so that we could buy in a friendly blue-collar suburb north of Minneapolis. My brother Tom lent us an especially large amount. With the muscle-power of some kind Bethel faculty and staff we moved to our new home in the summer of 1989. We were, and continue to be, abundantly thankful to God for this home in which we still live.

The Spirit Comes to Class

My teaching load allowed me time to breathe, and my classes were enjoyable. One classroom incident made a powerful impression on me, more so than any other in my lifetime of teaching.

I was teaching an elective course on certain aspects of the person and work of the Holy Spirit. In one session I was trying to guide the students through the perplexing issue of the baptism of the Holy Spirit. We considered the various views within the Christian churches, and the arguments for and against each position. I attempted always to adjudicate these matters under the authority of the biblical teachings, yet even with such a reverent approach God's people differ sincerely on what the teaching of the Bible really is. What did it mean to "receive the Holy Spirit," and how did one do this?

While we were having a lively discussion in class, one young woman spoke loudly, clearly, and with deep emotion: "Let. Him. In." Susan paused between each word, and put special emphasis on "In," crying out the word plaintively in two conjoined syllables that will stay with me forever. Then, just as she had said this, she put her head down on the desk and appeared to be crying quietly. The students and I ceased from whatever movements we were making and I just stood at my teaching post and allowed the silence to do its work.

After a while, if I remember correctly, I asked Susan what she meant by "Let him in." She replied, as best I can recall, that we were spending so much time and energy talking about all the details of Spirit baptism that we were failing to see God's obvious word to us: Let him in; invite the Spirit in; come to him in a condition of hunger, thirst, obedience, and receptivity.

I thanked Susan, whom I had come to know fairly well before this course, and tried my best to pull together the loose strands of our previous discussion. I affirmed Susan, especially for her deep longing to know God in his fullness, and to experience all of the Spirit's presence and power so that she might serve God mightily and bring others nearer to him.

I said to the class that Susan's desire was not just a longing that some Christians might experience, but that—no matter which words we use to speak about Spirit baptism—it was indicative of a deep hunger that every follower of Christ should have and experience more and more. I may have mentioned Jesus' words in Matthew 5:6 ("Blessed are those who hunger and thirst for righteousness, for they will be filled") and Luke 11:13 (". . . how much more will your Father in heaven give the Holy Spirit to those who ask him!"). I'm almost certain I reminded the class of the biblical teaching that every true child of God has been indwelled by the Holy Spirit from the time of regeneration, but that other ministries of the Spirit—such as teaching and filling—are blessings that may be repeated often in the life of the believer. I then dismissed the class with prayer. I think regularly of those solemn moments on the day when the Spirit came to class in such an unusual but welcome manner.

Heart Surgery

Because I had been so preoccupied with matters concerning our house in Dallas, two moves, writing projects, and my adjustment to teaching at the seminary, I neglected to have my heart tests for over two years. They were to have been done yearly after my experience donating blood in New Jersey.

In the fall of 1990, with no thought of this issue on my mind, I went one day to a primary care doctor to see whether I had a chest cold or something more serious such as the flu or pneumonia. This was my first visit to a doctor since our days in Texas, and when the doctor listened to my chest she startled me by exclaiming "Wow!" She was alarmed on hearing such cardiac regurgitation (backflow) and urged me to see a cardiologist immediately. My respiratory issue resolved itself in a few days and I set up an appointment to have my heart checked.

After meeting with the cardiologist and having an echocardiogram and some other testing, I learned that I would need open-heart surgery as soon as it could be arranged. I was stunned by this news and made plans with the dean right away. I would finish my fall courses in December, have the surgery on January 17th, and return to teaching for the spring quarter in mid-March. Dr. Erickson graciously arranged for other professors to teach my winter quarter courses.

I had the surgery done at the Mayo Clinic in Rochester, about an hour and a half south of our home. Because of the relative newness of this type of surgery in the United States (it had been developed in France) I was not able to have the operation in the Twin Cities.

My problem was that I had a serious mitral valve prolapse, which meant that as soon as the blood was pumped out of my left ventricle, to send oxygenated blood to the rest of my body, a large portion of the blood leaked back into the left ventricle. The mitral valve did not close tightly after each beat. The backflow of blood not only prevented sufficient oxygen from reaching my body but also caused my heart (left ventricle especially) to become quite enlarged, because it had to make room for the blood coming back into it.

Instead of replacing my defective mitral valve with a mechanical valve or a pig valve (the two most common surgeries at the time for the problem), the surgeon tightened my own valve (by utilizing an "annuloplasty" ring) and the leakage stopped. After several days of recovery and rehab in Rochester I came home.

At home I did my exercises and took the medications I was prescribed, but my recovery was slower than I had thought it would be. Because my chest had been cut open from just below my throat to just above my navel, the bone and muscle needed time to heal, and this could not be hurried. The return of strength to my body was a slow process.

As the date of my first class sessions approached, I determined to teach as scheduled. Returning to the classroom eight weeks after surgery, I came to realize, was a bit too soon. By the strengthening grace of God, however, I taught the courses and was glad I could.

I was, at this point, living in a girls dormitory. Or so it seemed. Joni had returned from three years on the East Coast, and she and Laurie had enrolled at Bethel College. Joni was majoring in social work and Laurie in nursing. A friend of theirs, also majoring in social work, came to live with us after finishing her first year at Bethel.

Joni, Laurie, and their friend Lori brought lots of energy into our home as they studied, worked, cried, played, and sometimes quarreled over the next several years until each one earned her degree. All five of us were busy, but it usually was a good kind of busyness. One more thing: for some mysterious reason the college boys came calling at the house from time to time to see how the three lovely young ladies were faring. How thoughtful of them!

Sabbatical

One benefit of being on the Bethel faculty was the school's policy of awarding sabbaticals. A sabbatical is a block of time—usually one or two quarters—during which the faculty member receives his or her normal salary but is not expected to teach or participate in committee work. The time is to be used by the professor for personal revitalization, reading important new books and articles in one's field, and researching and writing with a view to publication. The faculty member may also travel out of the country for research or teaching.

Usually the professor schedules the sabbatical adjacent to the summer break, so that the total block of time in which to work uninterruptedly might be as long as six months, or even longer. Neither school where I taught previously had such a benefit, and I was very grateful for the sabbaticals I now received.

Another benefit from Bethel that I had had at Prairie but not at Criswell was a teaching assistant (TA)—a student who helped with such tasks as research, certain kinds of grading, and giving assistance to students. With my sabbaticals and my excellent TAs (who were available also during sabbaticals) I was able to complete some writing projects that I hoped would be of benefit to students, pastors, and fellow scholars.

One sabbatical above all stands out in my memory. While I labored on my work as planned, I also spent a larger-than-usual time daily in the company of the Lord. I did not start my work first thing in the morning, because I knew that I would do better after the spiritual refreshing I so desperately needed.

This sabbatical was, and still is, the spiritual highlight of my life. Most of the days I entered my home office in the morning, sat down at my desk, and opened my Bible to the place where I left off the previous day. I then entered into communion with God for two or three hours, sometimes without a break or even moving from my desk.

What did I do for all those hours? Usually I started by reading the Bible, one book at a time, moving slowly and meditating while I underlined those words and verses that gripped me. Occasionally I turned to other places in Scripture that spoke of the topic I was dwelling on. I did not feel any compulsion to read a certain amount each day. On some days I re-read the section from the previous day, even doing this for several days in a row.

I was following Spurgeon's method: read until something in the text stops you, then meditate on that part until you think it's time to move on. One may read one or two chapters a day, or just one or two verses. The important thing is to hear from God and put into practice the Word of the Lord.

I did not usually do in-depth Bible study during these times, but lingered over the passage before me to discern God's instruction, conviction, warning, rebuke, and words of love, hope, grace, and encouragement to me.

Most of my special time with God each day, however, was not directly in the Bible. The Scripture of the day was always beneficial, of course, but not only in the words themselves but also in the way they launched me into glorious times of adoration, thanksgiving, and confession. God used these three realms of prayer and intertwined them powerfully to build me up in my inner person. I also spent time in intercession (prayer for the needs of others) and petition (prayer for my own needs), but focused mostly on the first three areas of prayer.

For one or two hours every day I was lost in adoration (worshipping God for who and what he is in himself), thanksgiving (expressing gratitude to God for everything—material and non-material—he has given to me and withheld from me throughout my lifetime), and confessing (bringing my sins into the light of God's holiness and asking for his forgiveness).

Concerning confession, I regularly asked God to show me my motives for doing or not doing certain things, and to rid me of motives that were not pleasing to him or beneficial to others. I prayed regularly the powerful prayer—attributed to David—in the book of Psalms: "Search me, God, and know my heart; test me and know my anxious thoughts. See if there is any offensive way in me, and lead me in the way everlasting" (139:23–24). I spent much time simply saying, over and over, things like "I love you Lord," "I praise you Lord," "I thank you Lord," "I trust you Lord," "I give myself wholly to you, Lord," "You are wise and good in all your ways."

I am having a difficult time putting into words those months of communion with God. I think of the apostle Paul's mention of a person (probably himself) who "was caught up to paradise and heard inexpressible things, things that no one is permitted to tell" (2 Cor 12:4).

I am by no means likening myself to this person, but I use these words to communicate somehow what it is to enjoy a taste of the heavenly bread and water that our Lord Jesus Christ offers to everyone on this earth who comes to him hungering and thirsting for righteousness.

In this life one may have a foretaste of the Marriage Supper of the Lamb in eternal glory. In the divine-human quest that is the life of every Christ-follower, we continually sense God's longing for fellowship with us and his arousing in us a longing for intimacy with himself. This reciprocity—this giving and receiving of eternal love that flows within the triune Godhead and then outward to and among all of God's people—is likely the closest any of us will experience of the heavenly life while living in these mortal bodies.

One more note: during these special sabbatical experiences I sensed the physical nearness of Jesus unlike anything I had ever known. Very often as I looked toward the wall next to my office door (about six or seven feet from my chair) I "knew" immediately that Jesus was standing there, giving his blessing to me and my work and especially assuring me—by his calm, comforting presence—that he will be with me always.

I did not see a physical form, and I knew there was no material substance there, but a few times I walked to the "presence" and hugged him. I felt a bit odd hugging the air, but I knew Jesus knew what was in my heart. I no longer hug the air, but from those special sabbatical experiences to the present I have been aware of the mysterious presence of Jesus in the same location, whenever I sit quietly at my home office desk in order to commune with him.

CHAPTER 14

Adventures in Theology

Declining Health

IN THE YEARS FOLLOWING my 1991 mitral valve surgery my heart was still not functioning well. I moved along like a car on the interstate highway with a governor spring on the gas pedal holding me at 50 miles per hour. I should have been able to drive at 70 or 75, and I wanted to do so. But, even though the surgery stopped almost all of the backflow of blood, the previous severe regurgitation had left my heart so enlarged that the left ventricle was hindered significantly in its ability to pump. The hope had been that, after the surgery, my heart would return to its normal size and strength. But this did not happen.

In this weakened condition I adjusted to a new pattern of life: frequent visits to the cardiologist for echocardiograms and other tests, experimentation with a number of drugs that were supposed to strengthen and regulate my heart, a pacemaker followed by a pacemaker/defibrillator, and a growing realization that my physical stamina was lessening—gradually but noticeably.

At times I had expected my bodily strength to plateau at a level from which I could live and work reasonably well, but my heart condition continued to worsen. I tried not to dwell on my health issues, but committed them to God and gave myself to the tasks before me.

The major task before me, of course, was teaching my students. They were a blessing to work with and my classes were progressing well. Even though I often had to return to my office after class and lie on the carpet for thirty minutes or so (putting a "Please do not disturb" sign on my door), I was very grateful for the privilege and responsibility of having a part in the education of these women and men of faith.

Another privilege I had was to belong to certain scholarly societies and organizations that would help me do my work better. I would read their journals and materials and attend their meetings as much as my strength would allow.

It had been some 20 years since I attended that life-changing 25th anniversary conference of the Evangelical Theological Society, and I continued to be active in the society. I had also become a member of the American Academy of Religion, the Society of Christian Ethics, the Evangelical Philosophical Society, and several other academic societies. The meetings of the ETS, EPS, and AAR were always profitable to attend, as were the meetings of the SCE, although I was seldom able to go to the SCE events.

Listening to the papers presented by established—sometimes world-renowned—scholars as well as by younger, upcoming scholars was almost always beneficial, and I was thankful to be able to present a paper myself from time to time. The discussion and networking between sessions and at mealtimes was sometimes as valuable—if not more valuable—than what I learned from listening to the papers.

I hesitate to single out anyone, but one scholar in particular had been very influential in my life and thinking ever since the 25th ETS Conference. Clark Pinnock, the often controversial theologian who obtained his doctorate in New Testament under F.F. Bruce, had written or edited major works on scriptural revelation, divine sovereignty and human will, and trajectories in contemporary theology that had affected me significantly. Even though he changed his position quite dramatically on these and other issues, and even though I clearly disagreed with him on several major areas of theology, I valued him as a very perceptive, honest, and unafraid scholar, as well as a sincere friend and brother in Christ. I will always be grateful for the interest he showed in me and the encouragement he gave to me from as far back as my teaching days in western Canada.

Many years after my early involvement with Clark, Judy and I stayed overnight with him and his wife Dorothy in their home in Ontario. They were gracious hosts, or course, and Clark took Judy and me to a special revival meeting at the Toronto Airport Vineyard Church. This was surely the most unusual "revival" service Judy and I had ever attended, and we could easily see—and hear—why the prolonged series of meetings at this church and similar "revival" meetings throughout North America had been receiving extensive media attention during the previous months. We witnessed such spectacular phenomena as people falling, jerking, barking, laughing, and simply lying stretched out and motionless on the carpet while the speaker and the musicians continued to call on the Holy Spirit to accomplish his work in the hearts of all who were seeking him.

Because of a prior commitment, Judy and I had to leave in the middle of the happenings in the auditorium. Clark told me later that he did "fall in the Spirit" backward and that he was caught by the assigned "catchers," but he also said that he did it voluntarily, and could have resisted the impulse if he so chose. One thing I had learned from my extensive studies of Clark's life and writings was that he was a man consistently concerned about the ministry of the Holy Spirit in the lives of people, starting with his own life. After all, his doctoral dissertation under F. F. Bruce was titled "The Concept of the Spirit in the Epistles of Paul." [1]

Christians for Biblical Equality

Another organization that I have been a member of, since its beginning in 1987, is Christians for Biblical Equality. (For years previous to the founding of CBE I was a member of the Evangelical Women's Caucus.) CBE is an organization of Christian men and women who believe that the Bible, properly interpreted, teaches the fundamental equality of believers of all ethnic groups, all economic classes, all age groups, and both men and women, based on the teachings of Scriptures such as Galatians 3:28: "There is neither Jew nor Greek, slave nor free, male nor female, for you are all one in Christ Jesus."

In addition to a solidly orthodox statement of faith, CBE holds to certain core values, including the following.

- Believers are called to mutual submission, love, and service

- God distributes spiritual gifts without regard to gender, ethnicity, or class

- Believers must develop and exercise their God-given gifts in church, home, and world

- Believers have equal authority and equal responsibility to exercise their gifts without regard to gender, ethnicity, or class, and without the limits of culturally defined roles. [2]

---

1. A study of Pinnock's life and thought up to 1990 is my chapter "Clark H. Pinnock" in *Baptist Theologians*, edited by Timothy George and David S. Dockery (Nashville, TN: Broadman, 1990), 660–84. The same article, with minor differences, appears in the *Christian Scholar's Review* (March, 1990), 252–70. A thorough, masterful account of Pinnock's theological pilgrimage is by Barry L. Callen, *Clark H. Pinnock: Journey Toward Renewal: An Intellectual Biography* (Nappanee, IN: Evangel, 2000).

2. CBE website: www.cbeinternational.org.

During my childhood and teen years I had both nuns (we addressed each as "Sister") and priests (addressed as "Father") for teachers. While a few of the nuns and priests were unquestionably troubled individuals (as I was), they were on the whole fine men and women. I respected both the nuns and the priests as persons and as teachers. If I had been asked who were "better" as people and teachers, I would have answered "Neither. They are equally good."

As a student at Prairie Bible Institute I had mostly male teachers in the classrooms and male preachers in the Prairie Tabernacle pulpit. But the primary Bible teacher (Ruth Dearing) during my freshman year was one of the major reasons I decided to return for my sophomore year. In addition, the women who preached from time to time in the Prairie Tabernacle (especially the fiery Mary Morrison of the Faith Mission of Scotland) made a strong impression on me, as much as the best male preachers did.

During my nine years at Prairie, the issue of male-female leadership in society, ministry, or the home was seldom mentioned, except with regard to missionary service, since a large majority of all missionaries were women, and a large number of them were single women. When the issue was considered it was usually raised by the president, L. E. Maxwell.

I can still remember Maxwell's remarks on the apostle Paul's instructions to wives and husbands in Ephesians 5:21–33, where wives are told to submit to and respect their husbands, and husbands are told to love their wives as their own bodies and "just as Christ loved the church and gave himself up for her." After considering the passage as a whole Maxwell concluded with the following summary (my paraphrase): "Wives, pay attention to what the Bible tells you to do, not what your husbands should do. And husbands, pay attention to what the Bible tells you to do, not what your wives should do. Each of you focus on what the Scriptures are saying to you, not to the other. Husbands, the Bible does not say to make sure that your wives submit to you and respect you; wives, the Bible doesn't say to make sure that your husband loves you as they love themselves, and as Christ loved the church. Each of you concentrate on what you are to do." In his book, *Women in Ministry*, written with Ruth Dearing, Maxwell remarks concisely, "She would be a strange wife indeed who would not respect a husband who loves her as Christ loves his church! (Eph 5:25)."[3]

With regard to public speaking ministries for women, whether married or single, Maxwell urged that the qualifying criterion should be giftedness from God rather than maleness or femaleness. He writes, for example,

3. L.E. Maxwell with Ruth C. Dearing, *Women in Ministry* (Wheaton, IL: Victor, 1987), 140.

of Mrs. Jessie Penn-Lewis (1861 to 1927), an English speaker and writer whom God used greatly for many years.

> While most of her ministry was in England, she also had speaking tours in Sweden, Russia, Finland, Denmark, Canada, and the United States. Many times she spoke at Keswick conferences in England and Scotland. Dr. R.A. Torrey, introducing her at the Moody Training Institute in 1900, described her as "one of the most gifted speakers the world has known. . . ." Not only did Mrs. Penn-Lewis minister in speaking but also in her writings. . . . Christians the world over have been signally challenged and led into a life of victory through her penetrating messages on the Cross in the life of the believer.[4]

Christians for Biblical Equality enthusiastically affirms both men and women equally in the home, society, and in ministry. Women as well as men should be welcomed equally in leadership, teaching, and pulpit ministry based upon clear evidence of their Christian character and the gifts of the Holy Spirit working through their lives.

Those who are aware of CBE know the above-mentioned concerns of the organization. What may not be as well known, however, is that CBE is just as concerned and active with regard to the welfare—physically, psychologically, spiritually—of women and girls around the world who are suffering terribly from abuse of all kinds: rapes, beatings, murders, and other horrors such as trafficking of their bodies, simply because they happened to be born female rather than male.

For many years I have been a big fan of CBE and the wise, godly leadership and maturity demonstrated by its members and associates, not only in its international and regional conferences, but also in its excellent publications, *Priscilla Papers* and *Mutuality*. Due to serious health limitations, unfortunately, I have been involved only a small amount with CBE, but I greatly respect the current President, Mimi Haddad, and her gifted and faithful colleagues in their vital service to the church of Jesus Christ worldwide. Their mission fields and potential ministries are vast, yet as God provides they will, I believe, continue to grow and serve relentlessly those women and girls (and men) who continually cry out for justice, mercy, and the God of all grace.

4. Ibid., 109–10.

Hell

I have always taken statements of faith (theological beliefs) very seriously, and I never, to my knowledge, signed one with which I disagreed. Church memberships and invitations to join a school faculty and other Christian organizations (such as ETS and CBE) are often contingent upon the applicant's agreement with the doctrinal position of the group. In some cases one's signature is required, even yearly. Faculty members at Bethel Seminary are also expected to support the school's Affirmation of Faith.

One of my theology electives at Bethel was titled, "Contemporary Issues in the Doctrine of Salvation." In this course we considered such topics as universalism (everyone, even Stalin and Hitler, will eventually be saved), annihilationism (everyone who is not saved will go out of existence sometime after death), the "second chance" offer of salvation after one dies, and the eternal destiny of those who die without ever hearing about the way of salvation in Jesus Christ.

One of the major considerations about which the course materials revolved was the concept of hell. Each of the doctrinal areas just mentioned is an issue of concern precisely because each may offer a way of alleviating our mental and emotional distress when we contemplate the never-ending torment of the lost, no matter how evil they were on earth.

Hell is an extremely unpleasant subject to think about for many believers in Jesus Christ and for many non-believers. It has been labeled as morally repugnant by many. If there were no solid basis for the doctrine in the Scriptures, a Christian could gladly dispense with it. It would no longer be an "embarrassment" to the gospel of grace, as many (including theologians, religious leaders, and past and contemporary popular writers) have considered it.

There I was, teaching this course on salvation and its opposite, damnation. Not only in my childhood but also as an adult I had often thought about the issue of hell. Even though I struggled with certain aspects of the doctrine as traditionally stated, I accepted the basic concept because I knew it was biblical. I was not free to embrace the more beloved teachings of Jesus ("God so loved the world") while rejecting the "hard" teachings of Jesus (the "perishing" he spoke of in the famous John 3:16 verse just quoted).

But what about Bethel's statement of faith? Was that biblical? The last article of the statement reads:

> We believe in the personal and visible return of the Lord Jesus Christ to earth and the establishment of His kingdom. We believe in the resurrection of the body, the final judgment, the

eternal felicity of the righteous, and the endless suffering of the wicked.[5]

The last six words were the ones that troubled me. Was I to agree with an idea of never-ending, conscious, physical and mental torment, where sufferers ("the wicked") knew they would never, ever escape from this horrifying existence, with never a time—even a second—to have a brief easing of the most crushing and painful experiences in some fiery, wretched, God-forsaken torture-chamber?

All professors at Bethel had to affirm the doctrine of hell as expressed in the last six words of the statement of faith, but not necessarily in the gruesome description just given. If a faculty member could not agree to the words in the statement without mental reservation, that teacher should resign from Bethel, even if no one else knew that he or she did not accept the doctrine as worded in Bethel's doctrinal statement. No one at Bethel ever mentioned such a policy in my hearing, nor did I ever see it written, as far as I can recall, but to me it was a matter of conscience to follow such a policy.

Because of my inner turmoil I made an appointment to see one of the key leaders under whom I served. He welcomed me and we sat down across from each other in comfortable chairs. I got right to the point: Did those who wrote Bethel's doctrinal statement intend to convey the idea of *conscious* anguish in hell? Or might they have accepted some kind of "suffering" that consisted primarily of separation from God but without conscious agony as we usually think of suffering.

His response was—as I feared it would be—that the framers of the document no doubt thought in terms of conscious suffering. I thanked him for his time and excused myself. It was a very brief meeting and I was grateful that he asked me no questions. He probably sensed where I was coming from, but he wisely and graciously allowed me the space to struggle and think. He trusted me to do the right thing.

But what was the right thing? I went to the Scriptures to see what they actually taught, and whether I could honestly remain on the faculty. I told no one of my struggles. I can't remember the specific texts I studied, but quite likely they included the following. (I quote each here apart from its context to introduce the basic thought, but for deeper study I always consider a text in light of its context, just as I consistently teach my students.)

> At that time your people . . . will be delivered. Multitudes who
> sleep in the dust of the earth will awake: some to everlasting life,
> others to shame and everlasting contempt (Dan 12:1–2).

5. Bethel University website: www.bethel.edu.

> Then he will say to those on his left, "Depart from me, you who are cursed, into the eternal fire prepared for the devil and his angels. . . ." Then they will go away to eternal punishment, but the righteous to eternal life (Matt 25:41, 46).

> This will happen when the Lord Jesus is revealed from heaven in blazing fire with his powerful angels. He will punish those who do not know God and do not obey the gospel of our Lord Jesus. They will be punished with everlasting destruction and shut out from the presence of the Lord and from the glory of his might. . . (2 Thess 1:7–9).

As I studied these and other biblical writings anew it was obvious to me that the Scriptures spoke of a coming judgment when God will determine the everlasting condition of every responsible person who ever lived. There are only two groups mentioned. Whatever else one may say, the idea of some individuals being permanently separated from God and his people came across clearly to me from the Bible.

But what about the word "suffering"? This was what troubled me most. While the term is not used directly in the above Scriptures, it is implied. And since other Scriptures (such as Luke 16:19–31) support the concept, I had to conclude that the condition of the lost involves some kind and degree of suffering.

I put all of these ingredients in a large stewing pot in my mind and stirred them deliberately and slowly. I mixed them with liberal amounts of prayer and willingness to believe and teach the truth, wherever it led and whatever the consequences might be.

Finally, even though I was not able to comprehend the doctrine of hell to anything near my satisfaction, I concluded that I could live with the Bethel Affirmation of Faith. While the words "endless suffering" made me (and still make me) cringe, there was enough uncertainty about them, to my earthly mind at least, that I could accept them.

What did the word "endless" mean to the lost? The concept of time in a seemingly (to me) timeless state—in both the realm of blessedness and that of destruction—left me baffled (and still does). How do we know our earthly notions of time and the sensation of the passing of time will correspond to human experience in the afterlife? How can we know that our earthly feelings of suffering (often linked with the fearful anticipation of a long time of such anguish) will correspond to the sufferings of the lost who may not have any awareness of the passage of time, if there is such in the next life?

I thought through other aspects of this huge objection to Christianity and concluded two things. First, however bright we may be or think we are, we will never be able to put into words a clear, unambiguous explanation and description of the unbeliever's experience after death. There is no need for us to make detailed statements about the specifics of that life when our information is so partial.

Second, however we think about the eternal destiny of the lost, and however we may wish to (understandably) soften the concept of hell, we must conclude that the Bible teaches a future judgment in which there will be a permanent separation of human beings into the two categories considered above. We may deny this fact and call it a relic of an outmoded pattern of Christian belief, or avoid preaching on the doctrine in order to have a truly "progressive" church, but if we do so we will need to acknowledge what we are doing: selecting which parts of the Bible we think might most comfort and attract people and build the church, while setting aside the hard teachings.

In such a case we would be placing ourselves above the written Word of God, and may be considering ourselves "wiser than God" by not declaring "the whole counsel of God." I wanted no part of such a ministry, and continued (and continue to this day) to accept the doctrine of hell (the nature of which I am very unsure), knowing that the Judge of all the earth will do right (Gen 18:25).

Bible, Theology, Ethics

Even though, as a theologian and ethicist, I worked with the most difficult issues in the realm of human thought, I loved what I did. Whether a given day's class focused on the divine and human natures in the one person of Christ, or the basis for the doctrine of "original sin," or the position of the early Christians on whether it was right to join the military, I found each topic highly interesting and (to the surprise and delight of many of my students) very pertinent to the issues of everyday life.

As I wrote earlier, in my beginning years as a Christian, while a student at Prairie and Calvary, I concentrated on the study of the Bible. Of course I also continued to pursue theological studies, since biblical research inevitably raises theological questions. But during my years teaching at Prairie and especially while serving as a pastor in New Jersey, I gravitated increasingly toward theology. While I continued to love the detailed study of the Scriptures (and always will), I became more and more concerned about the need to pull together the results of my biblical studies into a more coherent whole than what I had.

I thus began to move more toward "systematic theology" as I sought to understand more fully and consistently such topics as humanity in the image of God, the incarnation of the Son of God, and the interaction of God's grace with human response. I felt that, for me, systematic theology was more difficult than biblical exegesis and exposition as I had practiced these, because I had to integrate, for example, my research in the book of Hebrews with my theology of the trinity. Systematic theology required that I take the step—sometimes a major sequence of steps—from the study of a Scripture text on prayer for healing (such as Jas 5:13–18) to the theme of prayer for healing throughout the Bible, church history, and the experience of people today.

While I knew that a flawlessly constructed system, integrating the major themes of Scripture and all serious theological thought with human experience—past and present—is not possible on this earth, I nevertheless attempted to develop, if only in my mind, a framework on which to hang all major religious themes, especially those within Christianity. I wanted a biblically-grounded set of beliefs, and a way of thinking and acting, that would serve not only me but also those to whom I minister, as free as possible of paradox and with the assurance of God's guidance to navigate the sometimes calm, sometimes stormy, seas of life.

A further chapter then began to open. While continuing as a pastor in New Jersey, preaching the Scriptures and developing my theology more fully, I was realizing increasingly my need to grapple with the ethical issues of the day. This was now a further step in my quest to develop my intellectual gifts as fully as I was able. I was interested not only in decision-making as such (whether this or that practice is right or wrong), but in laying a better foundation in my mind for understanding the moral life: how one goes about living the good life and how one makes decisions in situations of apparent moral conflict. It was through this unfolding process that God led me to pursue Christian theological ethics at Drew University, as explained earlier.

After I studied a given Bible text and drew from it its intrinsic and immediate truth, I sought to integrate this content in my developing theological framework. I then moved to the third level: searching for the everyday applications and implications of these findings for life in an unjust and unmerciful world—a world that offers no encouragement to walk humbly with God (Mic 6:8). I have always been grateful for God's sequence of leading me in my educational life as a believer: spirituality, missions, and Bible at Prairie; Greek and Hebrew studies at Cavalry; and theology and ethics at

Drew. I would not have chosen this route beforehand, but I thank God that his ways are higher than my ways.

Liberal-Evangelical Dialogue

Studying at Drew and teaching at Criswell and Bethel had well prepared me for a new kind of classroom experience. A theology professor (Dr. Don White) from another seminary (United Theological Seminary of the Twin Cities) and I developed a new course titled: "Liberal-Evangelical Dialogue." To our knowledge nothing of this sort had been tried previously between our two seminaries.

United was the liberal seminary and Bethel was the evangelical seminary. We had some very fine textbooks that seemed to have been written with our course in mind.[6] We limited the enrollment to twenty students: ten from each school. Dr. White and I sat next to each other with the students in a circle, and we professors started off each class session (three hours one evening a week, alternating between Bethel and United campuses) with our own interaction on the topic for the week, such as the nature of God or the concepts of sin and atonement.

This was the most intense and direct portion of the class time, because Don and I each presented and discussed our beliefs on the topic. We were not afraid to state our views and ask hard questions about each other's perspectives. We often disagreed and we had no problem admitting that. I was more blunt in pointing out what I saw as the inconsistencies and weaknesses of Don's views than he was of mine. Even so, we always spoke respectfully to each other and often agreed to disagree.

After Don and I discussed the topic of the day, we opened the discussion time to the students. A question might be addressed to me or to Don or to both of us. We then took a break, after which the students met in small pre-assigned groups consisting of some United students and some Bethel students. Each group remained together during the course. Finally, for the last segment of the class day, we came together again and shared with one another what issues had been raised among each small group.

When the course came to an end, neither Don nor I could think of any negative aspects of the experience. Each "side" learned new things about the other from the students and the professors, especially those of the other

---

6. Textbooks used in the course: Clark H. Pinnock and Delwin Brown, *Theological Crossfire: An Evangelical/Liberal Dialogue* (Grand Rapids, MI: Zondervan, 1990); David L. Edwards with a Response from John Stott, *Evangelical Essentials: A Liberal-Evangelical Dialogue* (Downers Grove, IL: InterVarsity, 1988).

seminary. Some stereotypes were broken down and we all recognized our need to discuss theology and ministry with openness, honesty, kindness, and a hearty dose of humility.

We could adjust to one another's views, however, only so far. No one was expected to soften his or her beliefs for the sake of class camaraderie or Christian unity. We felt fine disagreeing, because each particular issue, with the opposing views, was set out quite clearly in the reading assignments and in class. Scholars had done in print just what we were doing in class.

The one issue to which we kept returning again and again was—as might be expected—the basis and authority of our beliefs. I was particularly concerned that we not stray from awareness of the grounding of our ideas and statements, lest we should be simply spinning ideas out of our own heads and hearts according to our own desires. I stressed that evangelicals regard the Bible as the inspired, trustworthy, and authoritative Word of God. It is our highest and final authority for theological beliefs and guidelines for living in a world whose values and patterns of conduct hang shakily on a flimsy thread of relativism, opinion polls, and "following one's heart."

In one class session, as I was emphasizing the need to hear the biblical teachings on the topic, Don asked, "Why the Bible?" He remarked that he considered the Bible to be an important work of literature in the same way as were the writings of Shakespeare or other great literary masterpieces. His dual religious emphasis above all was love and justice, but he had no solid grounding for this conviction. He spoke of it as seemingly self-evident.

In spite of our differences, Don and I got along very well. With our wives we visited each other's homes and ate out together at times. Because, judging by the students' course evaluations, the course had been so successful, Don and I taught the class twice more—every other year. One year we even received a grant from the Association of Theological Schools that enabled us to invite visiting scholars—both liberal and evangelical—to the class sessions and to have the sessions filmed and broadcast on local public television several times.

Only because of my declining health did we have to discontinue this course. I will always be grateful to Don for his willingness to participate in this valuable experience for students in such a gracious manner.

PART THREE

Pursuing the Strength to Suffer Well

CHAPTER 15

Quiet Desperation

Serving and Struggling

DURING THE 1990S, ALTHOUGH my heart and body continued to weaken, I pursued my teaching and other activities with enthusiasm. I loved my students and my work and believed God wanted me to be doing the things in which I was involved. I was busy creating some new courses and improving existing ones, as well as co-editing a two-volume textbook set on Christian ethics with my faculty colleague, Dr. David Clark.

I also received invitations to serve as the interim preaching pastor in several churches: one for nine months and two for about a year-and-a-half each. I had enjoyed this kind of ministry in New Jersey while working on my doctorate and enjoyed it in Minnesota also. Judy always went with me when I preached, and when I taught Sunday morning and evening lay courses in churches. In the lay courses I would teach perhaps four to six weeks on such topics as bioethics, sexual ethics, Christian holiness, and the epistle of James.

I was especially privileged to perform the marriage ceremonies for our daughters: Laurie to Rick in 1994 and Joni to Greg in 1995. While my father and brother did not attend (nor were they present at my wedding), my sister Rosemary, her husband Joe, and their three children traveled from Pennsylvania to celebrate with us. Judy's parents and some of her siblings came also. Our "near-daughter" Lori moved out at the end of 1995, after which Judy and I began the life of empty-nesters.

While I was blessed and grateful to be able to participate in family activities and serve in the churches, seminary, and world of scholarship, my life and service became more and more difficult due to my declining health. As I moved through the last decade of the twentieth century I struggled increasingly just to get through each day.

Judy and I drove together to our places of work since Bethel was along the route from our home to Bethany Baptist. (Since our wedding in 1967 we have been able to live with only one car—or none; public transportation, car-pooling, walking, and adjusting our schedules to fit one another's have enabled us to save considerably over the years.) Each morning, as Judy backed out of our driveway and we headed to our offices, I sometimes said to her, "I feel like I have put in a full day's work already." Rising, shaving, showering, eating, dressing, and whatever else needed doing sapped me of most of the strength I had; climbing into the car used up the rest.

Another example of my condition at this time (I know this will be very hard for some to believe) has to do with the necessity at times of using the turn signal while driving. I remember distinctly several occasions in which I was driving when, because of the weakness throughout my body, I did not push or pull the lever when I should have. If I needed to change lanes, for example, I found it easier to turn my head and use the mirrors to see whether the next lane was clear, rather than expend the energy to push or pull the lever. I remember saying to myself at those times: "I've got to be in a very sorry state to have descended to this." I still did, of course, use the lever when I felt it was really necessary.

I did not benefit from the drugs I was prescribed. My cardiologist was very knowledgeable, but all he could do was order regular echocardiograms and try different medications. Nothing helped. I cut back on the non-essential aspects of my ministry. Reluctantly, I resigned from my final interim pastoral ministry. One service on Sunday mornings was difficult enough, but two services eventually became out of the question. I grew aware, especially as I was preaching during the second service, that something within was holding me back from the usual intensity I experienced while preaching. When I came to the point of longing for the end of my sermon I knew I had to step down.

Another means of cutting back was my decision to ignore my home email account. I continued to use my office account because it was directly related to my work. But home email was one more project to take my meager energy. I asked Judy to keep my inbox cleared out, and to inform me only when a really important message arrived. As it turned out this decision lasted a whole year, and I loved the freedom of mind and body it gave me.

Two activities, standing and talking, became especially troubling for me. In combination with my constant problems with breathing and bodily weakness, these two aspects of life gradually rose to the top of my health issues over which I had some immediate control.

Throughout the 1990s and early 2000s I determined much of what I did, or intended to do or not do, based on my previous (very familiar) reactions to these two activities. I tried to avoid them in every way I could, with standing being my greatest concern. Walking was not as difficult, but after five or ten seconds of standing I began to look for somewhere to sit. Sometimes I first had to lean against a wall if I saw nowhere to sit, but because I would otherwise soon faint, I hurried somewhere to sit down or lie down. Standing *and* talking together doubled or even tripled my weakness.

I worked hard to fulfill my responsibilities throughout those years, sitting on a stool much of the time while teaching. I also attempted to attend the annual meetings of the American Academy of Religion and the Evangelical Theological Society. These trips became so difficult, however, due to such issues as standing and shuffling along in the airport ticket-counter line, that I eventually had to cease from these very enjoyable and very beneficial activities.

At the last professional meeting I attended I was sitting on a sofa in a large mostly-open area by the doors to the outside. Dozens of scholars were waiting for their shuttles to the airport, as I was. Most of them were standing and busily talking. I saw one of my former teaching assistants in conversation about 25 or 30 feet away. He did not look my way. I very much wanted to get up and walk to him since I hadn't seen him for years. But I knew the energy it would take to go to him, wait until he saw me, and then stand and talk, even briefly. Sadly, I stayed where I was.

Just a few feet from me, at a right angle to my sofa, sat a scholar working on his laptop. There was someone sitting between us. I saw his name tag (Max Turner) and I immediately wanted to meet him. He was doing some of the best work at the time on spiritual gifts, but I would have had to stand, lean over his laptop, introduce myself, and thank him for his very fine work. I simply sat there and looked at him.

Another incident took place in an elevator. I was at the University of Minnesota Hospital when a distinguished-looking man entered the elevator. There were two other people, I think, standing with me. I knew right away who he was because several years earlier he and I had been interviewed on a local television program. He was a bioethicist at the U. of M. medical school and the two of us had been interviewed concerning the then-recent cloning of Dolly the sheep. He looked at me with a note of recognition on his face, but I averted my eyes. I remember thinking that he could speak to me if he wished, and I would have surely talked with him. But I was so exhausted I just stood there, aware of his looking at me. I reached my floor and walked out of the elevator.

After each of the above incidents and numerous others I felt both uncomfortable and sad, but I simply felt so weak that I had nothing to give and plenty to lose. In every such case that I can think of, if I had been sitting I would have eagerly entered into conversation, at least for five or ten minutes.

Talking Heart Transplant

During these years I had occasionally asked my cardiologist about the possibility of a heart transplant, since I did not have the more common condition of clogged, cholesterol-filled arteries. Bypass surgery or stents were not helpful for my condition, which was an enlarged heart that was becoming less and less capable of pumping my blood.

With regret, the doctor said that my heart was not bad enough for me to be placed on the transplant list. There were simply too many people in a worse condition, many of whom would die before a suitable heart became available for them. I grew more and more concerned about the ability to do my work, but I totally understood and agreed with the policy on heart transplantation.

I resumed my teaching at the seminary concerned with one matter above all (after my overarching desire to glorify God): to give the students a high-quality, profitable experience in my courses. I set aside everything I could to attain this major goal. I was zealous to lead my students through a life-changing experience with each course, not only intellectually and professionally but also with God and others relationally. I refused to lower my expectations, because I knew I served a mighty God who was able to accomplish mighty things.

One of the most important Scripture passages throughout my lifetime (I selected it to post with my Prairie yearbook photo as a graduating senior) was 2 Corinthians 12:9–10, which includes these words from the Lord: "My grace is sufficient for you, for my power is made perfect in weakness."

I had no idea thirty-five years earlier when I chose this remarkable text, the extent to which it would sustain me many dozens of times in the years to come, including now, in these days of emerging crises. I simply trusted that this text was speaking of one of God's "great reversals"—in this case that the weak are really the strong. Because I was weak—very weak—and I knew it, I trusted that God's power was being made perfect in and through my weaknesses. I was a weak professor of theology and ethics expecting God to accomplish his powerful work in every class through me. And I believed he did just that.

Yet my physical body continued to be weak, and growing weaker. At one of the appointments with my cardiologist I felt such a sense of urgency that I once again asked if I could be recommended to be considered for a heart transplant. This time, to my surprise, he went to work on my behalf and got me scheduled to be examined by the heart transplant team at the Mayo Clinic. Thus began a new chapter in my life.

On February 12, 1998, Judy and I drove to the Mayo Clinic in Rochester, Minnesota. This was our first visit to the Clinic since 1991 when I had my heart valve surgery. We had a very full day of testing and consultations with cardiologists to determine my eligibility to be placed on the heart transplant waiting list.

The outcome was that I qualified for a transplant. However, after a nearly two-hour discussion with the main transplant cardiologist assigned to my case (there were four such cardiologists on my team), Judy and I felt that I should not pursue the transplant at this time. Our decision was based on the information we received during our long consultation with the doctor. He informed us that the immunosuppressant drugs that I would have to take for the rest of my post-transplant life often lead to health complications—sometimes serious ones—in the transplant recipients.

Because my body's immune system would be trying very hard (as it should be) to reject and destroy the foreign object (the new heart) that had invaded my body, I would need to take powerful medications daily to suppress my immune system. With a weakened immune system and the side-effects of multiple drugs, transplant recipients are more susceptible to a broader range of diseases than are people with a healthy ability to fight foreign objects and conditions. Those with a transplant have higher rates, for example, of high blood pressure, infections, liver damage, pain, bone deterioration, memory loss, and certain types of cancer. In addition, large numbers of recipients battle with depression, no doubt due—at least in part—to the drugs.

Five years after transplant, 30 percent of the recipients have died. The doctor said what I was to hear a number of times in the years ahead, namely, that the person who receives a transplanted heart is trading one set of problems for another—trading one disease for another. Of, course, the new heart usually saves the recipient's life—for a time. The patient's life will almost always be improved quantitatively (by living longer) but possibly not qualitatively, to the extent that he or she had hoped for.

Judy and I, as well as the cardiologist, were comfortable with my decision not to move forward at the present time with the battery of tests and procedures that I would need to prepare for the surgery. But the doctor encouraged me to keep the transplant option open, and to contact him any time I wanted to revisit the issue. Judy and I drove home with a sense of relief that I would not be taking such a momentous step, at least for a time. We were grateful that God had given us peace about the day's proceedings.

Nevertheless, my reasons for requesting the evaluation at Mayo Clinic remained the same. I returned to my work at the seminary determined by God's grace to do my best one day at a time and trying not to dwell on my health issues. But the issues kept surfacing—every day. The pervasive lack of inner strength, seemingly in every cell of my body, and frequent, severe headaches were the two issues beyond my control that hindered me most of all. These I could not manage in the way I could adjust my standing and speaking.

Searching for Healing

I called for the elders of our church to pray for me, according to the instructions in the fifth chapter of the epistle of James. They graciously came to our home, read Scripture, sang hymns, put oil on my forehead, then placed their hands on me while they took turns praying for my healing. These were high-quality Christian people and I very much appreciated their gifts of time and genuine concern.

As the days went by with no change in me, and the registrar needing to finalize the course schedule for the coming academic year, I went to speak with the Dean and Provost of Bethel Seminary, Dr. Leland Eliason. He listened carefully and sensitively to my concerns, and after some discussion we agreed that I would reduce my teaching to 75 percent of the normal faculty load in the coming year. My salary would be cut by 25 percent, but I knew without any doubt that I should take this course of action, starting August first.

I had been taking vitamin, mineral, and other nutritional supplements for years, but now I studied such products more closely and consulted with some knowledgeable people in the field. As a result I increased both the quantity and (supposedly) quality of the items, longing for something—anything—to improve my health so that I might avoid a transplant. I was not happy about the high cost of these supplements, but my medications were surely not helping. Perhaps they were actually part of my problems!

Another part of my quest for healing—or at least improvement—was to intensify my prayer for healing. I studied the Scriptures in a fresh way and read materials that argued seriously the case for "healing in the atonement" and the necessity for me to "claim my healing" by faith.

I watched television healers and teachers, but I was most struck by the missionary evangelist T. L. Osborn who spoke sincerely, in an extensive interview, about the very large numbers of sick people who had received physical (and spiritual) healing during his long years of ministry.

The stories—one after another after another—flowed so believably from his mouth that I thought to myself: this man is either a phenomenal liar or a speaker of truth. I chose to believe the latter (and do to this day). His words and demeanor clearly had, to me, the ring of truth.

I attended different churches and services and several times walked forward to receive prayer for healing. I continued to study the Scriptures that I believed were pertinent to my situation, such as the following words of Jesus recorded in Mark chapter eleven:

> Have faith in God. . . . Truly I tell you, if anyone says to this mountain, "Go, throw yourself into the sea," and does not doubt in their heart but believes that what they say will happen; it will be done for them. Therefore I tell you, whatever you ask for in prayer, believe that you have received it, and it will be yours. And when you stand praying, if you hold anything against anyone, forgive them, so that your Father in heaven may forgive you your sins.

I tried to follow every part of this text and every part of other key passages such as James 5. While watching the television healers I once put my hands on the television screen as the preacher instructed, just where my hands would "touch" the preacher's hands while he prayed, but nothing happened.

Time went by and I continued to trust in God's promises such as Genesis 18:25; Isaiah 26:3; Romans 8:28; 2 Corinthians 12:9–10 and Philippians 4:6–7. These were not Scriptures on healing, however, but texts that told of the assurance God's children may have in the midst of *any* kind of trial. They do not promise the external change we may be seeking in our health or other material matters, as Mark 11 and James 5 seem to do, but they do promise the peace and comfort of God while we endure the suffering.

I wanted healing, however, not only the grace of endurance, and occasionally I fell from my position of trust. Here, for example, is my journal entry for March 30, 1998:

> I seldom get angry at God but yesterday I did. I have been having such bad headaches lately and every day I battle with one. I don't know why this is happening, and yesterday I felt irritated at God for not giving me some clear revelation about what the cause is and what I should do about them. I desire wisdom to know what to do about the overall problem or condition, and what to do each day with each individual headache. Nothing seems to help. I asked God to forgive me. I trust him even though I am perplexed and sometimes cast down.

One saying attributed to Martin Luther has helped me at such times: "It is better to shake your fist at God than to turn your back on him." Another thought that I picked up over the years contains similar wisdom (I can remember only the general sense, not the words):

> Even though you may be arguing forcefully with a person face to face, you are giving time and effort to that person because you consider him or her important. But if you simply walk away, you are showing that the person is not worth bothering with. If we are contending with God, let us not walk away from him. Striving with God directly says that we at least value and respect him, even if we disagree with him at the time. But if we have once come to know God in truth, we insult him gravely when we consider him irrelevant.

CHAPTER 16

On and Off the List

On the List

DURING THE SUMMER OF 1998, by the empowering grace of God, Judy and I took a major trip by air. We visited Santa Teresa, New Mexico (to see our daughter Joni and her family), Tucson, Arizona (to see my father) and Phoenix, Arizona (to see Judy's parents and other relatives).

Five days after returning home, Judy left to attend her family reunion in California—another nine-day trip. I was not able to accompany her, but spent time in prayer and reading 1 Chronicles and John Wesley's *Journal*. I also spoke on the phone with the father of one of my students. The man had received a heart transplant years before and we discussed the pros and cons of his experience. Although he had had post-transplant difficulties due especially to the drugs, he urged me to move forward toward the transplant.

As I was seeking God for direction regarding this crucial decision, I turned to Wesley's *Journal* for February, 1744—the place where I had last left off reading. His entry of February 17 referred to Daniel chapter three, giving the words of the three Hebrew young men to the king: "Our God whom we serve is able to deliver us from the burning fiery furnace. But if not, we will not serve thy gods, nor worship the golden image which thou hast set up."

In my journal for that day I wrote that these words were very helpful to me, and that God seemed to be saying: "I am able to keep you from needing a transplant, and I am able to obtain one for you. But whatever I do, it will be good. Even if I give you a new heart and you have multiple complications, I will be with you. Remain loyal to me."

A short while later I read John Wesley's advice to a Mr. Viney, who came to Wesley seeking direction. Wesley's advice was: "If you go back, you are welcome to go; if you stay with me, you are welcome to stay. Only, whatever you do, do it with a clear conscience, and I shall be satisfied either way."

After reading these two journal entries from Wesley, I felt strongly that God was saying to me: "Stop delaying. Call the doctor now." So I did. I requested, with fear and trembling, that he move on with the formal procedure of having me tested further in order to be officially placed on the transplant list.

On August 26, 1998, after three full days of testing and evaluation in Rochester, and numerous tests in the Twin Cities before these, I learned that the Mayo Clinic heart transplantation team of doctors had put me on the transplant list. My journal entry for that day:

> It hit me like a ton of bricks to hear this. I expected that for some reason or another I would not qualify. The wait on the list is at least two years. I am somewhat fearful, but I have total confidence in God.

I then received a pager to wear all the time, so that Mayo Clinic would be able to contact me right away when a heart became available.

For the next two years I served as best I could in the tasks before me, teaching a 75 percent load with a minimum of committee work. My writing ministry, such as it was, had mostly ground to a halt. In April of 1999, I prepared a report for an upcoming appointment with the Mayo doctors. Following are some excerpts from my report:

> The best summary of my symptoms is that I always have with me a feeling of having to "push" my way through the day. This is never absent, although at times it is somewhat less than usual and at other times it is worse. But it is always there. . . . I feel as though I am pushing a wheelbarrow load of rocks all the time. At times the ground is fairly level and at other times I am pushing uphill. This feeling is with me whether I stand, sit, or lie down, whether I am physically active or not.

> It is only right that those in Status One and the more severe cases in Status Two [in which I was] should receive a heart before me. I understand, in a small way, the difficult decisions the transplant team faces concerning [those] who should receive a heart and when. And I am very grateful for the excellent care I am receiving from the Mayo Clinic doctors, nurses, and their colleagues. Most of all I thank God for the complete peace of mind, freedom from worry, and joy of heart while I live each day with my heart failure.

A Happy Death

During the fall of 1999, around the world, interest and anxiety were accelerating because the end of the millennium (as popularly understood) was approaching. Many self-appointed prophets—especially the doom and gloom types—were warning, without foundation, of terrible things that could happen when "Y2K" arrived (Y2K stood for "Year Two Thousand").

One fear that had a scientific basis concerned the millions of computers around the world whose internal workings were supposedly not designed for the calendar turnover from December 31, 1999 to January 1, 2000. The fear was that computers everywhere would malfunction in such major ways that—internationally and nationally—economic and governmental systems would be in chaos, and unable to function when the new year arrived. Activities involving national security, bank transactions, retirement funds, accounts receivable, and numerous other financial matters would probably be disrupted severely and for quite some time into the new year. As it turned out, the effects of the calendar change were minimal, due to the diligence of scientists and technicians around the world working throughout the previous months to prepare machines and systems for a smooth calendar turnover.

I mention these matters to illustrate the "millennial fever" that was in the air as Y2K approached. As one would expect, those who focused on Bible prophecy and the return of the Lord influenced some Christians toward believing that Christ would return in the year 2000. My father was one who was so influenced, and he expected this grand event to occur on the first of January.

When the Lord did not return on January first, my Dad began to go downhill physically. I believe this was due, to some extent, to the fact that Christ had not come back to earth. He began to lose weight rapidly and became progressively weaker, so Judy and I flew to Tucson to see him. He still had his sense of humor, was still able to wheel himself around the halls of the care center, and was able to sit with us on the back patio, looking for the turtle and the bunny who lived in the shrubbery around the courtyard. We also made arrangements with the management of the care center concerning the details of Dad's care and eventual death.

One week after we returned home, Dad died. I learned that he suffered for only about two or three days before God took him, and that he likely was on morphine for the last two days.

I was not prepared for him to die so suddenly, however. I thought we might see him one more time, perhaps in June. I went to teach my class the next morning but after about a half-hour at the office I asked a friend to drive me home. I simply could not focus on the coming class or other work because of thinking about Dad. I came home about 10:00 am and spent the day in a kind of fog while making phone calls about Dad's cremation. There were no tears. (I can count the number of times I have cried in my lifetime—as far as I can recall—on two hands and still have some fingers left over.) I was very grateful for Rosemary and Joe's willingness to travel to Tucson and take care of Dad's room and other final matters.

Dad was 88 when he died. This was the man whose head was plunged into a toilet bowl by his mother when he was little, and who left the last of his foster homes in Pennsylvania at the age of 14 to ride the rails and work out West wherever he could during the years of the Great Depression.

This was the one who was definitely "not like other men," but who was as honest and intense about doing right as anyone I've ever known. This was the man who came to Christ at the age of 50 and, eight months later, saw me come to Christ by urging me to read my Bible, since I wouldn't listen to anything he said.

This was the one who always "loved a good argument" but never learned how to respect and consider the views of others when those views were different from his. This was the man who said goodbye to his wife after 35 tumultuous years of marriage and never saw her again, as far as I know, for the rest of his life. (The name of the church in which they were married: Our Mother of Consolation.)

I considered Dad's going home to be a happy death—happy for him and for all who knew and loved him. For 38 years he lived as a man possessed. And he was—possessed by the Spirit of God in him. Although he had, to the end, many of the ragged edges he had acquired throughout his earlier yeas of rough and tumble living, he loved God mightily and served God—in his sometimes curious ways—passionately.

On one of my last visits with Dad as I sat on a chair next to his bed, he looked at me, smiled, and said, "I've had a GOOD life." I was taken aback by his comment! This man—unwanted as a child and unloved as a husband—was truly glad for the course of his "good life." He also had a good death, and, I'm sure, a grand entrance into the glorious presence of his Redeemer. No one there is scolding Dad for singing "Amazing Grace" too loudly, nor is anyone discouraging Dad from coming to mid-week prayer meeting while still in his work clothes.

Alone

That summer Judy and I drove to the Mayo Clinic for further evaluation. As we expected, I was removed from the transplant waiting list after having been almost two years on the list. According to recent tests there had been a small measure of improvement in my heart functioning, and there were too many others in much worse shape than me waiting for a heart. Judy and I felt good about this decision, because we knew what a huge difference in our lives the transplant would make.

Even though I had had some improvement, and even though I felt a bit better than I did two years earlier, my shortness of breath and accompanying fatigue continued to plague me daily. I wrote the following in my journal soon after being removed from the list:

> I feel very much alone in life. This is not due to anyone's failure to be there. Judy is absolutely wonderful in every way and Joni and Lori are totally supportive. I have a very loving, caring family and have no complaints about anyone on earth. But I know that others cannot really understand my situation. I cannot and do not expect them to. They surely do try. I do feel alone in the sense of having to live with something that is my personal burden to carry in life. I am *very* weary of this. I would much rather go to be with God or be healed. It is this in-between state that is very difficult. Yet I know that many, many people have a much more difficult life.

For the next three years I lived and served God and my students as best I could. I was able to accept some preaching invitations and to travel some to see family on both East and West coasts. I was helped greatly during this time by reading the Bible and numerous books by men and women of God. These were not books primarily about suffering and how to live with it, but were mostly about living with God and for God every day. These were powerful books on living and serving in the fullness of the Spirit, such as *The Memoirs of Charles G. Finney,* Charles Spurgeon's *An All Round Ministry,* John Piper's *The Dangerous Duty of Delight* (a condensed version of his *Desiring God*), *War, Peace and Nonresistance* by Guy Hershberger, and *The Life of God in the Soul of Man* by Henry Scougal.

Shortly before reading these I had been greatly helped by the works of W. Phillip Keller, such as *Triumph Against Trouble*. In addition I benefited much from *The Joy of Listening to God* by Joyce Huggett, *Destined for Glory* by Margaret Clarkson, *Helps to Holiness* by Samuel Brengle, and *The Writing Life* by Annie Dillard.

These works and a great many others excited me, strengthened me, instructed me, and drew me deeper into the very heart and mind of God. I saw in a new way his yearning for me to be consistently spiritually-minded, trusting, and compassionate in a desperately needy world.

As much as I profited from the Scriptures and these writings I still felt—as stated above—quite alone because of my congestive heart failure. I know it was difficult for others to understand how I felt—both physically and emotionally—since I was teaching my classes (sitting on a stool, as mentioned above), walking around the seminary, and even preaching occasionally.

From time to time I wrote up a brief handout for those who stopped me in the hallways at the seminary or church, explaining briefly my health situation. I chose this way of communicating with friends, concerned students, and colleagues because I got exhausted relating even a brief account of my condition. I even came to wait until most of the students were in classes before I walked to my mailbox or used the library, in order to encounter as few people as possible. I almost always ate my lunch in my office, with the door closed. It was not that I did not want to talk, but that I did not want to stand in the hallway. But I did have a desire to sit and talk with those who could sit with me and not be rushed.

Most people seemed to want a brief summary (sometimes on the run) of how I was doing, and I realized that this is the way I also related to those in difficulty, at least some of the time. I decided that I would never again ask someone "How are you doing?" unless I was ready to give time and concentrated attention to the person's response. If I did not have this time to give I would, as I passed people in the halls or elsewhere, say things that did not require an answer, such as "Good to see you, Kevin" or "Have a good evening, Jennifer," if it was near the end of the school day.

One time I felt so alone that when I was finished teaching for the day I walked slowly by the offices of faculty members, seeing if anyone might have the time and inclination to talk a bit. I was not looking for a long conversation, but something more than a brief interaction about our classes or other professional activities.

Some office doors were closed, as mine usually was, and I did not knock on them. At the open doors I tapped and peeked in and said "Hi." I didn't say why I had come, because I did not want the person to feel obligated to talk. I think I said something like "Working hard, I see," or "Keeping busy?" The person looked at me as I leaned on the door frame. They said something and I said something.

If I sensed an opening to a bit of a conversation, I sometimes sat down in their office and said something more. It was not nearly so exhausting to talk sitting down. But I was only hinting that I had a need for a listening ear and perhaps a prayer together. I was not explicit, so the faculty member looked at me with uncertainty, and with an obvious desire to get back to the work at hand before I stopped by. (Professors do not just sit at their desks waiting for students or other professors to visit.) I then excused myself and moved on.

These were fine men and women—every one of them a friend. I didn't feel the least bit slighted. It was such an unusual thing I did that I likely would have reacted the same way and probably did in the past. I know if I had knocked on the door of any one of them, said I was hurting and asked them to pray for me, everyone would have gladly done so. If he or she was leaving right then for class or an important meeting, they would likely have arranged to get together with me as soon as possible. I did not feel hurt, but I did feel sad and alone.

A couple of times I phoned John Piper, a friend, local pastor, international Christian leader, scholar, and author of many important books, and asked if we could have lunch together. On one occasion, after we had ordered, I asked John if he wanted to know why, specifically, I had asked him to lunch. He asked why, and I said something to this effect, "Because I'm desperate; I feel like I'm dying of thirst; I wanted to be with someone who also had a deep thirst for God." We talked of God, sin in the life of a believer, holiness, speaking in tongues, physical healing, and faith according to James 5 and Mark 11. I am not a close friend of John and his wife Noël, and I have major theological differences with John, but I value each one highly and benefit each time we are together.

Running Out of Time

Because my heart rhythm was presenting problems, I had to have an AICD implanted in the wall of my chest. While I had had a pacemaker for years, this was a defibrillator-pacemaker that would shock my heart or pace my heart as needed.

This device had saved many lives and I was grateful to have it, even though the electro-physiology team had problems implanting it and then re-implanting it. Because the electrical leads were not attached correctly in the manufacturing process, I spent the entire night in my hospital bed twitching and jerking uncontrollably from jolts of leaking electricity until the doctors removed the original device and put in a different one the next day. I did not notice any improvement from the AICD, but I was at least in a safer condition.

As I turned the pages on my wall calendar month after month, and as I struggled to teach my courses while finding every day more difficult than the one before, I developed a serious problem sleeping. Each year previously, in order to help me breathe while I slept, I had been increasing the number of pillows that lay under my head. Judy even bought me a foam rubber wedge on which I slept to hold my head up still higher. The pillows were piled on top of the wedge.

After a while, however, this elevated sleeping arrangement no longer worked. I simply could not get enough breath, yet I had to be alert to teach the next morning. Out of desperation I started sleeping in a reclining chair in our living room. Even with my upper body almost upright, however, I woke almost immediately after getting to sleep, many dozens of times during the night. Because my heart had become so enlarged, it hardly had any pumping power left. My body was receiving so little oxygenated blood that I jerked awake as soon as I feel asleep. The sense of suffocation made me sit up as straight as I could and deliberately concentrate on one deep breath after another until my exhaustion pulled me back to sleep. I then woke with a jerk and the cycle repeated itself, over and over.

Finally I developed a "concoction" of ingredients—all legal but probably not all that would be approved by my doctors—that helped knock me out for longer periods of time. Yet I sensed that my self-developed potion could not prop me up much longer. My heart, I felt, would not keep working in this strange manner for long.

I had been told by the Mayo doctors that I did not qualify to be kept on the transplant list any longer, and this left me confused, disappointed, and even desperate. As I got out of the recliner each morning after another fitful night I asked God for the strength I needed to teach my classes well that day.

My journey of quiet desperation was taking me closer to a point of crisis again. A few excerpts from my journal will throw some light on my condition.

> July 22, 2002. I am not sure why, but my fatigue seems to have worsened over the past 4–5 months. This has been discouraging. But I will trust God for his daily strength.

> May 2003. Recently my cardiologist said my heart was "severely enlarged, severely dysfunctional and end stage" (by "end stage" he means that there is nothing else prescription medications can do to help).

> June 11, 2003. The past month or two have been the worst I have ever been physically. The weakness throughout my body has become much worse and I don't know what God is doing.

July 13, 2003. Judy and I had our first meeting at the University of Minnesota Heart Transplant Center in Minneapolis, with Dr. Andrew Boyle, one of the transplant cardiologists. We met with him for about 1-1/4 hours. I had phoned my long-time Twin Cities cardiologist 2–3 weeks earlier, taking him up on his offer to look into the transplant possibility again. Because of the long ride to Rochester we decided to pursue the transplant option in the vicinity of our home rather than at Mayo Clinic. The U. of M., which did more heart transplants than Mayo year after year, had an excellent reputation with this surgery and worked in close collaboration with the Mayo Clinic doctors.

Dr. Boyle, after looking at my records and test results, said that I have a 50–50 chance of living for one year if I keep on as I have been, with no change in my treatment. And there is a zero chance of living two more years. This was startling to hear! As a result of this meeting, they will be scheduling a number of very important tests soon, including an angiogram and a right heart catheterization. When these tests are concluded, the transplant team will meet to decide the next step.

With this news, the medical part of my quest intensified. For decades, since the months following my conversion to Jesus Christ, I have known that, in my pursuit of truth and salvation, God had gone before me in his unceasing quest for me. Whatever I had done in my searching had not been of my initiative, but of God's. God spoke to me through his Word and my conscience, and I responded, but even my responses were prompted by him.

The same was true, and still is, of my search for spirituality and my search for the grace to suffer well. In my journal entry for July 13 once again, I wrote these concluding words: "Even though this is a very difficult time for Judy and me, it is pure joy to trust in God. I give him the glory for the fact that I have no fear. I place myself totally in your hands, O Lord!"

CHAPTER 17

Waiting for a Heart

Bridge to Transplant

ON JULY 21, 2003, Judy and I walked into the University of Minnesota Hospital where I was scheduled to have several surgical procedures in the heart catheterization lab ("cath lab," as it was commonly called). I thought I would go home that evening. However, as the day progressed I learned that I would be staying overnight, and longer. It turned out that I was hospitalized for six days.

During my stay in the hospital I had the scheduled procedures in the cath lab, but I also had more advanced work done. My cardiology team inserted a "Swan catheter" and a "Hickman catheter" in my neck and chest to help connect my heart to a battery-powered pump that continually infused a powerful drug called "milrinone" (accent on the first syllable) directly into my heart, as a "bridge-to-transplant."

The most seriously ill patients waiting for a heart have some bridge to keep their hearts beating until a heart becomes available. Some patients must live for weeks or even months in the hospital while waiting for a donor heart, and some die during this waiting period because their heart can no longer keep going, even with a bridge.

The bridge I received was ideal for me, however. In fact, its effect on me was remarkable. The milrinone was a clear liquid in a clear elastic bag that I replaced every two days. The bag hung in a pouch on my right hip and a device automatically pumped the drug directly into my heart. The bags had to be refrigerated and were very, very expensive. It was no small thing that my health insurance covered the costs, and to this day I still feel deep gratitude to God for his gracious provision.

When I was released from the hospital on July 27 I felt an energy that I had not known for years. The pervasive weakness within me for so long had become strength. I could move about, breathe, and talk with an ease that was wonderful. Most of all, I could sleep once again. Beautiful, peaceful sleep!

If ever a medication deserved the name "miracle drug" it was—at least in my case—milrinone. On the first night after coming home from the hospital with the pump I slept in our bed, not in the recliner. Somehow my body was now receiving oxygen at a level sufficient enough for me to sleep and to move throughout the day with much more energy than I had had in quite some time.

On the List Again

Soon after I received the pump Judy and I met with Dr. Boyle. He told us that I was now on the transplant list once again. When I was previously on the list I was at status 2, not likely to be called. Now I was at 1-B. The only higher status is 1-A, for those so bad they need to live in the hospital all the time until (and if) they get a heart. I also learned that among those of us at status 1-B, I was number three on the list. Since, at that time, the University of Minnesota did an average of three transplants per month, my time could come quite soon.

Some other pieces of information interested Judy and me greatly. Dr. Boyle said that if I had waited two to three months longer before getting my milrinone, it would have been too late for my body to receive a donor heart. My body would be shutting down and wouldn't be able to accept the new organ. He also said I would have been dead within a year if I had continued as I was.

Another interesting piece of information was that the nearly two years I spent on the waiting list through Mayo Clinic accrued to my present total waiting time. This was why I was now so high on the list and could be called very soon. With this knowledge, and with the major difference the milrinone had been making in my level of energy, I wrote the following words in my journal for August 13, 2003.

> I feel like the richest person on earth. I simply cannot express in words the deep joy and delight in God and God's wisdom and goodness in my life. In spite of my numerous sins God has blessed me beyond measure. I desire to live fully for him, every minute of every day, until he calls me home.

> I have been praying for the man or woman who may soon die—the one whose heart I will receive. May that person and his or her family be hearing your voice even now Lord, and be responding to you.

For the next several months I enjoyed my increased level of energy. I liked being able to be out of the house more, especially trimming bushes and trees and doing some planting in our yard. On one occasion I even took my electric chain saw and climbed a tree close to our house—one that I cut back regularly to keep the branches from scraping our roof.

As I was up in the tree I was aware that I now had two cords I needed to avoid cutting: not only the electric cord for the saw but also the dangling plastic cord that delivered the miracle drug to my heart. Fortunately I was able to accomplish the job without a crisis. As I look back now I realize it wasn't the wisest thing to do.

Hidden Danger

From the time I received the milrinone pump, even though I felt much better, I was at risk for my life. The danger, which increased steadily until I received a new heart, was due to the way the drug actually improved the pumping ability of my badly enlarged heart.

In the simplest terms my cardiologist used the example of a horse pulling a heavily-loaded cart. As the horse became more and more weakened by the heavy load it was pulling, the driver whipped it more and more to keep the horse moving. The whipping worked for a while, but eventually the horse collapsed and died. The doctor said my struggling heart was like the horse, and the milrinone was like the whip. However the drug actually works when it enters the heart chambers, it acts on one's heart muscle like a whip on an exhausted horse. The horse (my heart) is not made to be abused repeatedly by the whip and sooner or later the horse cannot lift another foot. Its life is over.

The milrinone was my wonder drug for the moment but my heart was actually becoming worse as the drug kept "whipping" it. The milrinone was not a long-term bridge to transplant, and my risk of death increased steadily the longer I was on the drug. After my transplant, Dr. Boyle told Judy and me that he was "on pins and needles" until I received a new heart, because of the likelihood of my heart simply giving out—no longer responding to the drug. He also said that my heart was the most enlarged he had ever seen, and that it had doubled in size from the dimensions it had when normal.

As time passed my ranking on the heart transplant waiting list—for this region of the country—was raised from third to second in the type A blood group. The two major criteria used to determine whether a heart is a likely fit for a patient are the blood type and the size of the heart. (A tissue-typing test was also necessary, but the Rh factor did not matter.) Just as a large person would not do well with a small heart rattling around in his or her chest, so a slender person like me would not be able to receive the heart of a large person.

Even with these criteria met, however, the final decision as to whether the donor heart will be implanted in a given case can only be made after the transplant surgeon inspects it visually. If something does not look right the donor's heart must be discarded and the patient sent home. Fortunately, until the surgeon gives the go-ahead the patient has not yet had their chest opened nor even received anesthesia. The situation here described—going home without a new heart—is called a "dry run."

I had to go on disability in August of 2003 because—if the law of averages held true—I was getting close to transplant time. I therefore did not teach during the fall quarter, nor would I teach again until I recovered from the transplant surgery—if I received a new heart.

Another factor in my decision to go on disability—in addition to the law of averages—was my gradually decreasing strength of body. I was being kept alive by my wonder drug, and I was surely doing better with it than before—especially in my breathing and sleeping—but as the weeks went by I became weaker and weaker. As the exhausted horse could not endure the punishment much longer, so my whipped heart was reaching its limit of endurance. I did not have the strength or the stamina to teach.

Dry Run

In mid-October I had a "dry-run." I was at home when the hospital phoned about noon. I had a strange feeling go through me when I heard the words: "We have a heart available, one that might possibly be suitable for you." I phoned Judy right away at the church office and she came and drove me to the hospital.

It took the nurses and other medical professionals six hours to prepare me for the surgery. Since a donor heart should not be out-of-body for more than three hours, I assumed that I was phoned right away after the accident that took the life of the donor, and that the donor's body was kept alive for some time before the heart was removed.

After being prepped and waiting to be wheeled into the operating room, after lying for hours on a flat, narrow, table-with-wheels, and after having had my chest shaved and various IV's inserted into my arms, the surgeon came to see me. He said that the donor heart was damaged and would not be suitable for a transplant. This was, of course, a disappointment, but I was glad the doctor made the decision he did. I certainly did not want another poor heart. It was late that night when Judy and I drove home. Getting ready for bed I asked her, "Did this day really happen?" A few days after returning home from the dry-run, I wrote the following in my journal.

> As I was being readied for a possible transplant I said to God that I did not want to come off the operating table alive unless I would make a significant impact for the kingdom of God during the rest of my life (There is a small percentage of heart transplant patients who die during the surgery, or within the first few days after the surgery.). . .
>
> But I must let God determine what "significant impact" means. I cannot judge how influential this or that factor may be. If I am "merely" to be an encouragement to Judy, Joni, Laurie, and their families, and to a few other friends and relatives, then I must accept that. I do long, however, to also make an impact through writing and speaking, as God gives me strength. And if I may honor my Lord and extend his kingdom through further teaching at Bethel Seminary, then I want to return to the classroom as well. I simply desire to do God's will every day—to not lose one day for the promotion of his great glory and the extension of his kingdom.
>
> Judy is my dearest friend on this earth, and our love gets sweeter every day I know her. She is the best life-partner anyone could have, and I will be eternally grateful for her—God's greatest gift to me other than his full salvation.

Four days later I added a bit more.

> Because of a bad head cold I stayed home from church this morning. Although I feel miserable, I was blessed greatly by reading the last chapter of Keith Drury's book, *Holiness for Ordinary People*. In that chapter are powerful testimonies from men and women hungry for God and greatly used by God: Catherine Booth, David Brainerd, William Bramwell, J. Wilbur Chapman, Charles Grandison Finney, John Fletcher, Billy Graham, Dwight L. Moody, Phoebe Palmer, Evan Roberts and Oswald J. Smith.
>
> Thank you, dear God, for giving me a deep hunger for you and the extension of your kingdom. As Dwight L. Moody said, "I really felt that I did not want to live any longer if I could not have this power for service. I kept on crying all the time that God would fill me with His Spirit."

CHAPTER 18

Transplant and Rehab

A New Heart

IT WAS SUNDAY, NOVEMBER 16, 2003—my 60th birthday. I did not go to church that morning since I felt especially without strength. Our daughters and their families came to our home after church to share dinner with us and celebrate my birthday. As we were enjoying our time together the phone rang. It was about 4:00 pm and it was the hospital calling, telling me that they would have a heart for me about midnight. I would need to be at the hospital between 6:30 and 7:00 pm. Here is my journal entry just before Judy and I left for the hospital.

> God knows whether I will return to this house or not. If I do, I hunger and thirst for God's glory to be shown through me the rest of my days on earth. While Judy was at church this morning I was in turmoil of soul over this very thing. I don't want to waste my life! I just bought John Piper's book, *Don't Waste Your Life*, and it expresses the longing of my heart.

We had plenty of time to get to the hospital (a 30-minute ride) and therefore Judy had no temptation to speed. I did miss my birthday cheesecake made from my mother's recipe (my favorite dessert), but the phone call changed my priorities in a big hurry!

We walked into the hospital, checked in, and right away the transportation staff wheeled me to a private room. After I undressed, the nurses and other medical staffers began the extensive routine of getting me ready for the surgery, the same as they did for my dry-run and for my mitral valve surgery at Mayo Clinic almost 13 years earlier.

The nurses shaved my chest and abdomen and painted them with antiseptic. I think it was blue. They put a saline drip IV into my arm to keep me hydrated. They took blood—lots of it. They put other IV lines in me; I think one of them was an antibiotic drip. They hooked me up to a heart monitor, an oxygen monitor, and a blood-pressure monitor. All the while they had to work around my milrinone pump and the elastic bag and cord.

The nurses regularly checked my vital signs and put medications into me as needed through the IV's. The person from anesthesiology came and made sure that an IV line was ready for me to be anesthetized. The only thing bothersome in all of these procedures was getting the IV in the back of my hand. I have had this done at that location on my hand dozens of times throughout my lifetime and it is never, ever, pleasant.

There was also the paperwork: forms to read and sign, and lots of questions to answer as the staff person went down the required list. The doctors, residents, fellows, interns, and (I think) medical students also came, introduced themselves and then asked many questions, often the same ones since these white-coated men and women did not all come at the same time. I have to admit I did become weary of repeating the same information over and over to my interrogators. Because this was a teaching hospital, however, I understood this was a valuable part of the students' training.

Finally they wheeled me into the operating room. I think it was somewhere around 11:00 pm. My very capable transplant surgeon was Dr. Liao, assisted by Dr. Kim. These two highly skilled specialists—with Vietnamese and Korean lineages respectively—were the human instruments God used, along with a battery of excellent nurses and technicians, to perform the complex and delicate surgery.

The staff transferred me to the operating table. Although I cannot remember, I'm almost certain I asked for one or two pillows to be placed under my knees, because my lower back hurts more than a little when I lie on a flat surface for very long. (There is, for good reason, no mattress.) In fact, I'm quite sure I asked for the same comfort measure during my hours in the preparation room. Operating rooms (and cath labs) are always cool, so I likely asked the nurses for more toasty warm blankets from time to time. (They keep an oven full of them!)

With the pillows under my knees, the warm blankets over me, and the capable nurses hovering over me, I was given the anesthesia and was sent off to some parallel universe in a very comfortable frame of mind—and body.

From what I can piece together, the team opened me up about 1:00 am, and the actual implant surgery lasted from 2:30 to 6:30. Judy, Joni, Greg, Laurie, Rick, and Pastor Bruce Petersen waited and prayed for me during the long night in the waiting room provided for the family of the patient.

I give God great praise for his keeping me free from anxiety from the time we received the call at home until I drifted off for the operation. Judy tells me that she also was at peace during the time of my preparation and surgery. She was so exhausted she slept through much of it. I'm quite sure that this God-given peace was due at least in part to the fact that Judy and I knew that there was no other medical solution to my end-stage condition.

Dozens of relatives and friends had been alerted by phone and email and asked to pray before we even left for the hospital. With so many praying, including the small band in the hospital waiting room, the comforting truth that God does all things well for his children, and the good reputation of the heart transplant program at the University, we did not experience the worry that we certainly could have otherwise.

Beginnings of Recovery

I remember nothing from the day after surgery, although Judy says that when she and the family were allowed to see me somewhere around mid-morning, I was awake. Judy's sister Diane in Portland, Oregon, and her husband Denny had been doing a fantastic job—along with faithful friends at Bethel, Bethany Baptist, and elsewhere—communicating to scores of God's people around the world about the details of my operation.

In one of Diane and Denny's emails to our prayer partners, soon after Judy was allowed to see me, Diane wrote: "Of course the next 48 hours are very critical and he will be in ICU. Judy will stay with him the whole time. Judy said that he looks awful but medically speaking he is doing well. They did have to give him blood transfusions, but only minimally so, due to the fact that there was so much scarring. His recovery will be longer than originally expected because of the additional scarring." I believe the "scarring" was from my previous heart surgery.

I remember very little from the next couple of days because I was so heavily drugged and slept much of the time. The doctors had told me previously that the two biggest dangers after a transplant are infection and rejection. The drugs I was receiving orally and through the IV's were—in large measure—to prevent these two lines of attack on my new heart.

After a few days, a tall nurse came to my bedside, smiled, and pulled the drainage tubes—at least five or six of them—out of my chest and abdominal areas. I'll never forget when she stood at the foot of my bed, reached forward until she was holding the several large diameter tubes, and then pulled them all as one, so swiftly and smoothly that they were out before I barely realized what was happening. There was no pain, just discomfort.

My next task was to start walking a few steps at a time. I have always found this to be difficult after major surgeries. The pain, weakness, and unsteadiness I felt when I tried to walk made life rather unpleasant. Three days following the surgery I still felt wretched. I distinctly remember being very frustrated because I did not seem to be getting any strength back. Fortunately, as the hours and the days passed by, I became stronger and the pain became weaker. On Tuesday, November 25, they let me go home. I got to listen to my new heart for the first time just before I was released.

Denny, my brother-in-law, sent a very detailed email message to my praying partners. Following are a few parts from his report.

> We spoke briefly with Bob himself. He said that there is no way to finish his recovery there in the hospital. He is so tired of being in that bed, and they keep coming in for all of the different things they have to do. But he said that it is not easy to get out of a major hospital. It is bad enough to get in (making sure all of the insurance permissions, etc., are in order), but worse getting out. It seems like you have to be cleared by every housekeeping person, almost to the point of how to groom your middle toe. They figure it will be well into the afternoon before they actually go home. . . .
>
> Romans 8 has sustained Bob tremendously, the whole chapter including our salvation, God working all things for our good, and the presence of the Holy Spirit. They have a lot yet before them. Five days a week (Monday-Friday) they will have appointments at the hospital. The rest of today will be taken up with just getting settled at home.

When I was finally released I went with Judy to the hospital discharge pharmacy. When the attendant had filled the order and brought it to me I was both stunned and amused by the size of my order. It was a large paper shopping bag like the ones used to carry groceries from the store—and it was full. I received probably about a dozen different medications in all sizes and quantities of boxes and containers. After the ride home Judy and I were alone for the first time in nine days. The quiet was wonderful!

Two days later it was Thanksgiving Day. Here is part of my journal entry written at 6:55 am.

> Today is Thanksgiving Day. And what a one it is. I received a new physical heart in the early morning hours of November 17. I received the heart of a [teenager]—a very strong heart! . . . God has been good in all ways. It was not easy recovering in the hospital, but I had excellent care. Judy and my precious family have been wonderfully supportive during this time. . . . Everyone (family) is coming today for Thanksgiving dinner—for a short

time. . . . *Thank you*, Lord, for my new physical heart, and for my new spiritual heart given to me on Thanksgiving Day 41 years ago! I will never cease to praise you!

Later that evening after our loved ones had gone I sent an email report to family, friends, and colleagues. Here are some excerpts from the message.

The recovery will be long. The surgery was a brutal assault upon my body. I will need to follow cardiac rehab guidelines carefully for quite some time to rebuild lost muscle mass especially in my legs. That area and the arms get hit hardest after a heart transplant. God will give me strength. I use the treadmill at home, and do other exercises and take tons of pills every day. I expect, if all goes well, to be back in the classroom in March 2004. . . .

I am getting biopsies of the new heart every week for the first four weeks, and then less frequently after that. The biopsy—performed through a catheter in my neck—is the only way the doctors can know for sure if my body is rejecting the new heart. I am still very weak, and I get worn out after very little activity. . . .

Probably my lowest point came in the hospital on Thursday, November 20. I couldn't see that I was making any progress. I wondered if I even wanted to go on. It was too hard to try. But God was at work, and here I am now.

Another chapter of my GraceQuest had ended, fittingly, on Thanksgiving Day. A major new chapter—one that has continued to the present day and will continue to my last day on earth—had now begun. I had no idea how unexpectedly and persistently difficult this final phase of my life would be. But God had brought me through the previous 60 years by his grace, pursuing me when I was not pursuing him, and I had no doubts at all that he would pursue me, love me, and stay close to me no matter what lay ahead. I knew that his grace would be sufficient for me, and that even this knowledge was a gift of his amazing grace.

Learning the Routine

As a 60-year-old with the heart of a teenager, I started my 90 days or so of scheduled rehabilitation with considerable optimism. My rehab would include physical exercise three times a week at the hospital, frequent biopsies, tests and doctor appointments quite often, and swallowing a hefty fistful of pills, capsules, and tablets every day.

Whenever I left the house I wore a pale-yellow porous paper mask over my nose and mouth, held in place with an elastic band around my head. This was to prevent nasty viruses and bacteria from getting into my body and causing trouble. Because my immune system was greatly suppressed, I was far more susceptible to harmful intruders than the average person. As I mentioned previously, I learned that the two major problems faced by heart transplant recipients, and the two leading causes of death, are infection and rejection. I was glad that I had no serious difficulties with infection, and after a couple of months I no longer needed to wear the masks. (In fact, to this day, except for two bouts of pneumonia, I have had practically no problems with infection; I rarely even get a cold.)

Dr. Boyle strove to maintain a proper balance between, on the one hand, giving me too little immunosuppressant medication, which might lead to rejection of the new heart (because my immune system would be doing exactly what it is supposed to do—kill off any foreign objects or substances), and, on the other hand, giving me too much, which might lead to infection (because my immune system would be suppressed too much and thus unable to fight off harmful invaders such as dangerous viruses and bacteria.)

Many weeks Judy drove me to the University of Minnesota Hospital every day, Monday to Friday. We spent a lot of time there for the first three months, and got to know the underground tunnel system very well. The doctors, nurses, technicians, and other staff who treated me were all high-quality men and women, regarding both their professional skills and their demeanor. (To the present day, with only a few exceptions, my opinion is the same. I have been well cared for and am deeply grateful for the hospital personnel.)

I wrote to the donor's family and thanked them for the precious gift of their loved one's heart. It was an awkward letter to write. I said I would be glad to meet with them at any time. I thought they might want to listen to their loved one's heart by putting their ear to my chest or listening with a stethoscope. I have never received a reply, and was told that this was sometimes the case. The pain of loss is just too much to bear. The correspondence was indirect—through the transplant program. I never knew the donor's name and the family never knew mine.

I was adjusting gradually to my new life. I did not experience, however, any boost in energy now that my old heart was gone and my new one was functioning. In fact, I was weaker than when I was on the milrinone just prior to the surgery, although with the transplant I no longer was at the edge of death and no longer had the milrinone equipment strapped to my body.

Because of my ongoing lack of strength my doctor made the decision to implant a pacemaker about six weeks after the transplant. Fortunately the pacemaker increased my energy level, although it seemed strange that my new teenage heart would need such a device. Ever since that surgery I have used a pacemaker.

At one point during the early weeks after my transplant, my five-year-old granddaughter Katie asked Judy some very serious questions. "What did they do with Grandpa's old heart?" Judy said they had to throw it away. Then Katie started to cry. "Where did Jesus go? Does Grandpa have to ask Jesus into his new heart?" Judy answered these and similar questions carefully and patiently, and Katie seemed to be satisfied.

As mentioned above, I had frequent biopsies in those early months. The purpose for these was to see if my heart was experiencing any rejection; this was the only way to determine rejection. For each biopsy, after having been prepped and put on hold—often for two or three hours or even more— I was wheeled into the cath lab, switched to the operating table, and hooked up to IV's and other devices. The cardiologist then cut out several pieces of my new heart to be studied in the laboratory.

About a day after the samples were snipped from my heart I received a phone call from my transplant nurse coordinator, giving me the results. The words I most wanted to hear, and often did in those early months were "no evidence of rejection." Sometimes, however, there was evidence of rejection. In these cases Dr. Boyle either changed my medication dosages or prescribed a different—or additional—medication, depending on the "grade" I received that indicated the degree of rejection.

In some cases the rejection was so severe that I needed to be hospitalized and given large amounts of steroids through an IV. I was hospitalized six times in 2004 alone. In some not-as-severe cases of rejection I was able to stay at home and take large amounts of steroids (prednisone) orally. After a week or so I had to go back and get another biopsy to see if the rejection had increased or lessened. One nurse told Judy and me, "We give you a new heart and then take it away piece by piece."

Once, when Dr. Boyle was preparing to begin my biopsy procedure, he asked me what kind of music I would like to hear. I replied, "Cuban or Afro-Cuban." A nurse put some on. Dr. Boyle then made the incision in the right side of my neck and began to insert the sheath into my major neck artery. The sheath is a long, thin, flexible tube that the doctor slides through the length of the artery toward my heart. Once it is in place the very thin catheter, with snips on its end (to clip the small pieces of the heart for biopsy), is then inserted into the sheath and directed to the locations in my heart from which the samples are taken. Usually five or six specimens were removed, one at a time.

On this occasion Dr. Boyle was having a very hard time getting the sheath to move through my artery. (He later told me I was "dry as bone.") As he was struggling and pushing, I noticed that the very lively Cuban music seemed to be getting louder and louder, and the tempo seemed to be increasing more and more. Both the volume and the tempo seemed to be intensifying in proportion to the amount of effort Dr. Boyle was exerting. Finally he got the sheath in and relaxed briefly. As he relaxed, it seemed to me that both the volume and tempo of the music eased off, and he then performed the procedure without further incident.

Either my experience with the music was all in my own mind, as I was empathizing with Dr. Boyle, or the original music had been performed for a while at the more intense level, which was then coming across on the cath lab sound system at the very time Dr. Boyle was struggling most. Perhaps it was some of each. Whatever the cause or causes, I experienced these moments as the most humorous incident in all of my cath lab procedures. It brings a smile to my face and mirth to my inner being whenever I recall this surreal incident of synchronized music and medicine.

Sometimes, at the same time as the biopsy, the doctors would cut an incision in my groin area and insert a catheter to the arteries around the heart. This was to perform an angiogram, which showed what was happening inside the arteries. Some of the time the doctors also did a right-heart catherization to study the pressures between my heart and my lungs. On all occasions in the cath lab the medical team took many vials of blood. (Throughout my ongoing recovery I have frequently had 10–12 vials of blood taken from me at one time.)

Whether I had some or all of these procedures, it was always a long day for Judy and me. On occasion I had to be checked into the hospital instead of sent home, due to complications from the procedures. I clearly remember one occasion when the procedures were completed by mid-to-late afternoon, yet the nurses did not get the bleeding from my groin artery to clot until about 1:00 in the morning. Such was my "new normal."

With so many hospital stays—usually several days at a time—I had some interesting experiences. Judy sent a lengthy email message to our prayer partners in September of 2004, detailing some of my experiences during one of my hospitalizations for acute rejection. I had just had a setback and needed to stay one more day in the hospital.

He is scheduled to come home tomorrow, Sunday. Yesterday Bob's spirits were very good and he had at least three opportunities to share the love of God with others.

One was a nurse who poured out the story of things she was struggling with and needed a word of encouragement toward Jesus. One told him she and her husband decided to go to church because they felt their children needed some kind of spiritual foundation . . . and one was a Muslim man.

The man came into Bob's room to change the sheets, etc. and ended up closing his door and spending over an hour talking to Bob. He said he wished he had been born a Christian instead of a Muslim. That gave Bob a wonderful opening to share the good news of being "born again" with him.

When the man was going to take Bob's temperature he put the thermometer under Bob's arm instead of in his mouth, because he wanted Bob to be able to continue to talk to him! What an encouragement it was to see God work in someone so spiritually hungry. See what your prayers have accomplished!

In the hospital, if I was awake and had the strength to talk and if the circumstances were favorable, I would enter into conversation with the different workers that came in and out of my room. Sometimes I chatted with my roommate, if I had one. Much of the time, however, I was simply too weak. Many, many hours Judy sat quietly in my room: reading, resting, and praying while I slept. She almost never left my side.

CHAPTER 19

Struggle and Redirection

Support Group

IT WAS A FULL-TIME job to work on my recovery according to the doctors' orders. Judy took off three months of work in order to drive me to all my appointments and to care for me at home. I was scheduled to return to the classroom in March of 2004, so I wanted to be in top condition, to give my best to the students.

I was increasingly bothered, however, even after receiving my pacemaker, with the slowness of my recovery. While I spoke to a number of groups who invited me to come and talk about my transplant experience, I was not growing in stamina as I had hoped I would, and needed to, if I was to teach my two spring quarter classes. Even worse, I had such severe headaches (quite likely intensified, at least in part, by my medications) that I would be incapacitated many hours at a time—16 hours on one occasion.

There was a support group that met once a week at the hospital for anyone who had had a heart transplant or was waiting for one. Family members were invited also. Judy and I attended two or three of these sessions, in which attendees (ideally) volunteered their experiences—good and not so good—in order to give empathy, find empathy, and perhaps receive some specific help for their particular struggles from those who had been transplanted longer. The sessions were especially beneficial to those waiting for a heart.

In my case, however, the support group was a major disappointment. I was definitely not doing well, so when Judy and I went to the group on one occasion I was hoping very much for some help. The kind of help I was looking for was not medical advice, but some indication of where I was on the recovery spectrum in relation to the 20–25 others in the room.

Was my recovery at 12 weeks, 15 weeks, or however far out from the transplant, typical of the average recipient at this point, or was I doing better or worse on the whole? If I was doing about the same or better, I could move toward teaching in March with more confidence than if I was not recovering as quickly as most.

When I had the opportunity to say a few words along this line, and ask if others had felt as lacking in strength as I was at this point, one man with a pony tail who had been transplanted years before shot me down, or at least that's how I felt. He said emphatically that a person with a heart transplant can do anything any other person can do, even climb mountains. He said it was all in one's head.

It may be that another person or two made some comments after those of Mr. Pony Tail in reply to my concern, but if they did I have no memory of them. All I remember is feeling hurt and disappointed and, yes, angry. When the meeting ended one kind man took me aside and assured me that most of the people in the room had had, or were having, a difficult time recovering—quite a bit more than they will say in the group setting. I thanked him for his empathy, walked out, and never returned to the "support" group.

In the Classroom Again

Although I continued struggling with my two major concerns—bodily weakness and severe headaches—I went ahead and prepared the syllabus for the Christian Social Ethics courses I would begin teaching toward the end of March. Fortunately, I would teach two sections (30–35 students in each) of the same course, so I had only one preparation for each two class sessions. In addition, I had taught this course many times before. I also built a "safety net" of several colleagues who agreed to teach for me at short notice if I should not be able to teach on a given day due to my condition.

As it turned out, due to health setbacks, I taught only six of the ten weeks. Yet I did all of the grading, while my gracious "safety net" colleagues taught the other four weeks and did a solid job according to the students. My teaching assistant, Laura Gilbertson, coordinated the courses and guided the students very capably, especially during the times I was hospitalized or otherwise too sick to teach. At the conclusion of these two courses I could say confidently, with praise to God, that the students had a valuable introduction to Christian Ethics.

I was scheduled to teach a theology course that summer but my health was still poor. Because I did not want a repeat of the previous quarter I knew that I should not attempt the task. Because of the commitment I had made to teach, however, I could not see a way out. To my great surprise God provided through a dear friend the means to have someone else—someone very competent—teach the course.

Leaving Bethel

I went on short-term disability once again, and did not teach in the fall of 2004 or the winter of 2005. I had to return to the classroom in March of 2005 or go on long-term disability, which meant I would need to take early retirement. Thinking of this prospect jolted me hard.

In facing my decision, three lines of thought were converging and colliding in my mind. First, I greatly loved the students, the subject-matter, and the classroom experience, and did not want to retire from that special ministry to which I had been called, and to which I had devoted most of my life. Second, I was very concerned about my monthly salary payment coming to an end. I would qualify, I hoped, for permanent disability, but this would nevertheless mean a significant drop in income for the coming years. Third, with great disappointment in the downward trajectory my recovery had taken, I knew it would be in the best interest of the students, and in my own best interest, to step down.

It was this third factor that led me, after much serious thought and prayer, to submit my letter of resignation. No one suggested this, but I could see no alternative. March 1, 2005, would be my last day as a faculty member of Bethel Seminary. In making my decision I felt no pressure of any kind from the President of Bethel, Dr. George Brushaber, the Seminary Provost, Dr. Leland Eliason, or my department dean, Dr. David Howard Jr. They could not have been more understanding and supportive.

I was able to spend some time on the seminary and college campuses for several months after my retirement, since my office would not be needed by someone else until August 1. This helped make the transition from office to home easier for me both physically and psychologically.

The Bethel community (including the staff and faculty at Bethel Seminary San Diego) invited me to a number of farewell occasions at which I, among others, was given great encouragement (and lots of hugs) before moving into a very different phase of my grace quest. My 17 years at Bethel had come to an end, and I was profoundly grateful for the students, staff, faculty, administrators, trustees, alumni, and loyal friends who had made my ministry at this fine institution both enjoyable and, I trust, fruitful.

I knew I would keep in touch with some of these men and women in the years to come, but I also knew that my teaching career—at least in a formal, professional capacity—was now over. I still remember, on my last day on campus, walking out of my then-empty office, down the stairs to the hallway, and out the front door to meet Judy at our waiting car. It was late on a warm July afternoon and there was no one around. As I seem to recall, neither Judy nor I said much of anything as we rode slowly through the campus, past the beautiful trees, to the highway and home.

Adapting

A new life lay before me, one with many unknowns. One thing I did know, however, with certainty, was that the God I knew personally as my Redeemer, Sanctifier, Counselor, and Friend would never abandon me. Nor would he lessen his interest in and care for me now that I was "retired."

From my earliest years as a believer I had heard and heartily accepted the notion that Christ's disciples never retire. I continued to believe this strongly. No matter what label would be used to indicate my position in life, I would never retire from actively serving my Lord in any and every way I could, as he gave me strength. My title would be different, but my longing after the fullness of God's grace flowing into and through me, to as many needy people on this planet as possible, would, I trusted, never abate. My grace quest after God, due to his always-prior grace quest after me, would only intensify. I believed and felt these truths deeply.

As the days and weeks went by, away from the people and concerns of Bethel, I had difficulty focusing on much of anything except my health issues. With Judy serving in our church office five days a week, and with our children and their families (always loving and supportive) needing to attend to their numerous responsibilities, I was alone almost all day every day. I never minded this, however, and never felt lonely. I enjoyed having visitors on occasion, and I enjoyed being alone with the Lord as well.

I have been neither a television watcher nor an internet searcher. I have used these technologies at times for entertainment or information, and have benefited from them, but on the whole I find it difficult to sit for long in front of either screen.

I have enjoyed our neighbors, however, both before and after the transplant. Although my time with them has never been extensive, because of my health, Judy and I value them highly, and we have some good memories of times with them and with those we now refer to as "former neighbors."

Our end of the street has had at times a very delightful "international" character. We have lived alongside of or across the street from Hindus from India (an arranged marriage), Catholic Latinos from Mexico and other

Central American countries (most being immigrants without documenta-
tion), Sunni Muslims from Yemen, Shiʻa Muslims from Iraq (fleeing for
their lives, literally, from Saddam Hussein) and American Muslims. We
made a point to meet each of these families and spend time with them as
circumstances allowed.

Each family came to us, stayed several years, and then moved away.
The Yemenis moved back to Yemen so their children could learn the Qurʾan
in Arabic—the only real way to learn this sacred book. The Iraqis moved
to Texas, the Hindus to another area of the Twin Cities, the Latinos back to
Mexico or other Central American countries, and the American Muslims, I
think, elsewhere in the Twin Cities area.

We read from the Qurʾan and the Bible while eating with our Sunni
friends and we ate Indian food with our Hindu friends on Thanksgiving
Day. (For the first time in her life, dear Sona cooked turkey, so Judy and I
could have traditional American food along with her curry and rice and
boiled eggs!) We ate with our Shiʻa and Latino neighbors, and I sat on our
front step with the American Muslim man discussing a book he was writing
about women. The Sunni man from Yemen, during one conversation we
were having about family, actually said to me shortly after his father had
died, "You are my father!" In almost all respects our lives were enriched
from our interactions with these neighbors. We miss them, but our present
neighbors are also enjoyable and very kind, even though I seldom see them
anymore due to my medical complications.

Painful Decisions

One thing I needed to do after leaving Bethel was to cut the size of my library
significantly. With my seminary office books piled in boxes on the floor next
to my home library shelves, I had several thousands of books to go through
and decide which to keep and which to give away. I could not possibly make
enough space for all of them. While I had invested a small fortune (at least
for Judy and me) in my personal library over the years, I had no desire to sell
the books I had to part with. I wanted to give them away.

To my delight I learned of an organization close to our home named
East-West Interknit, run in a very professional and Christ-centered manner by a missionary named Annette Jones. This servant of the Lord, now
widowed, uses her home and garage as a base from which to ship valuable academic books and journals overseas to help build solid theological
libraries in evangelical Bible colleges and seminaries. These are schools with
proven, effective programs and successful alumni, who need to grow their

libraries for accreditation purposes, but are in such poor countries that they have great difficulty in buying the necessary high-quality books.

After several weeks of painful sorting and culling my library books I gave hundreds of valuable books and journals to Annette, along with a small donation for the shipping costs. Some of these items had been very good friends and valuable tools for decades, but our parting was made less painful by the knowledge that these materials would be used by God to extend his reign over the earth. Men and women students under the guidance of capable, national teachers would use these books and journals in their training to become Christ's ambassadors for many years to come. (In the years since that initial culling I have brought together two more shipments for Annette, and am blessed often by the realization that my books, carefully chosen over several decades, are now tools in the hands of God's servants in Ghana, Haiti, India, and other exciting places around the world where the Lord is growing his church.)

While I was compelled to downsize my library due to space concerns, the major criterion for choosing which books to go and which to stay had to do with the projected usefulness to me of this or that item in the years ahead. The selection process, therefore, was very difficult. (And each additional culling became even more difficult, because each time I tried to keep "the best of the best" for future use.)

The struggle of selection revolved around the uncertainty of my future health. While I had accepted the fact that my classroom ministry was over, I was hoping that my learning and writing ministries would continue the rest of my days. If so, I would need my tools and companions to write with the highest quality the kinds of materials God would lead me to write.

Like all of us, however, I could not know the future. If my health worsened, would I even have the ability or desire to focus on the many topics that interested me? I knew that, whatever life held, I should keep my most valuable works (especially key reference volumes) on the Bible (including the biblical languages), theology (including apologetics), ethics, church history, my Wesleyan materials, the spiritual life, and—the most important categories for my personal growth (outside of the Bible)—biographies and autobiographies.

I gave away some large reference sets, such as my 38-volume set of writings of the church fathers, my 10-volume *Theological Dictionary of the New Testament*, and my 12-volume *Expositor's Bible Commentary*. I gave these away, in part, because their removal instantly created a large amount of shelf space which I badly needed, but also because I knew how helpful these and other sets would be to the students and their schools' accreditation goals. (To the present day, however, I miss being able to turn to these sets.)

Missionary Outreach

The involvement with East-West Interknit fueled my ever-present interest in the outreach of the gospel, to the end of the street and to the end of the world. Starting with our student days at Prairie and continuing to the present, Judy and I have come to know a large number of choice missionary servants of God in many nations. Some of these we have supported by prayer and finances for decades.

One of our favorite mission agencies, founded in the 1970s by a good friend from Prairie days, is Action International Ministries (ACTION). The founder, Doug Nichols, and his wife Margaret, were appalled at the desperate condition of the thousands of street children in Manila and determined to do something to help them. Because they did not see others working with these orphans and outcasts wholistically—addressing hunger, poverty, gang life, drug use, lack of education and work skills, and selling oneself sexually in order to survive—they began a very fruitful, many-faceted ministry with these street children in Manila that continues to the present day, not only in the Philippines but in other countries as well.

Doug has also had a longstanding concern for the approximately 41,000 devoted pastors and Christian workers in the Philippines (as well as the many thousands in other lands) who have little or no training in how to study and understand the Bible, Christian theology, and the skills of preaching and ministry. These workers cannot afford formal training or more than a few books. In many cases, they can barely feed their families.

Because of this serious lack of training Doug has developed a significant literature ministry through ACTION, and Christian Growth Ministries (CGM) in the Philippines, by which high-quality books and booklets are distributed to hundreds of little-taught but highly motivated pastors and Christian workers each year. If at all possible, these servants of Christ are taught what is in the books and (in the case of Study Bibles) how to use them in their daily work. The books and booklets are either donated by scholars, pastors from wealthier countries, or published by the mission itself.

I have been privileged to serve God in a very small way through this literature ministry. *Serving by the Spirit: Spiritual Gifts and Spiritual Preaching* (available in Spanish as *Sirviendo por el Espiritu*) and *Praying by the Spirit* (with Jane E. Spriggs, and available in the United States in a slightly modified edition titled *Heart Cries*) are two small lay-oriented books I wrote for ACTION and published with CGM in cooperation with ACTION.

I mention these publications to illustrate how God has been encouraging me by giving me a small ministry of writing for the kingdom during my recent years of poor health. I am filled with joy whenever I hear that one or both of these little books has been distributed to needy Christian workers in pastors' conferences in many lands. I am also heartened when I learn that one of these books, or some other item I wrote previously, perhaps decades ago, has been helpful to men and women in their personal lives and public ministries.

CHAPTER 20

Relapse

A Shocking Revelation

As HEALTH ALLOWED, DURING the months following my retirement from Bethel, I served God by writing, by praying, and by encouraging fellow believers in their own ministries for God. My biggest preoccupation, however, to my dismay, concerned my ongoing health difficulties.

With doctors' appointments, tests, procedures, adjusting to new medications and dosages, frequent trips to the emergency room (sometimes in our car and sometimes in an ambulance), hospitalizations due to serious bouts of acute rejection or diverticulitis (a condition of the digestive system), skin cancer surgeries, and the surgeries needed to repair several inguinal (groin area) hernias, working with my health issues had become a full-time job. I even developed steroid-induced diabetes, and had to give myself shots of insulin every day. I could no longer speak of my post-transplant condition as a "recovery," since I was gradually worsening, not improving. It was more of a relapse than a recovery.

In addition to the above I struggled to adjust to other issues on a daily basis: severe headaches (the worst), nausea, light-headedness, hyper-sensitivity to sudden noises, trembling of my hands, bodily weakness, and other side-effects from the medications I was prescribed.

I even developed a ventral (incisional) hernia a couple of inches above my navel, a condition that sometimes occurs after a patient has had major thoracic surgeries using the same line of incision. My two open-chest cardiac surgeries caused a weakness, and then a break, in my abdominal wall. Because the tear is inoperable, I wear all the time a wide elastic belt around my torso, held together with Velcro strips.

November 28, 2006, was a day I will never forget. It clearly was my most important day since the transplant. I had recently had my three-year testing in the cath lab, along with other tests, so Judy and I met with the doctor to learn the results. During an unexpectedly long (two-hour) consultation late in the afternoon, Dr. Boyle explained to us that my numerous attacks of acute transplant rejection had now led to permanent rejection. I now had a serious disease known as chronic transplant vasculopathy.

This disease had been developing for some time, but now was full-blown. It was not reversible, either on its own or through any known treatment. It would eventually take my life unless I died of some other cause first.

My immune system, after trying vigorously with repeated attacks for three years, had finally found a way to overcome the unwelcome invader—the foreign heart—lodged in my chest. Even though highly suppressed, my immune system never gave up on its major assignment to destroy the enemy.

There are sixteen or so arteries that bring oxygenated blood into the heart muscle. The heart is a bodily organ of its own and needs to be nourished in order for it to pump oxygenated blood to the rest of the body. My immune system had been gradually inflaming the arteries that carried fresh blood to the heart muscle. Silently and steadily the entire length of each artery was being narrowed to such an extent that, eventually, no fresh blood would get through. Some of my arteries, for example, were blocked 25–50 percent, some 75–99 percent and one 100 percent.

Some arteries are more critically important than others, but the vasculopathy was progressing—to a greater or lesser degree—throughout almost all of the cardiac artery system. The disease cannot be alleviated by the commonly known bypass surgeries or stents because these procedures target certain sections and places in the vessels, whereas the vasculopathy inflames the entire length of the artery.

When I asked Dr. Boyle how long I could expect to live he said maybe three months, maybe three years, maybe many years. There was no way to predict accurately. When I asked how I would die, if I died of this disease, he said there would be a series of small heart attacks or one big heart attack, or both. Because the nerves to my heart had been cut in the transplant surgery, I would not feel pain if I were having a heart attack. I would have other indications, such as profuse sweating and much more difficulty in breathing.

Judy and I left the clinic stunned. Judy drove us home as she had done many dozens of times before. As when we drove away from Bethel after my last day in the office, our words were few and our thoughts many.

As time passed, Dr. Boyle brought up the possibility of a second heart transplant. He said I would qualify, and I was quite sure my health insurance would cover the costs. We had a family conference—Judy and I with our two daughters. After a week or two going back and forth in my mind, and praying for wisdom, I declined the offer.

There were two reasons for my decision. First, I had learned that second heart transplants are usually not as successful as first ones, with respect to the subsequent quality of life. Why would I agree to go through the very difficult transplant and recovery process again, even though it might add more years to my life? The prospect of an even worse outcome was not a pleasant one at all.

A second reason for declining the offer had to do with the sense of excessive privilege I felt. I had had this concern before my first transplant, but it was now much stronger. If I chose another transplant, I would be receiving a second heart while many others were waiting for their first, and some would die before receiving one.

In addition, the extremely high costs seemed almost sinful in light of the basic medical care desperately needed by the hundreds of millions of poor and suffering people around the world. Some friends told me not to worry about the costs, because my insurance provider surely was not going to give the money they would save (by my declining a second transplant) to help with desperately needed medical care in other nations.

The thought of such staggering costs, however, troubled me greatly. As I often taught the students in my biomedical ethics classes, just because something *can* be done (with modern medical science) does not mean that it *should* be done. After some brief times of second-guessing my decision to decline, I settled into a position of rest on this matter.

Hospice

I continued to do poorly through December and the winter months, and in the spring of 2007 I looked into the possibility of hospice care. Hospice is a very beneficial and compassionate system of care for those who have been told by at least two doctors that they likely have no more than six months to live.

The patient may live at home if at all possible, if there is at least one family member or friend who is able and willing to care closely for the patient. If the person's condition worsens considerably, however, they may be moved to a hospice care center to live until passing away. I heard that almost everyone who enters hospice care is in the system until the time of death, and that the average length of time one spends in hospice is ten days!

Another important aspect of hospice—one to which the patient or their power of attorney for health care must agree—is that the patient cannot be pursuing remedial care. The patient receiving hospice care cannot, at the same time, be looking for a cure through ongoing medical treatment. If the patient wishes to pursue such a course of action, he or she needs to leave the hospice program.

Hospice care is palliative only. The nurses, social workers, chaplains, music therapists, massage therapists, and whoever else attends to the patient in their home or in the care center (one may choose all of these attendants or just one or two) are there for one reason only: the easing of pain and suffering and the comforting and soothing of the person during their final journey on earth.

I qualified for hospice in all of these respects and was accepted into the program, able to live at home. A nurse, a social worker, and a massage therapist visited me regularly, and were very kind and very professional. We even had our share of laughs.

I could have anything and everything I wanted, within reason, including narcotics for pain, since the purpose of the program was not my healing but my comfort. I tried the narcotics but, as I had learned in years past, they do not help me. After a brief high, if there is even that, I develop a horrible headache. So it does me no good, only harm, to take such substances for a bad headache or for any other pain!

Just weeks before I entered hospice my brother Tom died of heart failure at the age of 64. After a very troubled life—fueled by much anger and rage—he found rest at least. His bitter resentment against our Dad continued until the last couple of years before he died. He said to me, a few years before his death, "That man, Art Rakestraw, ruined my life." In his later years he began to move more and more closely toward a clearer understanding of the cross of Christ. He had had an extremely difficult time accepting God's absolutely free gift of forgiveness for himself.

During a three-month stay in a Seattle jail (due to an incident of rage in which no one, fortunately, was injured), Tom came to an understanding of the saving work of God. He told me that every time he walked by the jail after his release he thanked God for those months in prison. There he had come to know the Lord. Once again Rosemary and Joe kindly took care of Tom's final matters, as they did with those of Mom and then Dad. They are truly God's servants.

Now that I was in hospice I became increasingly concerned about doing something meaningful for the rest of my life. I had no desire to lie around and do nothing as long as I could work even a few hours each day, or if need be, each week. I sought the Lord for wisdom and direction, with confidence that he would give me a project—something that I could look forward to each day—that would glorify him and help as many people as possible for time and eternity.

While praying for some worthwhile project through which I could be loving God and loving neighbor, God gave me two projects and two valuable assistants—one for each project—to help Judy and me in these new tasks. To my delight, within a few weeks of being placed under hospice care, both projects were up and running.

Our friend from Bethel Seminary, Abigail Miller (now Sengendo), suggested I start a blog and offered to set it up and manage it. Thus began "The Benediction Project" (now "The New Benediction Project"). I write only about one article a month, but am grateful for the modest influence this vehicle has had around the world. Compared to the immense number of blogs on the internet, my postings are but tiny blips on the radar screen. But for those they have helped I am thankful.

Another friend from the seminary, Jane Spriggs, encouraged me to write the book on prayer that I had been considering but knew I could not do without additional help. (This is the book I referred to earlier.) Jane offered major and valuable assistance in several ways, and by the end of 2007 we had nearly completed the book. As indicated above, the small book was published both in the Philippines (2008) and in the United States (2010). Judy, Jane, and I have been encouraged by the feedback we have received concerning the ministry of this simple little book.

In early December I had a big surprise. My overall health condition during my time in hospice had seemingly improved slightly! With so many friends and family praying, with the huge relief of being free from doctors' appointments, tests, and procedures, and with the excitement and motivation from the blog and the book, I came to a point at which I was no longer eligible for hospice care.

It's not that I was better in any measurable ways, but I did not seem to be dying! I clearly did not feel any better than I did eight months earlier when I entered hospice, but hospice care was intended to help terminally ill people only during the last six months of their lives. Because I had gone past the time limit I was removed from hospice. I was bewildered and (although it sounds strange) disappointed.

Longing to Die

I wanted to die. I wanted to finish the prayer book and die. I did not want to keep living the way I had been living. Even though I was blessed and enthused because of the blog and book projects, I found these to be hard work, especially the book. My health problems were the major concerns of my daily life, not the writing as I would have preferred. Every day I struggled with the lack of bodily strength, shortness of breath, pain, light-headedness, and other side-effects of the medications.

I had mixed feelings when I took down the 2007 calendar and hung the one for 2008. According to the previous medical data, the probability was that I would not be alive on January 1. Yet I was alive, even though I was not overjoyed to be facing another year. I managed to find some excitement, at times intense excitement, from the likelihood that I would be home with the Lord by the end of the new year. If I lived to November, I would have my five-year transplant anniversary. Then I could go home. According to the national statistics concerning those who receive a heart transplant, 90 percent are alive one year after the transplant, 70 percent are still living after five years, and 50 percent after ten years. For those who had their transplants at the University of Minnesota, however, the last figure is 60 percent.

By the grace of God I moved cautiously through 2008. Surely it was by God's empowering presence because this proved to be the most difficult year of my life to that point. I was past four years out from transplant, which in itself was good. But I was living with a permanent, progressing, untreatable, deadly disease of the coronary arteries. I had been in and out of hospice and had tried oxygen to supplement my breathing, both to no avail.

I had become so debilitated from the continual, severe headaches that I agreed to be hospitalized in order to find help. After being tested in a number of ways and after several doctors considered my case, I still had no answers. I remember lying on the hospital bed looking up at 16 eyes and 16 nostrils staring down at me, when these white-coated medical personnel (some were interns and residents, I think) decided the best course of action for me was to go to a certain advanced pain clinic.

For several weeks I visited the pain clinic and, after more testing, was treated in several ways, mostly with shots—large ones. On one occasion I stood with my back to the doctor while a tall, strong nurse stood in front of me, holding her hands on my forehead. The doctor inserted a very long needle in the soft, hollowed region in the center back of my neck. He pushed the needle hard at an upward angle toward my frontal lobe, while the nurse pushed my head toward the doctor. It hurt, but somehow the nurse's strong hands on the front and sides of my head (even while I watched her wince) comforted me until the doctor withdrew the needle.

On several other occasions I had to lie flat on a table (there was a hole for my face) while a doctor gave me a number of painful injections in the back of my neck and upper spine. After weeks of being treated at this clinic and finding no lasting help, I discontinued the treatments.

I visited an acupuncturist, chiropractors, and massage specialists, and had (years before) spent six months under the care of a highly-trained headache specialist, but to no avail. The specialist referred me to a biofeed-back practitioner, but this approach was not helpful to me. (I now take no medication at all or an over-the-counter remedy when I get a bad headache. The pills sometimes help, sometimes do not, and sometimes make the pain worse, so I try to endure the headache as long as I can, just as it is.)

Sustained by the Word

One bright spot—actually 26 bright spots—gave me light throughout 2008. In January I felt that I should write a series of articles to post on "The Bene-diction Project." I wrote on the "Top Twelve Scripture Texts"—my favor-ite Bible verses or passages that had sustained me more than any others throughout my years as a follower of Christ. I wrote on one text each month, in this order: Philippians 4:6–7; James 1:5–8; Genesis 18:25b; Romans 8:28; Isaiah 26:3; Philippians 4:13; Matthew 11:28–30; Micah 6:8; James 4:8; Ne-hemiah 8:10; Galatians 5:22–23; and 2 Corinthians 12:7–10.

I wrote 26 articles on these 12 texts, obviously covering some of the passages in two or more parts. I had memorized and meditated very often on these Scriptures, and it was life-giving (though energy-draining) to put my thoughts down in written form. By the end of 2008 I was both excited about finishing the series and utterly exhausted from the project. I finished and posted the 26th essay late on December 31st, New Year's Eve.

Following is the last paragraph of that last article, concluding my thoughts on 2 Corinthians 12:7–10—the well-known verses on Paul's "thorn in the flesh."

> As we close the old year and begin 2009, may we all draw our strength from the grace of Christ. The days ahead may be dif-ficult, but the power of God is mightier than any and all thorns sent from the evil one. "He said to me," wrote Paul, "My grace is sufficient for you, for my power is made perfect in weakness." May we all be "benediction projects" to the Lord himself, to all we know, and to some we do not yet know, for it is in so doing that we receive benediction beyond measure.

I had no idea while writing the above paragraph how desperately I would cry out for the truth and experience of these very words in the new year—actually in just a few short hours!

CHAPTER 21

Worst Days Ever

An Enemy on the Move

DURING MY JOURNEY THROUGH the latter half of 2008 I was starting to face a new enemy. I did not recognize it right away, however, because it moved in as silently as it did steadily.

This foe would show itself to be more of a problem—*much* more so—than the headaches, the shortness of breath, and my other symptoms combined. This enemy was not only becoming very bothersome and difficult to live with, but it was becoming dangerous—and deadly!

As always, the grace of God was there to sustain me, even though I was unfamiliar with and unprepared for the new adversary in my life. I would surely need the sustaining grace of God in the days ahead because, as I would come to find out, this new enemy was not moving upon me alone. It had a partner, and together they worked to bring me down—to destroy me!

I found myself saying to Judy quite often, "I don't want to live." She then would reply, "You mean you don't want to live like this." I struggled to answer her, and usually agreed: I did not want to keep living with my health as it was. As the saying goes, I was sick and tired of being sick and tired.

But as I tried frequently to express my troubled thoughts I did not add the words "like this." I simply said, "I don't want to live." Judy kept trying to help me express what I really meant to say, but I knew deep down that I was saying just what I meant to say: I didn't want to live any more.

Judy's thought in itself was correct: I didn't want to live like this. The difference in our thinking (as I look back years later) was that Judy had hope that I would improve, whereas I had no such hope. We each had hope in God—strong hope—that God will always do what is best for his children (as *he* determines "best"). He will always work all things together for our "good." Judy's thinking, however, encompassed the real possibility that my

189

health would improve, but I felt rather strongly that God did not have this in my future.

Thinking Matters Through

I had two reasons for thinking that my health would not be improving. First, and far above the second, was that I came to accept the situation of the apostle Paul as my own. In a remarkable passage from his second epistle to the Corinthians, Paul wrote the following:

> Therefore, in order to keep me from becoming conceited, I was given a thorn in my flesh, a messenger of Satan, to torment me. Three times I pleaded with the Lord to take it away from me. But he said to me, "My grace is sufficient for you, for my power is made perfect in weakness." Therefore I will boast all the more gladly about my weaknesses, so that Christ's power may rest on me. That is why, for Christ's sake, I delight in weaknesses, in insults, in hardships, in persecutions, in difficulties. For when I am weak, then I am strong (12:7–10).

When I say that I came to accept Paul's situation as my own, I am not referring to Paul's first sentence. His thoughts about being kept from conceit and his "thorn in the flesh" being "a messenger of Satan" had to do with his personal circumstances, not mine. Furthermore, there is no agreement among Bible scholars concerning the nature of Paul's "thorn." Most agree that it was not necessarily a physical condition. It did involve, however, some kind of prolonged affliction—physical, psychological, relational, circumstantial—from the evil one that tormented him. In fact, his "thorn" may have involved one or more of the categories listed at the end of the above text.

After his first sentence, however, Paul expressed precisely what I felt God was teaching me about my situation. Paul's words, of course, referred to his own circumstances, but God applied them to me and comforted me greatly through them. (This use of Scripture is the same as that which the people of God have been practicing for millennia, as when, for example, the psalmist wrote of his own personal situation, yet his words have offered comfort and guidance to multitudes in similar situations.)

Paul's words that struck me most were those saying that he pleaded with the Lord three times to take the thorn away. God chose not to do so, however. He left Paul with the affliction even though it was a messenger (Greek *angelos*, the basic New Testament word for "angel") of Satan, and even though it tormented Paul! God had something better for Paul, as he wrote, but the horrible thorn remained, quite likely until the last day of his life—his day of martyrdom and glory!

Although this entire passage of Scripture comforted me greatly—the passage I chose to put under my Prairie yearbook picture over 40 years earlier—I kept thinking of the "three times." If Paul knew when to stop asking God for deliverance from his tormentor, perhaps I should do likewise.

It was not that I saw Paul's "three times" as a divinely ordained requirement for me, but that when I read his words and prayed about them, I felt that Paul's acceptance of his situation was the response that God was asking of me. I no longer asked (or ask) God for healing, and I had (and continue to have) great peace about my decision.

The second reason for thinking that I would not be improving was the factual medical data of my condition. The angiograms showed continuous progression of the vasculopathy, such that the arterial pathways bringing oxygenated blood to my heart tissues were steadily becoming more and more narrow. The disease my immune system devised to kill my heart was working continually to close the cardiac arteries completely.

When I asked the specialists how I was able to keep living with my vessels allowing little or (in some cases) no fresh blood to arrive at my heart muscles, I was amazed at the answer. There were numerous very small arteries called "collaterals" that, with signals from the brain, began to grow from healthy arteries toward the heart. In a very fine stream these tiny vessels transported the blood and kept the heart tissues from dying.

These collaterals are present incipiently in all people, but are not usually needed. I asked if these vessels will get the vasculopathy disease eventually and the doctors said, "Yes." I then asked if totally new collaterals would grow to take the place of the diseased previous collaterals that were keeping my heart alive and the doctors said, "No."

This information, along with other health factors, added to my willingness to follow the apostle Paul's approach to his thorn in the flesh. "Three times I pleaded with the Lord to take it away from me," Paul said. But God replied, "My grace is sufficient for you, for my power is made perfect in weakness." Paul concluded his remarks on the thorn with these words: "For when I am weak, then I am strong."

I knew, of course, that the Lord could heal me completely—even instantly—with one act of his will. Health conditions could never stand in the way of God's choice. I also believed that often-repeated prayers for God to work in a certain way, when offered in humility and submission to his sovereign will, are never ignored by the Lord. For me, however, I found great comfort in adopting the attitude of Paul and receiving for myself the remarkable words of the Lord to him.

I now accepted the high likelihood that, after five years of battling with my transplanted heart, I would not be improving—not in this life. This realization in itself did not crush my spirit. Rather, I felt free from having to pursue healing or even major medical improvement, because I did not believe these were in God's plan for me. If God willed otherwise I would welcome such gifts with gladness. I did not wish pain and suffering—not for a minute. I sought every day to find whatever relief I could from the afflictions I faced. In a sense, I was back in hospice, at least in my acceptance of palliative care only. It was nice to have a "plan"—an overall approach to my health situation.

Naming the Enemies

My "thorn in the flesh" was taking on a new face, however, in addition to the more strictly cardiological dynamics inside my body. Even though the acceptance of my condition was (and is) a very good feature of my thought world, I struggled with the fact that I had to keep living—day after day after day—for however long God wanted me here on earth.

Because of my daily health problems, as stated previously, I did not want to continue living. As Judy was reminding me of my true feelings as she saw them ("I don't want to live like this"), the fact was that I really did mean, "I don't want to live." While I sought to rely on the strengthening grace of God as presented in Paul's "thorn" account, there was something working upon my mind and soul and trying steadily to overtake me.

Finally I was able to name this beast: depression. As I heard myself saying daily, "I don't want to live," God brought to my mind the issues of hope and hopelessness. I knew that hopelessness—due to the relentless nature of my daily condition as well as a feeling of uselessness—was the root of my depression. And because I had no hope of my health problems lessening to any significant extent in this life, I wanted to die. And not only that, my creeping depression came with a partner that often accompanies it: anxiety!

The worst was upon me during the latter months of 2008 especially, when I started thinking of taking my own life. At first I quickly dismissed such thoughts when they arose. As time went by, however, I felt more and more drawn by this new and attractive option—one I had never thought of, except as an academic or counseling issue, during my entire lifetime. A soon and quick death could really be the solution, I thought! Both the never-ending uncertainty of my longed-for death and (especially) the never-ending round of daily difficulties, depression, and anxiety would come to an end immediately with an act of my will. I had no specific suicide plan but I had ideas that I entertained at times, always very briefly.

I did not tell Judy about my suicidal thoughts to keep her from worry, but because I continued to say to her, "I don't want to keep living" and "I want to die," she urged me to see a mental health professional. I told her I could fight this depression by myself, with God's help, and that some counselor—some stranger—could not offer me anything more than I could read in a good book on depression.

I asked God several times to take me home, but he refused my request. Three servants of God in the Bible—Moses, Elijah, and Jonah—also asked that they might die, but God refused their requests also.

As mentioned above, on December 31, 2008, New Year's Eve, I posted my final blog piece for the year about 10:30 pm. It was the second of two articles on Paul's "thorn in the flesh" account. I had fulfilled my commitment (to myself, and, in a sense, to my blog readers) to explain the twelve Scripture texts that had most helped me during my Christian life.

I was utterly exhausted both physically and emotionally, not just from the day's work but from the year-long project of covering the 12 texts in 12 months. I think I was in bed and asleep before the clock struck midnight.

I woke early New Year's Day—a day unlike any I had ever experienced or have ever experienced since. Judy was asleep, so I went into the living room and sat on the sofa. The following remarks are taken from my first blog posting of the new year, sent on January 22.

> The first five days of 2009 were the most awful time of my life, health-wise. I had never before known such anxiety. Even though I have struggled with anxiety both before and after my heart transplant of 2003, I have lived most of my life with no major problems with it. I never knew how real and frightening serious anxiety could be until recent weeks.

> It is hard, with words, to convey the terror of those days. (I say "those days" because, praise God, my last really bad day was January 5.) I'm not sure how to understand it all. But [in the morning hours of New Year's Day] I began to experience terrible fear within me—gripping my chest and abdomen, but definitely centered in my thoughts: thoughts of great apprehension, fear, and fear of fear.

> The "episodes" basically involved my sitting or standing in a completely overwhelmed state, fearing that I was not only losing control of a sound mind, but had actually lost it. I would cry out and say to Judy, "I can't take this anymore." I wasn't banging on

anything, or shouting out loud (but I was shouting in my mind), and didn't have any external symptoms except my frightened words and cries. Inside I was a wreck—crying to God for help but feeling under the grip of a terrifying force that seized me at the vulnerable edge of my fears.

What fears did I have? In part, accumulation of 25 years of heart problems, especially the past five since my heart transplant—with no medical hope of improvement—began to settle in me. But why now? I don't know for sure, although I have some ideas.

I do know that the fear had a lot to do with the future—not the far-off future but the fear of the immediate day itself, or the portion of the day still before me. I became terribly anxious about how I would spend my time. What would I do all day long? With my lack of energy becoming more of a problem each day, I can do less and less.

I had been having trouble sleeping and would wake as early as 2:00 am. To look forward to the long hours ahead would create such a sense of panic within me that I felt out of control. Each episode—lasting from 15 minutes to an hour or so—reinforced the apprehension about the next episode. I learned later that this was a classic pattern of apprehension—fear—adrenaline—further apprehension—fear, and so on. Adrenaline was pumping furiously during this cycle, and the more I fought the fear, the more I became filled with fear.

During some long nights and days I spent hours reading the Scriptures on anxiety, praying for some understanding of this "enemy" . . . that seemed to be lurking around each corner of the house (actually, lurking within my mind), waiting for the right moment to pounce. I said to Judy several times, "Something has to change. I don't believe God wants me to go on like this." I sensed strongly that something would soon change.

Finally, I did two things. One, which I had done several times before, was to follow James chapter five and called for the elders of the church to come to our home and pray for me. They did so gladly, and brought the church music team with them to sing. Another, which I had never done before, was to visit a mental health professional to discuss what was happening to me. Between the elders' prayers, the doctor's guidance and medications, a truly marvelous little book the doctor recommended by Dr. Claire Weekes, and the prayers of others, I began to understand and conquer the awful, awful fear.

Behavioral Health

I doubt if I will ever forget my first visit to a psychiatrist. While Judy was parking the car I walked with my small carrying case into the clean, pleasant, and well-lighted clinic building. On my left was a pharmacy, in the middle was a good-sized dental center, and to my right was a wide stairway. Above the stairway was a sign that said "Behavioral Health." This term was relatively new to me, but I felt sure I should go up the stairs.

As I climbed slowly, a distinct thought came to my mind: "Oh no, I'm going to see a shrink! Only other people do this!" I had no idea what to expect, but Judy and I had committed this appointment to the Lord, so I was not worried. In addition, Dr. Barbara Butcher, the excellent primary care physician Judy and I had had for many years, highly recommended to me the doctor I was about to see. I had (and have) great confidence in Dr. Butcher.

On the second floor I stopped at the "Behavioral Health" desk, handed the woman my insurance card, and said I had an appointment with Dr. Bruce Hermanson. She returned my card and handed me a clipboard with several pages of questions to answer. One page had on it the well-known, nine-question personal data inventory commonly used by mental health professionals. During the last two weeks, it asked, how many times have I felt that life was not worth living, felt nervous, anxious, and restless more than usual, and other questions like these. Before I had completed the paperwork a kind-looking man with glasses came into the waiting room and, learning that I was his next client, invited me to his office.

Dr. Hermanson was exactly the person for me. He asked key questions, listened carefully to my replies, related to me with genuine compassion and respect, and prescribed two medications in low doses. He assured me that I could contact him at any time if I needed to before our next appointment. He did not have me lie on a cot while he sat off to my side, behind my head, holding a pad and pen!

The doctor had no air of superiority about him and, although he was obviously very highly skilled, seemed to know well the therapeutic limits of his medical profession. I left his office knowing that we would do well together and thanking God for directing my ways.

As helpful as Dr. Hermanson and his prescribed medications were, I believe two additional factors that God used to bring significant healing to me during the first ten days of January were, as mentioned earlier, the prayers of the church elders and others, and the book by Dr. Claire Weekes.[1]

1. Dr. Claire Weekes, *Hope and Help for Your Nerves* (New York, NY: Signet, 1969; Afterword copyright Dr. Claire Weekes, 1990).

It would be quite difficult for me to overstate the value for my recovery of the small paperback by Dr. Weekes. Published in 1969, *Hope and Help for Your Nerves* has received extremely high praise from some of the most prominent specialists in her field. One wrote: "This book presents probably the best known therapy for panic-anxiety." Another said: "The books of Claire Weekes have done more to help phobic sufferers worldwide than all other treatment programs combined."

Because the book had helped me so much, I highlighted the key ideas of the book in my blog posting of January 30, 2009. Dr. Weekes presents four steps for dealing with serious anxiety, and I will briefly summarize them here.

Her first step is "Facing." Look at yourself and your emotions, she says, and note how tensely you are fighting the fears rising within you. *Do exactly the opposite!* Sit comfortably and do not shrink from the upsetting sensations. Face and examine the awful feelings. *Don't fight them.* By your anxiety you are stimulating an excessive flow of adrenaline which then produces the very sensations that are troubling you.

The second step is "Accepting." Be prepared to accept and live with your illness for some time, she writes. Your body has quite likely been through some very serious episodes, and *your nerves have been highly sensitized.* Small triggers may set off your sensitized nerves very easily, so be sure that you *truly accept* (not "put up with") your physical illness and symptoms. *This means 100 percent acceptance (not 99 percent) at the very peak of your crisis experience!* Try to live and work with your symptoms without paying them too much attention. The reason acceptance is such a key to recovery is that with this attitude, adrenaline and the sympathetic nervous system are not being triggered, hence there are no symptoms.

"Floating" comes next. "To float is just as important as to accept, and it works similar magic," she notes. Let "float" not "fight" be your slogan. Let the terrifying thoughts float away; picture them leaving your body. Realize *they are only thoughts; don't be bluffed by them.* Don't strive to relax, but simply let the thought of relaxation be in your mind. Calm breathing, where you allow your abdomen to move in and out with each breath (sometimes called "belly breathing") helps tremendously. The relaxation of your mind through facing and accepting will eventually bring the relaxation of your body.

The final step is "Letting time pass." Despite your new approach to your illness, your symptoms will almost certainly continue to return for some time—perhaps, at first, as acutely as before you learned these techniques. Dr. Weekes says that "your adrenaline-releasing nerves will continue to be fatigued and sensitized for some time longer, in spite of your new approach." Re-sensitization of nerves may occur at some future time, but because you have developed an inner core of confidence and strength you will pass through the fear. "Because this confidence has been born the hard way, from *your own experience,* you will never quite lose it. You may falter but you will *never be completely overwhelmed again.*"[2]

While Weekes is not writing from a religious perspective, the parallels between her four steps and the teachings of the Bible are remarkable! The steps she gives apply extremely helpfully to the struggles, temptations, anxieties, and other battles of the Christian life. As we face the problem squarely, accept the problem as being allowed (or perhaps, in some cases, sent) by God for his infinitely wise and good reasons, float with the (often awful) inner tensions while resting in God's love and care for each of his children, and letting time pass as we move through our daily responsibilities with trust and submission to God, we will ride out the greatest difficulties life (or the evil one) can throw at us.

Serious anxiety and serious depression—either one or the other or both—may afflict committed Christians as much as non-Christians. In my case they came together, but depression attacked me especially in the latter months of 2008 while anxiety seized me especially in the earlier months of 2009. However, during the six months or so of my mental health crisis, as I refer to it, these twin afflictions never left each other's side, even though each had its special time of attempting to dominate and destroy my mind, and me.

I marvel that, except for the first several days of January (and, to some extent, even during them), I was able to move through each day without hysteria or despair, and to appear outwardly to be of a sound mind. The battles with the twin terrors, which truly did terrorize me at times, took place within my mind. Only Judy knew, as much as a person can truly know another, the thoughts that were swirling about and colliding in my mind.

As alluded to above, I remember sitting on the sofa on the first day of the new year, before Judy awakened, screaming in my mind, "I can't take this anymore. I can't do it." Within minutes, however, there came to my mind strongly and clearly the powerful words of the apostle Paul—words that I had memorized over 45 years earlier—"I can do all things through Christ who strengthens me." Right away I stopped saying "I can't do this," because the biblical words—stated only once within my mind—silenced my truly desperate cries. The suddenness of the change in my mental attitude was remarkable, even as I think of it years later.

2. Ibid., 24–72.

CHAPTER 22

Emerging from Depression

The Price of Success

DEPRESSION WAS A MORE drawn-out, deep-down, and potentially deadly enemy than anxiety, although the anxiety I faced was, in no uncertain terms, very frightening. The above-mentioned book by Dr. Weekes deals almost entirely with anxiety. I wished that I had a whole book by her on depression rather than one chapter, although the ten pages she does have were helpful.

In my war with depression, however, I was not without other helpful written materials. I had no one book as I had for anxiety, but I found help in parts of a number of fine books. Some of these I had had in my personal library for many years. As always, the best books on serious personal issues are written either by those who have passed through the waters themselves, or (such as Dr. Weekes) who have been closely involved with the sufferers. With this in view, I wish to lift some comments from one writer who experienced depression far more serious that I have ever known.

In 1984, the English cleric and New Testament scholar, Dr. J. B. Phillips, published *The Price of Success: An Autobiography.*[1] There are 14 chapters in the book, but it is in the last chapter, "Light at the End of the Tunnel," where Dr. Phillips discusses his serious bout with depression. He was the author of many popular books on Christianity, but is best known as the translator of the highly successful and highly readable *The New Testament in Modern English,* first published in 1958.

His depression began in 1961, when he was 55, after some years at the peak of his success, and lasted for several years. Here are his words to give the setting, placed just before his first chapter.

1. J.B. Phillips, *The Price of Success: An Autobiography* (Wheaton, IL: Harold Shaw, 1984).

I was tasting the sweets of success to an almost unimaginable degree, my health was excellent; my future prospects were rosier than my wildest dreams could ever suggest; applause, honour and appreciation met me wherever I went. I was well aware of the dangers of sudden wealth and I took some severe measures to make sure that, although comfortable, I should never be rich. I was not nearly so aware of the dangers of success. The subtle corrosion of character, the unconscious changing of values and the secret monstrous growth of a vastly inflated idea of myself seeped slowly into me. Vaguely I was aware of this and, like some frightful parody of St. Augustine, I prayed, "Lord, make me humble—but not yet." I can still savour the sweet and gorgeous taste of it all—the warm admiration, the sense of power, of overwhelming ability, of boundless energy and never failing enthusiasm. I still do not regret it, in a sense it was inevitable, for I was still very young for my age. But it is very plain to me now why my one man kingdom of power and glory had to stop.[2]

Phillips writes that in the midst of all of this success, quite suddenly his speaking, writing, and communicating powers dried up. "I was not in a panic but I was certainly alarmed," he said. He took some time off from work, but then realized he had to cancel all speaking engagements for the rest of the year. In his words, "the feeling of being utterly drained of all emotion and desire persisted and I simply ceased to work." He had a number of medical tests but the doctors could find nothing physically wrong.

After a few months, during which I was not entirely idle, I found the mental pain more than I felt I could bear and I went as a voluntary patient to a psychiatric clinic not far from here. This was the point of breakdown, and after much hard thinking I have decided to write down my experience. My reason for writing this chapter is that it may help someone else who is depressed and in mental pain.[3]

I can only testify to the fact that it would have been of inestimable comfort and encouragement to me in some of my darkest hours if I could have come across even one book written by someone who had experienced and survived the hellish torments of mind which can be produced . . . . That is why I decided, however reluctantly, that this chapter must be written by someone who has experienced the almost unendurable sense of terror and alienation.

2. Ibid., 9.
3. Ibid., 197.

> Of course it is more than possible that most of my readers will never experience this particular Hell which life can inflict upon human beings. In that case, I beg you not to be unmindful of the unseen and often inexpressible sufferings of others. At least do not look down on those who are undergoing what seems to you to be purely imaginary terrors. And please have the charity to remember that most of them are fighting a battle of almost unbelievable ferocity just to keep going at all.[4]

Phillips then writes of what helped him most. While he believed there was no substitute "for the long unhurried conversations between the sufferer and the compassionate trained psychiatrist," he regretted that in his clinic the most a patient could expect in this respect was 10–15 minutes *per week*! He mentions "the use of drugs, which did me no good at all!" and continues, "the staff were kindness itself, but as far as I was concerned the daily contact with others who were suffering as I was did me more good than anything."[5]

> Much earlier, the late Leonard Browne had very easily and skilfully helped me to see that I was trying to please an exacting father. My life's drive, although I did not know it at the time, was to become so wonderful that I was beyond all criticism. The lack of love and security had to be compensated for by performance.[6]

God Who Understands

In his last few pages, Dr. Phillips makes some observations that help pull together much that he has been saying.

> I think, to be frank, that I can see the hand of God in all this. There will certainly be no VIPs in heaven and I think I can accept the fact that I am basically a perfectly ordinary person. To be made to realise this is terribly painful because the unconscious is thoroughly amoral and is determined to defend the *status quo* to the last. I don't think God minds hurting us, but I am absolutely certain he will never harm us. It may even be the assaults of the "principalities and powers" who seem to be allowed to pick their targets. I simply do not know. But I am

4. Ibid., 201.
5. Ibid., 202.
6. Ibid., 208.

improving steadily and I have gained much greater insights than I had in the days of health and prosperity.[7]

Phillips shares a final letter, one that he wrote in reply to a fellow sufferer—one of the many who wrote to him after learning of the suffering he had endured.

> I think prolonged suffering, whether it is mental, physical or both, tends to make us impatient, resentful, angry and frustrated; we begin to see the jaws of despair. . . . I never thought, for example, that I should ever know the type of despair that leads people to self-destruction. I know it now, but I am still firmly of the belief that it really solves nothing and is a cowardly gesture.[8]

> There is an almost inescapable loneliness about the experience of prolonged suffering. If we hang on, and of course we must, I am pretty certain that we shall emerge with a far more robust faith. I haven't even begun to "welcome" my afflictions, as St. James suggests in his epistle, but men and women have learned to do this and it must be possible.[9]

I have included the above selections from J. B. Phillips and Claire Weekes in order to help readers who suffer from depression, anxiety, or other psychological disorders. How might this information help? If nothing else, the sufferer can know that someone else truly understands how their affliction may seize them, grip them, dominate them, and possibly defeat them.

As I mentioned previously, one of the strongest longings I have had throughout my journey with heart failure—starting long before my psychological illnesses—has been to be understood as fully as possible by another person in this life. When kind people who were somewhat aware of my health difficulties would ask me, "How are you doing?" I almost always struggled with how to answer. Immediately I assessed in my mind whether they wanted the long answer (very few, if any, I assumed), the medium-length answer (maybe a few more, but still not many, I thought), or the short answer (what most probably wanted, so it's what I gave). I always welcomed (and usually wanted) follow-up questions, but these were few. I knew some wanted an even shorter answer, something like "Fine," "OK," or "Taking it one day at a time." I gave one of these super brief replies to those who were evidently in a hurry: either they didn't stop moving while walking past me

7. Ibid., 209.
8. Ibid., 213.
9. Ibid., 214.

and asking their question or they seemed to use "How are you" or "How're you doing" as a way of saying "Hello." One person actually said that this was the reason for asking their question of me, not to get any information. It hurt to hear this, but it stunned me more than hurt me.

The desire to be fully understood was almost as important to me as the desire to be healed of my condition. In fact, after I came to believe that it was not likely in God's plan to heal me, this longing became my strongest desire with regard to my health issues. As I write now, the alleviation of specific physical sufferings is more important than being understood, but for years the latter prevailed. Now that I realize my longing for full understanding by another is not attainable in this life, I am much more content. I no longer try very strenuously to answer, "How are you doing?" I am not bothered by the question anymore and even welcome it. I rest satisfied in the knowledge that my Good Shepherd knows everything and cares very personally about every pain and every sorrow.

Sensitivities

As the months and years have rolled by from 2009 to the present, I have gradually come to a place of acceptance and peace of mind with my station in life, although my contentment level is not always where it should be.

I have also been doing my best to reduce the number of visits to my various medical specialists, and have become more and more reluctant to have medical tests (except for lab work) or to check in to the hospital.

My reason for this reluctance is not because I have poor doctors. Quite the contrary—I have the very best in each specialty. But these highly-skilled men and women acknowledge that there is nothing more that they can do to bring substantial relief to me in my everyday struggle with chronic transplant vasculopathy.

At times they may, on the basis of lab-test results and my oral reports to them, make slight adjustments to my medications or prescribe a new one, but on the whole they simply monitor my condition and answer any questions I may have.

Above all (yes, I mean this), my doctors, nurses, and technicians are compassionate. There was a time during my post-transplant years when one of my most important doctors took a position in another city. I regretted this, but with some information from the nursing staff I chose another doctor in that specialty. After six months or so under his care I decided we needed to part. That he had helped many people over the span of his career I had no doubt. But I was at a point in my life that his abrupt, overwhelming manner became too distressing to me. Perhaps the difficulty was more within me than within him.

I phoned the transplant office and left a message requesting another doctor in that field. When a nurse called me back she asked, "What kind of doctor do you want?" I answered without hesitation or forethought, "Someone with compassion." I think she was surprised at my reply, but after a brief discussion we decided on my present doctor—a very knowledgeable, highly skilled, and very compassionate heart transplant specialist.

Notwithstanding my above experience, people who live with suffering, it seems to me, notice the kindnesses of others more than their rudeness or lack of consideration. Sometimes just a few words (or even the volume or tone of the words), a slight touch, or even a look may work wonders in the patient.

Throughout my life, especially during the years of heart disease, I have increasingly become very sensitive to those who suffer: physically, psychologically, spiritually, relationally or in any other way. As I walk through hospital corridors or store aisles and see someone in a wheel chair or using a walker, I feel an instant connection with that person. I sometimes breathe a prayer for him or her. And I always try to smile, although most of the time such a person is looking down, not up.

Recently I rode with Judy to one of the local big-box home-improvement stores to check on some electrical cord. We had parked in one of the disability spaces—as close to the door as one could park. No sooner had I walked from the car, through the huge open doors to the large space just inside the doors, that I said to Judy, "I have to sit down. You go ahead and I'll wait here for you." I felt as though I would collapse or faint.

Since there were no benches or chairs (notice how rarely, if ever, you see these in stores) I sat down on the floor, propped up against the wall with my legs outstretched. I watched the customers come and go through the doors, and was especially warmed when two younger employees—at different times—walked up to me and asked if I was alright, wondering if I needed help. I said I was OK and thanked them for their concern. Judy soon came and drove us home.

Even though Judy has always been a woman of God with deep trust in him and remarkable steadiness of spirit, I know that my physical health issues have weighed heavily on her. She thinks of and practices the truth of 1 Peter 5:7 often: "Cast all your anxiety on him because he cares for you." She just hands it over to God because she knows she cannot carry it. She has a wonderful and genuine joy in the Lord and seldom mentions how my difficulties affect her adversely, but she surely shares my suffering. How could one *not* share the other's suffering in such circumstances?

As stated earlier, it became clear to us in November of 2006 that, after three years of vigorous resistance from my body, I had permanent rejection of the transplanted heart. Because my condition continued to worsen, Judy in 2010 resigned from her position as office manager of our church. She had served extremely well in that capacity for almost 22 years and the church gave her a wonderful farewell celebration.

I regret greatly that I was not able to attend. Even before this very important occasion I had stopped attending church services and functions. It took quite some time before I came to this decision, but the utter exhaustion I felt before, during, and after a church service left me no reasonable choice.

We are still members of this fine church and I try to keep aware of the most important happenings. Judy continues to be very active in attending services, serving as an elder, and participating in other important ways. From time to time church folks stop by our home. I am always thankful for them and for others who visit, even though I am not able to give much of myself for long. At the present time, my available energy for a home visit is often no more than 15 or 20 minutes.

The Best Years

The years since Judy stepped down from her position at the church until now have been the best years for the two of us together, as a married couple, since the heart transplant. Surely I have been the best psychologically, and it seems to me that four factors in particular have contributed to this state of affairs.

One is that Judy's presence in our home most of the time is a huge comfort and source of blessing to me. We enjoy each other greatly and have ever since our honeymoon days in 1967. When we are together we enjoy much the same things, especially reading and (as I am able) discussion.

We spend time considering the articles from our daily newspaper and other publications, especially those from various Christian perspectives. We benefit much from talking about the things of God—both old and new—that fill our minds continually. We pray together several times daily (not long times but meaningful ones) and sometimes discuss the books we are reading and the portions of the Bible we have been spending time in lately. We pray every day for our children and their families. Our five delightful grandchildren—Chloe, Tommy, and Jack from Joni and Greg, and Ashley and Katie from Laurie and Rick—as well as their moms and dads are continually in our thoughts and prayers. We pray for our loved ones near and far, and for our friends both in our church and elsewhere. And we pray for the many we know who are involved in kingdom building all over the world. I must say, however, that conversation and spoken prayer, even with Judy, has become much more difficult during the past year or so. It exhausts me even to listen, because I still concentrate intensely. (I know no other way to listen.)

I very rarely leave home, and have been this way for several years. It is simply too exhausting to go anywhere except for an occasional brief lunch with Judy perhaps twice a month. I do, of course, go to medical appointments if I think that I absolutely must.

I am thankful that I enjoy our home and home life, although I confess to getting cabin-fever from time to time. I also admit to feeling great sadness when I see Judy drive off alone to worship services, shopping, social engagements, and other special activities that we used to share together.

Both Judy and I are deeply grateful, more than we can express in words, for our very kind and selfless neighbors who eagerly mow and trim our lawn, remove the snow (there's a lot of it here in Minnesota!) from our driveway and walks, and help us with various home-ownership tasks—outside and inside—we can no longer do. Other friends from church, Bethel Seminary, and elsewhere demonstrate the same remarkable spirit of kindness and generosity to us. We are indeed rich in many faithful and understanding friends, even though we cannot give back to them as they give to us.

A second reason these are my best years psychologically is that, as mentioned earlier, I am no longer looking for any help from the world of medicine. This has brought me great freedom of mind. To have my hopes raised and then dashed to the ground repeatedly is no longer a part of my life. I have no expectations of improvement, so I can't really be very disappointed any more in the medical sense, even though I continue to have the highest respect for and trust in my fine team of doctors, nurses, and technicians. The main times I do experience some disappointment is when I realize I am still alive, and may be for some time to come. I very much long to go home to glory. This disappointment, however, is not nearly as severe today as previously due to the factors being mentioned here.

Another element in my daily life that works wonders is in having a ready reply, as follows, to the depression and anxiety that occasionally still come around. "Why hello, former twin terrors, I can't say I'm glad to see you but you may linger a bit if you like. As you have learned by now, I will be ignoring you while I go about my activities. I know just what you are and you no longer frighten me. You are only thoughts—that's all. You cannot bluff me because I have you figured out. Pardon me while I think on those things that are true, noble, right, pure, lovely and admirable." I thank Claire

Weekes the psychiatrist and Rabbi Paul the apostle (in Phil 4) for giving me this very effective greeting to my once-mighty adversaries.

Finally, I consider these to be my best years psychologically since the transplant because God has given me a strong sense of mission. I have had such a calling since my conversion at the age of 19, but God has renewed this passion within me.

While I cannot go most places nor do most things, I can pray and give to expand the kingdom of God on earth. I can also work on writing projects that I believe are prompted by the Spirit of God. There is much about which I am very excited to write, as God allows me both time and strength. I now desire, most of the time, to stay alive, to flourish, and to serve people near and far by encouraging them to know God, enjoy God, love God, and love others enthusiastically with mercy and justice.

In these matters my spirit is very willing, although my body is weak. But even with my weaknesses I hope to honor God with a robust spirit until he calls me home. I have no interest in complaining or whining. I am now willing to stay in this earthly body, only because of God's never-slackening grace quest in my total being. My own perpetual pursuit after God's grace is being fueled increasingly by his daily assurances that my life still does have meaning—for time and eternity.

CHAPTER 23

The Mystery of the Quest

God's Silent Search

THROUGHOUT MY CHRISTIAN LIFE I have pondered the mysterious nature of God's quest for the hearts of men and women and boys and girls. That there is such a quest—one that extends to every person on earth—seems evident throughout the Bible. Referring to his soon-coming crucifixion, resurrection, and ascension, Jesus said to the crowds, "And I, when I am lifted up from the earth, will draw all people to myself." The apostle John, who records these words in his gospel (12:32), writes earlier of Jesus: "The true light that gives light to everyone was coming into the world (1:9)."

Also, as recorded in John's gospel, Jesus told the religious leaders who criticized him for healing an invalid on the Sabbath, "My Father is always at his work [his compassionate quest] to this very day, and I too am working (5:17)." To this Jesus added, "I am the bread of life . . . . that comes down from heaven, which anyone may eat and not die. I am the living bread that came down from heaven. Whoever eats this bread will live forever. This bread is my flesh, which I will give for the life of the world (6:48–51)." "For God did not send his Son into the world to condemn the world, but to save the world through him (3:17)."

Even to those who refuse to respond to God's quest, the apostle Paul makes clear the reality of that quest: "Or do you show contempt for the riches of his kindness, forbearance and patience, not realizing that God's kindness is intended to lead you to repentance (Rom 2:4)?"

Whether God is drawing those who are not believers in Christ, or seeking a closer relationship with those who acknowledge him as Savior, the workings of God's quest are surely mysterious. To Nicodemus the Pharisee Jesus said, "The wind blows wherever it pleases. You hear its sound, but you cannot tell where it comes from or where it is going. So it is with everyone born of the Spirit (John 3:8)."

While the God of the Bible is known for his openness, he is also known for his hiddenness. God both reveals himself and hides himself in mystery. In one remarkable chapter of Isaiah, which begins with the divine invitation, "Come, all you who are thirsty," God declares, "For my thoughts are not your thoughts, neither are your ways my ways. . . . As the heavens are higher than the earth, so are my ways higher than your ways and my thoughts than your thoughts (55:8–9)."

Life on earth for everyone involves mystery. Whether we are religious or not, Christian or not, contemplative or not, we are all aware of things mysterious. At least in the simplest sense of the word "mystery"—something unknown, kept secret, unexplained, or seemingly unexplainable—we all live with a sense of the mysterious, including our thoughts in the realms of spiritual knowledge and experience.

It is completely understandable that we live—to a greater or lesser extent—with some awareness of mystery regarding the secrets of the spiritual world. This somewhat hazy awareness is due, at least in part, to the qualitative and necessary distinctions between the divine and the human, the infinite and the finite, the holy and the unholy, and the creator and the creation. Regarding the last, how could we *not* have a sense of the mysterious even if only occasionally we stare into the starry heavens on a cloudless night, look intently into the searching eyes of the great apes, listen with our eyes closed to the soft wind speaking in the trees, or gaze out upon the ocean as the misty darkness descends over the never ending churning of the waves?

To a great many people the mysteries of the natural world overlap and intertwine with the mysteries of the spiritual world. Some people revere a high mountain or a very old tree, while others worship the entire creation or consider it the "body" of God. People who live with some religious beliefs and practices—almost all of the earth's population—develop some sense of the spiritual world through, among other influences, their contemplation of the natural world. Both the psalmist David and the apostle Paul write of this component of God's universal—and mysterious—quest for the people he created (Ps 19:1–6; Rom 1:18–20).

Humanity's Response

It was some time after I had come to know Jesus Christ that I began to think seriously about the mysterious ways that God brings people to himself. And it was some time after that search had been underway that I began to think seriously about how God works with his people after they have come to him. I came to see that God's quest after the hearts of his redeemed children is as insistent and intense as his quest after the hearts of nonbelievers. I also came to see that God's ways of developing faith and holiness in his redeemed are, just as with his work in bringing about the new birth, wonderfully—and sometimes painfully—mysterious.

One of the most remarkable biblical texts that conveys the truth of God's ever-present quest after his loyal children is found in the midst of the book of Second Chronicles: "For the eyes of the LORD range throughout the earth to strengthen those whose hearts are fully committed to him (16:9)." This statement of the Creator's eyes searching "to and fro" (the wording in the King James Version) to find and strengthen those who follow him is so encouraging and heart-warming that, it seems to me, it alone is sufficient to sustain God's people to the end of their earthly pilgrimage. I have this verse on my office wall, given to me years ago by my daughter Laurie, and I read it or repeat it from memory nearly every day,

While the way God strengthens us is sometimes evident, at other times it is mysterious. Just how does God work all things together for our good when we suffer, and how can we say he is strengthening us when we regularly feel great pain, experience serious bodily weakness, or live with constant emotional distress? In my own trials I have been greatly helped by reading that God uses our sufferings to produce in us perseverance, character, and hope (Rom 5:3–5). I rejoice that he "comforts us in all our troubles, so that we can comfort those in any trouble with the comfort we ourselves receive from God (2 Cor 1:4)." And I have been encouraged often by this exhortation regarding the perseverance that God's trials produces: "Let perseverance finish its work so that you may be mature and complete, not lacking anything (Jas 1:4)."

The above three biblical texts, as well as Paul's famous passage on his thorn in the flesh, teach that God uses our sufferings—if we respond trustingly to him—to develop our Christian character so we will be strong servants in his kingdom work. This teaching—found in numerous other places throughout the Bible—is truly glorious, and I don't know how successfully I would have dealt with my sufferings without these and similar Scriptures. I'm quite sure that I would have struggled far, far more than I have concerning the purpose of my sufferings—and my life.

But why do these Scriptures, as helpful as they are, not fully satisfy either my heart or my mind at the peak experiences of pain, weakness, and mental tumult? It is one thing to consider the problem of evil and suffering in its logical and theological forms, especially when the thinker is healthy and in good spirits, but it is a very different matter to consider the problem in its existential and personal forms in one's difficult daily life experiences. While I have found it very important in my life to think long and hard about evil and suffering as intellectual matters, I have found it even more important to ponder the issues with respect to my own personal struggles.

Yet, I wonder, can these two avenues of inquiry be kept apart, like two parallel highways, as the people of God travel steadily toward their eternal home? We are emotional beings as well as intellectual beings. We are soul and spirit, as well as body, and our quest for answers to life's biggest questions involves our whole selves. God gently (or not) arouses our sense of mystery and then reaches out to us in ways that are often imperceptible. We respond, perhaps in very slight degrees at first. But then, as God responds to our responses, we are encouraged by his grace to pursue our search for answers that we hope will satisfy us intellectually, emotionally, bodily, and spiritually.

Suffering, Pain, and Evil

Why does God allow suffering? More specifically, why does a perfectly good God allow truly horrible sufferings and pain in the world for so many people? Why does an all-powerful God allow some people to do horrendous evil to others for so long without striking them dead as soon as they begin to plan their cruelties?

In addition, why does God allow us and even exhort us to pray earnestly concerning specific matters that we long for, with what we believe are good motives, yet respond to our prayers in ways that, at times, leave us mystified? These matters of prayer and discerning God's ways of answering prayer have been a major part of my search for the grace to suffer well. Multitudes of others have gone before me on this search—a search that involves mind and body, soul and spirit.

Since the beginning of the human race, people who have had some idea of a Supreme Being who was said to be both good and mighty have struggled with the existence of evil, pain, and suffering. They have wondered, like Job, how to make sense of life and of God's ways, in light of terrible "moral evil" such as murder and theft (Job 1:15, 17), and awful "natural evil" such as death from lightning and tornadoes (1:16, 19) and severe pain and suffering from bodily illness (2:7, 13).

While Job was obviously struggling with his sufferings as a deeply personal and painful set of experiences (the "personal problem of evil"), rather than as a difficult philosophical issue (the "logical problem of evil"), he did raise serious questions about the purpose and worth of his life in view of God's seeming reluctance to come to his aid.

Those who are experiencing great suffering are not looking primarily, or at all, for some intellectual solution to their difficulties. They want personal and practical help, and if they are believers in God they want assurances of God's loving presence and care. But some sufferers are also bothered by serious intellectual questions about God's goodness and power in view of their severe condition. Why does God, who is supposed to be all-loving and all-powerful, allow his children to suffer, and suffer *so much*? Like Job they may say: "I have no peace, no quietness; I have no rest, but only turmoil (3:26)?"

It is good, then, for sufferers who have these intellectual questions, and for all of us who look over the earth and feel overwhelmed by the extent of evil, pain, and suffering, to have some answers, however imperfect, to our questions and the questions of others about the logical problem of evil, also referred to as the intellectual, philosophical, or theological problem of evil. I am using these terms interchangeably, as I am with the terms evil, pain, and suffering. While I recognize that helpful distinctions are necessary at times between the words evil, pain, and suffering, I have found that, in my personal experience with chronic illness, I need all three of these terms to adequately think about and explain my daily situation. The words often overlap and intertwine in my mind and experience, and in what follows I frequently use one term to stand for all three.

The Logical Problem of Evil

The basic conundrum involved in the logical problem of evil can be stated thus: It is not logically possible to argue successfully that God is all-good, that God is all-powerful, and that genuine evil exists. (Genuine evil is that which brings such horrific pain and suffering upon people that no possible benefit can be found for the sufferers, either in this life or in some future life.)

The argument allows that a great amount of pain and suffering in the world may have some positive purposes unknown to the sufferers, but insists that there is some evil—genuine evil—that is purely gratuitous (also referred to as dysteleological evil), with no possible good reason for allowing it. Did every single beating and death during the Holocaust, it may be asked, have some beneficial component to it (other than, in the case of death, the end of one's earthly torment)? Has every death from starvation on a parched wasteland in East Africa had some redeeming side to it? "Of course not" is the expected reply.

Some thinkers, including many skeptics and atheists, assert that the problem of evil as stated above is unsolvable, and therefore undermines the orthodox view of God as perfect love and perfect power. They seem to believe that a traditional Christian—a really thoughtful one at least—must give up one or more of the central claims of their faith in order to sleep well at night.

There is another, more familiar, way the quandary is stated. (1) If God is all-good he would never want genuine evil to exist. (2) If this all-good God is all-mighty he would never allow genuine evil to exist. (3) But genuine evil does exist. (4) Therefore, God is either not perfectly good or not all-powerful, which in either case demonstrates that the God of traditional theism does not exist.

Many who believe in a personal God of some kind offer a number of responses to this dilemma. Following are several attempted solutions, any one of which, if valid, will supposedly—according to their proponents—"solve" the logical problem of evil.

One view argues that, even though God is loving, there is a "shadow side" or perhaps even a "demonic side" in him that accepts and even seems to endorse some genuine evil. John Roth is a theologian who holds this view. "Everything hinges on the proposition that God possesses—but fails to use well enough—the power to intervene decisively at any moment to make history's course less wasteful. Thus, in spite [of] and because of his sovereignty, this God is everlastingly guilty and the degrees run from gross negligence to murder."[1]

We may imagine a three-legged stool called "traditional theism," supported by perfect love, perfect power, and genuine evil. Each leg must stand firmly (that is, be considered as true) if the standard theology of God is to be upheld. Reluctantly, Roth concludes that he must give up—or at least weaken—the historic doctrine of God's perfect goodness. He weakens this leg so much, however, that the stool collapses and does away—in his opinion—with the pesky logical problem of evil. However, even though God was seemingly complicit in watching 10,000 Jews a day go up in smoke during the Holocaust, Roth can still believe in God—a mighty God even if not the morally perfect God of supreme goodness he once believed in.

A second possible way to "solve" the problem of evil is to argue that, while God is perfectly good, he is not all-powerful. Contrary to Roth's view,

---

1. John Roth, "A Theodicy of Protest," in *Encountering Evil: Live Options in Theodicy*, edited by Stephen T. Davis (Minneapolis, MN: Bethany House, 1981), 16. This fascinating book contains five provocative approaches to the logical problem of evil, along with each author's critiques of the other four views, and the authors' responses to the critiques.

this position says that God is totally good and truly longs to end all evil, but he is not able to do so. If one is willing to weaken the leg of the stool named "omnipotence," so that the stool collapses, then the problem of evil will disappear.

A Jewish rabbi, Harold Kushner, in his very popular book, *When Bad Things Happen to Good People*, concludes that he must deny the historic Jewish (and Christian) belief in the almighty power of God. He writes: "I can worship a God who hates suffering but cannot eliminate it, more easily than I can worship a God who chooses to make children suffer and die, for whatever exalted reason."[2]

While Roth gives up the biblical teaching that God is love and Kushner gives up the biblical teaching that God is almighty, Mary Baker Eddy, founder of the Christian Science Church, "solves" the problem in a very different way: she asserts that genuine evil and suffering do not exist. If there really is no evil or suffering, then there is no problem to solve. God can be seen as both all-good and all-powerful, and then we can worship him without any troublesome questions about what he is really like.

In Mrs. Eddy's view, evil, sickness, death, and deceit do not come from the perfect God. If he did not create them—if they cannot be ascribed to him—it follows that they do not exist. But, Mrs. Eddy stresses, this is not to say that they do not seem real. The "only reality of sin, sickness, or death," she writes, "is the awful fact that unrealities seem real to human, erring belief, until God strips off their disguise."[3]

Christian Science does not deny the intensity of the human experiences of disease, pain, and suffering. When the early Christians were fed to the lions, it hurt, and they died. "But on a deeper level of perception, the Christians transcended merely physical death, for they knew they were even then coming into the fullness of their resurrected life. . . . The people who seek Christian Science healing do so because they experience pain; but the pain is not reality, and when they recognize its unreality, it ceases to hurt them."[4] This is why Christian Science refuses to rely on medicine.

2. Harold S. Kushner, *When Bad Things Happen to Good People* (New York, NY: Avon, 1981), 134.

3. Mary Baker Eddy, *Science and Health with Key to the Scriptures* (Boston: The First Church of Christ, Scientist, 1906), 472.

4. Pam Robbins and Robley Whitson, "Mary Baker Eddy's Christian Science," in *Christian Science: A Sourcebook of Contemporary Materials*, edited by Manager of Christian Science Committees on Publications (Boston, MA: The Christian Science Publishing Society, 1990), 17.

The Free Will Defense

Biblically-informed Christians know that to deny either God's perfect love or God's perfect power is heresy. We also know from our experience, from history, and from the Bible, that horrific suffering, pain, and evil really do exist. What then do we do with the logical problem of evil? How do we answer the very difficult questions that confront us? Must we admit that we cannot logically believe in, at the same time, all three legs of the stool?

Many Christian thinkers, led by the esteemed Christian philosopher of religion Alvin Plantinga, who recognize the serious challenge to orthodox faith posed by the logical problem of evil, offer a solution that even some ardent nonbelievers in God admit is logically successful.

Plantinga's project has not been to prove what God is like, nor to establish irrefutably that people should believe in the God of orthodox faith, or in any God. His project, rather, is known as the Free Will Defense (FWD), and is offered simply to demonstrate that the three orthodox beliefs—God's perfect love, God's perfect power, and the reality of evil—can be held together without logical contradiction. Plantinga's FWD is complicated, but here is his "preliminary statement" of it.

> A world containing creatures who are significantly free (and freely perform more good than evil actions) is more valuable, all else being equal, than a world containing no free creatures at all. Now God can create free creatures, but He can't *cause* or *determine* them to do only what is right. For if He does so, then they aren't significantly free after all; they do not do what is right *freely*.
>
> To create creatures capable of *moral good*, therefore, He must create creatures capable of moral evil; and He can't give these creatures the freedom to perform evil and at the same time prevent them from doing so. As it turned out, sadly enough, some of the free creatures God created went wrong in the exercise of their freedom; this is the source of moral evil. The fact that free creatures sometimes go wrong, however, counts neither against God's omnipotence nor against His goodness; for He could have forestalled the occurrence of moral evil only by removing the possibility of moral good.[5]

In what follows, theologian John Stackhouse offers a succinct and helpful summary of Plantinga's Free Will Defense.

---

5. Alvin Plantinga, *God, Freedom, and Evil* (Grand Rapids, MI: Eerdmans, 1974), 30.

THE MYSTERY OF THE QUEST

God desired to love and be loved by other beings. God created human beings with this end in view. To make us capable of such fellowship, God had to give us the freedom to choose, since love cannot be either automatic or coerced. This sort of free will, however, entailed the danger that we would use it to go our own way in defiance of both God and our own best interests.

For God to grant human beings free will was to grant us the awful dignity of making real choices with real consequences. If God prevents us from sinning, he is preventing us from truly free action. And if God constantly and instantly repairs our mischief, then it is likely that we would never face our sin and need for redemption.[6]

Plantinga's FWD has stood the test of time, before both Christian believers and nonbelievers. He acknowledges that his "aim is not to say what God's reason [for permitting evil] *is*, but at most what God's reason *might possibly be*."[7]

The existence of natural evils, such as hurricanes, tsunamis, and earthquakes, is also addressed by Plantinga. In his view, "*natural* evil significantly resembles *moral* evil in that, like the latter, it is the result of the activity of significantly free persons. In fact both moral and natural evil would then be special cases of what we might call *broadly moral evil*—evil resulting from the free actions of personal beings, whether human or not."[8]

Plantinga points to the logical possibility of the traditional doctrine of Satan (mentioned in Job 1) and his cohorts, and their rebellion long before God created human beings. With this doctrine, one can argue that since Satan's rebellion he has been "wreaking whatever havoc he can. The result is natural evil. So the natural evil we find is due to free actions of nonhuman spirits."[9]

While as God's people we receive these explanations with gratitude, we must keep in mind that all who venture into the mysterious realm of philosophical theology are using fallible, finite, human reasoning to attempt to examine the infallible, infinitely wise divine mind of the Supreme Being. In one sense it seems outrageous that any created being would attempt to investigate the mind and the ways of the Creator. But in our quest, if we stay

---

6. John G. Stackhouse Jr., "Mind Over Skepticism," *Christianity Today* (June 11, 2001), 74.

7. Plantinga, *God, Freedom, and Evil*, 28.

8. Ibid., 58–59.

9. Ibid., 58. Davis, in *Encountering Evil*, proposes another valuable approach to the logical problem of evil, similar to the FWD of Plantinga.

little in our own eyes, leaning on the always trustworthy Word of God and, with caution, the reasoning powers God has graciously given us, we may be profitable instruments in our Master's hands. This is my desire, and the desire of many millions throughout the world, until the end of our journeys on this earth.

> Oh, the depth of the riches of the wisdom
>> and knowledge of God.
> How unsearchable his judgments,
>> and his paths beyond tracing out!
> Who has known the mind of the Lord?
>> Or who has been his counselor?
> Who has ever given to God,
>> that God should repay them?
> For from him and through him
>> and for him are all things.
> To him be the glory forever!
>> Amen (Rom 11:33–36).

CHAPTER 24

To Maintain a Constant Victory

No Delay

I WANTED TO WRITE these final chapters with a rousing, triumphant tone, one that would stimulate and give strong reason for every reader to follow the Lord Jesus Christ wholeheartedly to the end of his or her life. While my deep desire and hope is to encourage everyone as just stated, my previously anticipated, idealistic note of triumph will need to be tempered by a more somber mood of realism. My current health situation prompts me to adjust my approach. I thought about waiting until I felt better before starting this chapter, but then decided to move forward for two reasons.

The major factor spurring me on is the growing awareness that I may never feel better than I do right now. In fact, if I project into the future on the basis of the past year of my life, the picture on the screen is of a man struggling even more than now to breathe, move about, and live with weakness and pain. I hope, of course, that this picture will never materialize, at least not for a long time.

If the above picture does become reality, however, I will reject (as I do now) the notion that one's thinking of such a possible path, and especially one's articulating it publicly, will contribute to (or even cause) such a decline. Some consider the following words of Job to reveal the serious lack of faith that led to his awful condition: "What I feared has come upon me; what I dreaded has happened to me (3:25)." To some, Job's mentally conceiving of such a dismal outcome actually brought it about. A thoughtful reading of the first three chapters of Job will demonstrate easily how erroneous such an interpretation is.

A second reason for deciding to continue with this chapter now is that God may use these words—coming, as they are, from a sometimes more troubled than triumphant mindset—to help others who are similarly troubled. If I waited until (and if) my physical health showed some improvement, even minor, and my spirits were more upbeat, I might lead some readers to think that I don't really understand the intensity of their suffering, since I am not really suffering all that much.

I decided I should write from my soul and experience now, not when circumstances—physical and emotional—are more comfortable. The book of Psalms, which is for many (including me) a powerful source of comfort when experiencing severe troubles, is also a repository of dozens of psalms of lament (over a third of the book) in which the writers cry out to God, not only for immediate tangible help but also for answers to their seemingly unanswered prayers and questions.

Over the millennia, God's people reading the psalms of lament have found solace and encouragement in knowing that others who sought God and the way of righteousness often suffered greatly—physically, psychologically, spiritually—while waiting for God to work on their behalf. Psalms 43, 69, and 88 are examples of such laments.

While I desire to be wholly realistic, I desire also to emphasize that my realism includes a consistent and life-giving "joy of the Lord" as well as a consistent and life-draining weariness with life. The joy and the misery are daily experiences—no day is without both—but I have to say that, by the overcoming grace of God, the joy—more often than not—rises above the misery. The joy does not push away the pain and other difficulties, nor does it suppress them. It lets them be, but infuses my soul with the awareness of God's very near and very comforting presence.

Intimacy with God

I write these words with the deepest conviction and genuineness I have, based upon over a half-century of experiencing God and over half of these years with heart problems. By the mutuality of God's never-ending quest after me and my comparatively minuscule response to God, I live a daily life of joy (not necessarily "happiness") and acceptance of my circumstances *because of the intimate presence of God in my thoughts, prayers, and activities throughout the day.*

While I know that this relationship with God is a gift of his amazing grace, I also know that such a relationship is *what God longs to give to (and experience with) every human being on earth.* Decades of wide and deep study of the Scriptures, and decades of knowing (or knowing about) numerous Christians—from all backgrounds and all corners of the earth—who live or have lived in intimacy with God, give me the confidence to make this assertion.

I trust that there is no boasting in the above words, but I am willing to take the "risk" of being considered spiritually proud if only I might point the way, for even one person, to the glorious experience of personally knowing God.

By "personally knowing God" I intend both halves of Jesus' "Greatest Commandment:" loving God with all of one's heart, soul, and mind, and loving one's neighbor as oneself (Matt 22:34–40). "Loving God" begins with our awareness of and acceptance of God's first loving us through Christ. As we respond to the pull of his grace and enter into the life of "loving God" wholeheartedly, we move out from this basis of daily communion with God to involvement with our neighbors, loving them in the same ways as we love ourselves. Anyone and everyone on our planet and on our street is our neighbor, and it becomes an integral and joyful part of loving God to discern and obey God's promptings concerning how best to love our neighbors as ourselves.

The life I am referring to does not just happen. I wish I could say that this "life of God in the soul of man" (to use the title of Henry Scougal's classic work) has been my uninterrupted experience since my early days as a Christian. I cannot claim anything of the sort, even though I have had all of the resources of the indwelling Holy Spirit available to me for holiness and power, as does every child of God (2 Pet 1:3).

I had to learn, and am still learning, that the graces and gifts of the Spirit are cultivated in us by God over time, as we seek him above all else and obey what we know of his will at each given moment. A song I learned soon after I became a Christian, "Trust and Obey," sums up my daily responsibilities. These three words are with me continually, sometimes several times a day. And I have found, as John the beloved apostle has written, "His commands are not burdensome (1 John 5:3)."

Reality

I would be less than honest if I ended this book leaving the impression that all is well with me, other than some physical problems. All is not well with me. I am not "doing OK" or "doing fine," even though I sometimes give one of these superficial replies to the question "How are you doing?" But, as I wrote earlier, it is very difficult to give the answer I want to give because (a) it would be much more than people want to know; most people (including me, some of the time), seem to be looking for a brief word or two about one's physical condition. In addition, (b) it would be a complicated answer, especially if I tried to avoid giving any wrong impressions. And, (c) it is very tiring to talk, although I still do to some extent as I am able.

As I have tried to explain earlier, my current issues are physical, psychological, and spiritual. While these areas, of course, greatly overlap and interconnect, they are still distinct to me as I go through my day. The physical difficulties, especially pain, lack of energy, and the struggle to breath, are with me constantly. I live with them because there is nothing else I (or the doctors) can do in the realm of the physical body.

The psychological arena is where most of my battles are being fought every day. While changes in my physical condition and variations in my degree of closeness to God clearly affect my moods (for better or worse), it is what takes place in the realm of my thoughts, my will, and my feelings that largely determines whether I am having a good day or a poor day. Above all, it is my will that governs what is allowed to linger in my thoughts. With my emotions, however, I experience only partial success in controlling them.

I remember saying to God angrily, very early one Christmas morning, "I don't like you!" I had awakened with terrible ankle/shin cramps and I could not walk them away for what seemed like forever.

Even with the strong will that God has graciously given me, I am aware that, at times, my emotions are largely—although not totally—beyond my control. Here is when I sense that functions, systems, and medications within my body are causing my feelings to fluctuate. Bursts (not necessarily audible) of irritation, impatience, frustration, disappointment, anger, and hopelessness take their turns trying to spoil my day. My sinful self, I have no doubt, enters into this melee. By God's grace I then seek to insert my will into the nasty situation and, with prayer, memorized Scriptures, and the passage of time, expel these unwelcome (and potentially very harmful) emotions.

If I were without God I doubt if people would want to be around me, and I doubt if I would want to be with myself—or with them. While most of my battles are fought in the psychological realm, the victories are won by means of the spiritual resources God has given to his people. In the words of the apostle Paul,

> [T]hough we live in the world, we do not wage war as the world
> does. The weapons we fight with are not the weapons of the
> world. On the contrary, they have divine power to *demolish*
> *strongholds* (italics added). We demolish arguments and every

pretension that sets itself up against the knowledge of God, and we take captive every thought to make it obedient to Christ (2 Cor 10:3–5).

When I struggle, as I do daily, I must keep in mind that God's children are involved, fundamentally, in a *spiritual* war, *not* a war of people fighting people. "For our struggle is not against flesh and blood, but against the rulers, against the authorities, against the powers of this dark world and against the spiritual forces of evil in the heavenly realms (Eph 6:12)." Our enemies, then, are not our bosses, co-workers, neighbors, relatives, or those we once considered friends. We may have serious issues with such people, but we do best to remember frequently that we are not really battling them, but the evil powers and spiritual forces seeking to use them to destroy us.

None of us needs to be held in bondage to these forces. Instead, Paul writes, "put on the full armor of God," which consists of truth, righteousness, the gospel of peace, faith, salvation, the Word of God, and prayer (Eph 6:13–20). These "weapons we fight with"—these seven pieces of "the full armor of God"—actually have the "divine power to demolish strongholds!" I have experienced this work of demolition against strongholds in my life, but I have found that this demolition work needs to be repeated over and over. The demonic forces begin erecting their next stronghold in me as soon as the previous one has been torn down.

These amazing teachings in 2 Corinthians 10 and Ephesians 6 are indeed life-saving and life-transforming, but they are not meant to be once-for-all remedies. They do not comprise some kind of spiritual warranty that we obtain and then put away in a drawer, forgetting about it except in times of crisis. These are real weapons we are to use daily against the forces of evil. They are not the only weapons, however. Also powerful are music, boldly speaking one's testimony, praising God out loud, and declaring victory through the blood and in the name of Jesus Christ (Eph 5:15–20; Rev 12:11).

Rose from Brier

This account of my life journey would be more than a little incomplete without reference to a book written by a missionary to India named Amy Carmichael. Though small in size, *Rose from Brier* has had a major influence on many sufferers—none, I expect, more so than me—since it was first published in 1933. Ms. Carmichael never wrote this as a book in the usual way. Rather, in her own words, the book consists of "Letters written originally to the Dohnavur Fellowship Invalids' League, but now shared with any ill who care to have this rose from our brier."[1]

Born in Northern Ireland in 1867 as the eldest of seven children, Amy Carmichael lived most of her adult life as a missionary to the Dohnavur area of South India. Her unusual work began in 1901 while she was doing itinerant evangelism. She came to know that little girls were sometimes taken and trained as dancing-girls for the Hindu temples, which meant a life of immorality and degradation for them. Wherever she could she saved children—boys as well as girls—from this fate. With her as "Mother," the Dohnavur Fellowship, affectionately known as the "Family," began.

The Family now consists of a large company of people from both India and other countries, men and women, married and single, whose common loyalty is to the Lord and Savior, Jesus Christ. Babies, children, young men, and young women are receiving care, education, and practical training for life.[2]

In 1931 Amy Carmichael had a fall that severely damaged her spine. She became an invalid and continued as such for the last 20 years of her life, being increasingly confined to bed. From her sickbed she labored at reading, writing, and directing the work at Dohnavur, authoring over 35 books during her lifetime. She died in 1951 after 50 years of service in India, and at the time of her death there were over 900 people in the Family.

Amy Carmichael came to know God intimately through her sufferings, and in *Rose from Brier* she expresses the most helpful thoughts about physical, emotional, and spiritual suffering I have ever read. I keep this book close by my bedside. Ruth Bell Graham, wife of the famous evangelist Billy Graham, said, "By far the best I have found" on the subject of living with serious illness. This little gem has been one of the top five books in my entire life from the standpoint of helping me live well.

I believe others may best understand why this book has been so beneficial to me in my sufferings if I quote—rather extensively—from her book. I long for my readers to be as strengthened by her words as I have been. (It will be helpful for readers to know that a "harrow" is a heavy frame with metal spikes or disks used for such work as breaking up clods of dirt or covering seeds. On a farm it may be pulled by a team of horses or by a tractor.) Following are some selections from her book; from time to time she includes one of her poems or songs.

---

1. Amy Carmichael, *Rose from Brier* (Fort Washington, PA: Christian Literature Crusade, 1973; first published 1933), 5.

2. Ibid., 199.

Properly speaking, this is not a book at all, but only a bundle of letters. They were written in pencil a little at a time; they could not have felt formal if they had tried. . . . [R]eading them through I am troubled to find them so personal and sometimes so intimate. It is not that I think the personal or the intimate interesting or valuable, but that I did not know how to give the comfort wherewith we ourselves are comforted without giving something of my own soul also. If I had waited till the harrow had lifted [i.e., till the sharpness of the pain had eased], perhaps a less tired mind would have found a better way. But then the book would have been from the *well* to the ill, and not from the *ill* to the ill, which I think it is meant to be—a rose plucked straight from a brier. . . .

All these letters have been written, as one of them tells, what time the storm fell upon me, not after the coming of the calm. [The "storm" is her serious fall; these letters were all written within the first two years after the fall.]

> The toad beneath the harrow knows
>
> Exactly where each tooth-point goes;
>
> The butterfly upon the road
>
> Preaches contentment to that toad.

There can be minutes when the toad is not properly grateful to the butterfly—no, not even if he comes dressed like a very good Christian. He is upon the road: he isn't under the harrow; he never was there.[3]

Before the Pain Has Passed

Such a minute came one morning when all I wanted was something which would help me to escape from myself; and there is nothing that can so quickly give this release as a book that takes me out of my own life into the lives of others. Just then the post came—"and a book packet!" said my dear nurse. Her voice with its note of expectation was as delightful as what we hoped would be the contents of that parcel. Eagerly she opened it and eagerly I watched her. . . . [Perhaps it would be some excellent literature]. But no—that fat parcel was full of tracts for the sick. I tried those

3. Ibid., 9–10.

tracts, but somehow they took me nowhere. This sounds most unmissionary; unhappily, it is true.

It was not till some time later, and after several similar experiences, that it struck me perhaps the reason was because they were obviously written by the well to the ill, to do them good; and so they could only flutter past like ineffective butterflies. But I found that things written by those who were in pain themselves, or who had passed through pain to peace, like the touch of understanding in a dear human letter, did something that nothing except the words of our eternal Lord could ever do.

So these letters purposely go forth from under the harrow *before* [italics added] the sharpness of the prod of a single tooth is forgotten. They go to some who are under far sharper harrows, and they carry all they can to them of sympathy that understands. They are not, or course, meant to be read straight through. . . . Nor will every letter fit every mood. Illness has its moods. But I hope that they will not irritate any poor toad. . . . They go to some who are disappointed. They hoped to be well long ago and are not well yet. This little song is for them, and then for the others, never forgotten, for whom the end of illness will be heaven.

Before the winds that blow do cease,

   Teach me to dwell within Thy calm:

Before the pain has passed in peace,

   Give me, my God, to sing a psalm.

Let me not lose the chance to prove

   The fullness of enabling love.

O Love of God, do this for me:

   Maintain a constant victory.

Before I leave the desert land

   For meadows of immortal flowers,

Lead me where streams at Thy command

   Flow by the borders of the hours,

That when the thirsty come, I may

   Show them the fountains in the way.

O Love of God, do this for me:

   Maintain a constant victory.[4]

4. Ibid., 10–12.

Amy Carmichael's "little song," just quoted, did not affect me with its full force until I read it a second time, and then a third. Each time I read it the remarkable yearning of the author sunk in more deeply. Unselfishly, she requests constant victory *now*, right *in the middle of* her pain and suffering!

She is *not* asking for prompt *relief* from the pain, but for an attitude of calm and even joy as she languishes in the parched, windy desert. She longs for this victory—*constant* victory—*before* the suffering goes away, either temporarily or when God calls her home. She desires to show, *from her state of pain*, the sources of water she has found for the thirsty who come her way. Because of her prayer (and book), her longing is my longing.

CHAPTER 25

No Easy Answers

Enforced Rest

BECAUSE OF THE POWERFUL impact of Amy Carmichael's book, *Rose from Brier*, on me and a large number of other sufferers, I have chosen to include some additional contributions from her work, at considerable length. These paragraphs take us deep into her personal problem of evil and her resolution of what is, in my view, the most difficult issue in Christian theology and Christian living.

> One day, after weeks of nights when, in spite of all that was done to induce sleep, it refused to come, except in brief distracted snatches, the mail brought a letter which discoursed with what sounded almost like pleasure on this "enforced rest," and the silly phrase rankled like a thorn. I was far too tired to laugh it off as one can laugh off things when one is well. So *this* was supposed to be rest? And was the Father breaking, crushing, "forcing," by weight of sheer physical misery, a child who only longed to obey His lightest wish?

> This word [enforced] had what I now know was an absurd power to distress. It held such an unkind, such a false conception of our Father. . . . But the Lord our Creator knows (and all who have ever suffered know) that pain and helplessness are not rest, and never can be; nor is the weakness that follows acute pain, nor the tiredness that is so tired of being tired that it is poles apart from rest.[1]

> Peace in acceptance: to my reading of the Scriptures, pain (like sin and cruelty) is the work of the enemy—"An enemy has done

---

1. Carmichael, *Rose from Brier*, 18–20.

this." If it were not so we should, I think, have no right to resist it. We do not resist our Lord; if it be His dear hand that "presses heavily" . . . then we could not and should not push it off, or try to slip from under it. All the wonderful easers of pain, which I believe are His gift, would be forbidden to us. Doctors and nurses would not be working with Him, but against Him. We hold to His words, "Ought not this woman whom Satan has bound these eighteen years be loosed from this bond?"[2]

I have not found . . . that illness makes prayer easier, nor do any of our family who have been ill tell me that they have found it so. Prayerfulness does not seem to be a flower of the spirit that grows of itself. When we are well perhaps we rather take it for granted that it does, as though what is sometimes called a "sick-bed" offered natural soil for that precious flower. I do not think that it does. A bed can be a place of dullness of spirit as well as of body, and prayer is, after all, work—the most strenuous work in all the world. And yet it is our only way of joining the fighting force. . . . So what can we do about it?

One night, soon after neuritis had taken possession of me from shoulder blade to fingertips, I could no more gather myself up to pray than I could turn in bed without the help of the Lotus Bud, who was my faithful night nurse. But I could read, and I opened on Psalm 109: "Do Thou for me, O God the Lord." Do what? It does not say. It just says, "Do Thou for me." And the prayer, so simple, so easy for a tired heart, had a delivering power. It delivered from the oppression of the enemy. "Now there was leaning on Jesus' bosom one of His disciples, whom Jesus loved;" it was like that.

And soon the prayer passed into the most restful kind of intercession, the only kind the ill can attain unto, for they cannot pray in detail and they may know little or nothing of the needs of their dearest. But He knows all, down to the smallest wish of the heart. So we do not need to coin our gold in words, we could not if we tried: we are far too tired for that; and He who knows our frame does not ask us to do anything so arduous: Do Thou for her, do Thou for him, do Thou for them, O God the Lord.

This word of peace had greatly eased my spirit, when a letter came from the Secretary of the Dohnovur Fellowship Invalids' League. She quoted from the letter of a Danish invalid too ill to pray as she longed to do: "This form of illness is very sad; but I

2. Ibid., 27.

am sure that God will [counsel] His children in such times to have all their joy in God alone *and not in the service for Him* [italics added], not in their own forces. Of course you are thankful for these things also; *but the heart of a child of God must be so, that God Himself is enough for it."* . . . "Understand Thou my softly murmured prayer" is Rotherham's rendering of Psalm 5:1.[3]

I have come to this: our Lord is sovereign. He may heal as He will, by an invisible Touch or by blessing the means (His gifts) that are used. He may recover the exhausted one, as Rotherham renders James 5:15, or sustain with words him that is weary, as He did St. Paul, and use those words for the [helping] of others. . . .

The more I study life as well as books, the more sure I am that there is a darkness folded round that riddle into whose heart of light we are not meant to see. Perhaps that light would be too bright for our eyes now. I have known lovers of our Lord who in their spiritual youth were sure beyond a doubt that healing would always follow the prayer of faith and the anointing of oil in the name of the Lord [as encouraged in the fifth chapter of James]. But those same dear lovers, in their beautiful maturity, passed through illness, unrelieved by any healing. And when I looked in wonder, remembering all that they had held and taught in other years, I found them utterly at rest. The secret of the Lord was with them. . . . "As for God, His way is perfect," they said. "We need no explanation."[4]

Why Is There Pain?

Amy Carmichael now moves deeper into the mystery of pain. I continue to quote at length (very unusual, I acknowledge) from her book because of her remarkable insight and gripping manner of expression.

This that I write now is meant only for those who are harassed by the existence of pain. . . . Why is pain at all, and *such* pain? Why did God ask Satan [in Job 1:8] the question which (apparently) suggested to the Evil One to deal so cruelly with an innocent man? Why do the innocent so often suffer?

[All creation, according to Romans 8,] "groans and travails in pain together until now." . . . O Lord, why? Why did You make

3. Ibid., 53–55.
4. Ibid., 113–14.

flesh like a field threaded all over with roads and lanes where burning feet continually do pass? Men, women, children, beasts, birds, and some of the water-creatures—why, knowing what was to be, did you make them so? And the spirit of man, tuned like a delicate stringed instrument to the lightest touch, why, when it was to be smitten as by red-hot rods, did You make it so? Why build the house of life with every door set open to the devouring flame? It is a poignant *Why?*

I have read many answers, but none satisfy me. . . . There are many poetical answers; one of these satisfied me for a time . . . but . . . we know, with a knowledge that penetrates to a place which those words cannot reach, that our question is not answered. It is only pushed farther back. . . .

No, beautiful words do not satisfy the soul that is confined in the cell whose very substance is pain. Nor have they any light to shed upon the suffering of the innocent. They are only words. They are not an answer.

What, then, is the answer? I do not know. I believe that it is one of the secret things of the Lord, which will not be opened to us till we see Him who endured the Cross, see the scars in His hands and feet and side, see Him, our Beloved, face to face. I believe that in that revelation of love, which is far past our understanding now, we shall "understand even as all along we have been understood."

And till then? What does a child do whose mother or father allows something to be done which it cannot understand? There is only one way of peace. It is the child's way. The loving child trusts.

I believe that we who know our God, and have proved Him good past telling, will find rest there. The faith of the child rests on the character it knows. So may ours; so shall ours. Our Father does not explain, nor does He assure us as we long to be assured. For example, there is no word that I can find in the Bible that tells us that the faithful horse, which man's cruelty has maimed, will be far more than caused to forget on some celestial meadow; the dog betrayed far more than reassured; or that the little anguished child will be gathered in its angel's arms and there [be] far more than comforted.

But we know our Father. We know His character. Somehow, somewhere, the wrong must be put right; *how* we do not know, only we know that, because He is what He is, anything else is inconceivable. The word sent to [John the Baptist in Matt 11], the man whose soul was among lions and who was soon to be done to death . . . though the Lord of Daniel was so near, is fathomless: "And blessed is he whosoever shall not be offended in Me."

There is only one place where we can receive, not an answer to our question, but peace—that place is Calvary. An hour at the foot of the Cross steadies the soul as nothing else can. "O Christ beloved, Thy Calvary stills all our questions." Love that loves like *that* can be trusted about this.[5]

It seems right that I include here a brief word—a further word—about my quest for the solution to the problem of evil—the logical problem and, especially, the personal problem. As I stated earlier, while these are two different problems, they overlap and intertwine to a considerable extent, at least in my mind and experience. It is one thing for us to accept gladly the Free Will Defense as part of the logical explanation of evil (and I need that piece), but we need something more—much more—to provide consolation while lying on the parched desert without water. The personal problem of suffering is far more intense than the logical problem when we are under the harrow.

Previously I mentioned that during my doctoral studies, before I could begin my dissertation, I had to pass four major comprehensive exams. One of these had to be a significant problem in theology from pre-Christian times to the present. I chose the problem of evil, partly because I had studied a fair amount in that field already and partly because it was one of the most intractable and most persistent theological/religious issues of all time—if not the most troublesome of all—both logically and personally. I had to know about every major issue, writer, and writing in this area of study.

The qualifying exams were usually graded with a "pass" or a "fail." At times a student received a "pass with distinction," and I happened to receive this grade for my exam results on the problem of evil. I say this only to accentuate something very important: in all of my hundreds of hours of studying on this highly complex and frustrating set of issues, even to the present day, I have come to the same basic conclusions as those of Amy Carmichael. (However, I have never expressed them as powerfully as she has.) We both conclude that there are no fully comprehensible or fully satisfying answers to the vexing questions that flow from the issues of evil and suffering—at least not to those suffering severely.

5. Ibid., 187–91.

In my opinion, no matter how many PhD's tackle these age-old issues, they will not offer more satisfying or more uplifting responses than those of Amy Carmichael. I am not saying that hers is the best set of answers ever given, but that I doubt there is a better set of replies to those individuals who feel crushed and/or tormented by their sufferings.

Chronic Illness

Some final words from Amy Carmichael are not only fitting but full of consolation for the most seriously ill.

> [This last letter also must] be to the ill, and especially to you, friend, whom I feel as though I [know], you who may not look forward to health. A letter came lately from one in a hospital for incurable patients. The address went to our hearts. Some who appear to live in such places do not really live there, they only stay there. They live under the open sky. The winds of God blow round them. But for some there must often be a closing in of earthly walls as they look forward, not to autumn with its golden flow, but to winter, stark winter.
>
> It was my nurse's thought that there should be something [in this book] just for these, and so this morning I spent an hour in spirit with them, and a word came [to me for them, from Psalm 139]: "He knows the way that I take. You know my downsitting and my uprising. You compass [surround] my path and my lying down."
>
> Has the day to be spent in bed? Or in chair? Or partly in both? Think of the Lord our God, being about our [lying] down. Does it not seem as though He were searching for a word to tell us how near He is? And if He be so near as that, what can we have to fear? Does our flesh [tremble] as [our] imagination, vivid as ever, looks on to what may be? But *Dominus illumininatio mea* must be true:
>
> When the will has forgotten the lifelong aim,
>
> And the mind can only disgrace its fame,
>
> And a man's uncertain of his own name,
>
> The power of the Lord shall fill this frame.

He who compasses our lying down today will compass our lying down tomorrow; our falling leaves will fall into His hand. "You have made summer *and winter.*"

How, then, can winter hurt us? It is for help, not hurt, a gentle preparation for a divine surprise. . . . And He who compasses our lying down shall encompass our uprising, so shall we ever be with the Lord.[6]

I have quoted extensively from *Rose from Brier* because Amy Carmichael's words express precisely my thoughts. I cannot improve on her way of presenting certain experiences of suffering, both hers and mine. I send them out to all readers who very much need them, or will in the days and years to come. May many be strengthened by them as I have been.

6. Ibid., 193–94.

CHAPTER 26

Gratitude and Grace

Being Grateful

ONE WORD CAME TO mind when I considered how best to conclude this book: gratitude. One dictionary defines gratitude as "being grateful" and then defines "grateful" as "feeling or showing that one values a kindness or benefit received." I am abundantly grateful, and I wish to show it here.

The English word grateful comes from the Latin word *gratia*, which means grace. *Gratia* may also mean charm, pleasantness, love, friendship, service, favor, kindness, thanks, and gratitude. I find it delightful to realize the close connections between all of these terms. It is certainly appropriate that our Lord is spoken of as "the God of all grace" (1 Pet 5:10).

There are several categories of God's gifts that I wish to thank him for publicly. I am what (and who) I am today because of these gracious benefits from the God of all grace.

People and Churches

I first think of the people I have known who have influenced me most. My father Arthur, my wife Judy, Judy's father Bernard and her mother Blanche, the president of Prairie Bible Institute, L.E. Maxwell, my New Testament Greek professor, Carl Hoch Jr., and theologian Clark Pinnock. Of these, only Judy and Blanche are still walking this earth. Without doubt, Judy and my father, in very different ways, have been most used by God to shape me.

There are so many others I could mention in addition to the above, but the list would be very, very long. I have a long and detailed memory of those whom God has used to shape me. I know without any doubt I would not be who I am today (whoever that is) without many remarkable people:

family, fellow students, teachers, co-workers, pastors, missionaries, writers, Christian leaders of all sorts, fellow scholars, former students, and a host of friends and acquaintances. My brother and sister, my daughters and their husbands, and my five delightful grandchildren have been especially important in my overall personal formation.

Churches constitute a related realm of influencers. While the Catholic Church had serious weaknesses, God prepared me for life by using that church to instill in me some important values and helpful thoughts about God. Other churches, from the small independent Baptist church that was instrumental in the conversion of my father and me, to our present home (since 1988) at Bethany Baptist Church, have been instrumental in building me up in my faith through worship, preaching, teaching, and service opportunities, and fellowship experiences with a large number of wonderful people. One of the most important concerns for our family whenever we moved to a new location was to find and become involved with a group of Christ-followers with whom we could worship, grow, and serve.

We never found a perfect church, but we were never searching for one. We looked for leaders who were godly, spiritually-wise, and humble men and women whose strong desire was not related to numbers and money primarily, but to the faithful, balanced, Spirit-led preaching and teaching of the Bible, the worship of God in spirit and truth, and the extension of the reign of God over the earth.

Schools

In addition to people and churches, I need to mention schools, both those I attended and those in which I taught. While I would have chosen a very different path for my years of formal education, I look back now and say, "He has done all things well."

Catholic schooling, from second grade through my sophomore year at St. Joseph's College, gave me a solid general education, especially in math and the physical sciences. I also learned that the Bible was the written Word of God and that Jesus Christ was the living Word of God in human flesh. Four years of study at Prairie, followed by three years at Calvary, laid for me a foundation in theology, biblical studies, writing, the spiritual life, and an active compassion for all peoples on earth.

My doctoral work at Drew University provided just the right context for me to study historical theology and ethics, and to pull together a number of strands of thought that I needed to integrate for the rest of my life and service. Above all, perhaps, was that the PhD studies confirmed in me a most valuable insight: how little I knew in the areas of theological and religious studies. If I had left Drew supremely confident of my mastery in these specialties, my time there would have been largely wasted and my subsequent teaching activities would have offered, at best, mediocre experiences for the students.

I have had the privilege of serving as a full-time faculty member at three schools, in addition to helping as a teaching assistant or adjunct professor in three other schools. However, my times of service at Prairie (five years), Criswell (three years), and Bethel (seventeen years) were, for sure, quite different from one another, as I have related previously.

The schools were different in their governance and administration, supporting constituencies, perception by the public, theological and ecclesiastical distinctives, and quality of faculty. But in all three schools I found that the students were very pleasant, easy to work with, respectful, eager to learn, and desirous of growing in all three essential areas of theological education: knowledge (the head), skills (the hands), and spiritual maturity (the heart). These thousands of students have probably contributed as much to my personal and professional development as I (I trust) have to theirs.

The task of helping to prepare men and women for ministerial life and service changed markedly from my beginning in 1970 until my retirement in 2005, but the typical student remained much the same in motivation, academic ability, and legitimate concern about God's sphere of service for them when their program of studies was over.

I look back now and see both weaknesses and strengths in my education, teaching methods, and spiritual condition. Everything considered, I am filled with much gratitude for the grace of God extended to me through a lifetime of study, service, and spiritual growth. Much of the time, when I hear of a former classmate, former faculty colleague, or former student, I experience a special joy from the Lord.

I also think at times of the solemn words of James, the brother of Jesus: "Not many of you should become teachers, my fellow believers; because you know that we who teach will be judged more strictly (3:1)." God willing, I expect to be a teacher in some manner until he calls me home. I long to be faithful to this sacred task, and to those whom I may yet influence for Christ.

The Word

A fourth gift from the ever-gracious heart of God is his Word: the living Word, the Lord Jesus Christ, and the written Word, the Bible. If we did not have a God who has revealed—and continues to reveal—himself, we would be groping and stumbling in the dark, unsure of who we were, where we were going, and why it even mattered.

John, the disciple who leaned on Jesus' breast at the Last Supper, writes in the first chapter of his gospel concerning Jesus as the living Word and the supreme revelation of the Father.

> The true light that gives light to everyone was coming into the world. . . . The Word became flesh and made his dwelling among us. We have seen his glory, the glory of the one and only Son, who came from the Father, full of grace and truth. . . . Out of his fullness we have all received grace in place of grace already given. . . . No one has ever seen God, but the one and only Son, who is himself God and is in closest relationship with the Father, has made him known.

For over half of my teaching years I studied the biblical words of Jesus in much the same way as I studied the words of Isaiah or Paul. I did not pay extra attention to the teachings of Jesus because I was taught (correctly) that "*all* Scripture is God-breathed, and is profitable. . . (2 Tim 3:16)." I did not think that red-letter editions of the Bible, in which the words of Jesus were printed in red ink, were a good idea, because the words of James, John, or Jeremiah were just as inspired and authoritative as those of Jesus, and should not be considered of lesser importance.

As I progressed in my teaching career, however, I began to see Jesus in a somewhat different light. I continued to believe strongly in both his full deity and full humanity, but I began to probe more deeply than I had before into the life and words of Jesus the man in relation to the triune Godhead. From a number of remarkable Scripture passages[1] emphasizing the genuine humanity of Jesus I noted in a new way that, even though he was the Lord of all, he was also fully human and lived on this earth just as we all do, except that he never sinned.

He was the God-man who had previously set aside the independent use of his divine attributes—such as omnipotence, omniscience, and omnipresence—and did great works, taught the people, and made decisions in the same way that his followers were to do when he was no longer with them: in complete dependence upon the power and wisdom of the Father (John 14:10–14, 30–31). His sinless condition meant simply that he never sinned. He did not switch into his "deity" mode when he was getting ready to perform a miracle, resist a temptation, or teach a lesson. While this is a controversial point, it appeared to me that Jesus did all things (or almost all

---

1. Such as John 5:19–20, 30; Philippians 2:6–8; Hebrews 2:9–18; 4:14–16.

things) during his earthly life not as the mighty God he was (and is), but as a faithful, obedient human being and child of his heavenly Father, just as believers today are to live as faithful, obedient children of our Father.[2]

Due to this fuller understanding of Jesus and a renewed awareness of the centrality of the Messiah throughout the whole body of Scripture, I have moved closer than ever before toward a Jesus-centered approach to every-day life and service, without diminishing, I trust, the equal prominence of the Father and the Holy Spirit. While I do not wear a "WWJD" bracelet, I do believe that "What would Jesus do?" can be a very helpful question, among others, to ask when facing a difficult situation. Since Jesus was the wisest person who ever lived on this earth, who received his guidance directly from the Father, I find myself now looking increasingly at the actions and words of this simple blue-collar laborer from the hills of Galilee.

Jesus, the living Word, had a mind saturated with the Hebrew Scriptures, the written Word. This body of literature was the chief means God chose to make himself known before the coming of Christ. In the approximately two thousand years since then the Bible, both Old and New Testaments, has served as God's unique revelation to those who read it with an open mind and a searching heart. The apostle Paul wrote to his spiritual son Timothy, ". . . from infancy you have known the Holy Scriptures, which are able to make you wise for salvation through faith in Christ Jesus. All Scripture is God-breathed and is useful for teaching, rebuking, correcting and training in righteousness, so that the servant of God may be thoroughly equipped for every good work (2 Tim 3:15–17)."

I believe that without my (Catholic) New Testament, especially the book of Acts and the letters of Paul, I would not have understood the way of salvation nor come to Christ when I did. Perhaps I never would have. I also believe that, without consistent reading and meditating in the Scriptures from the very beginning of my new life in Christ, and seeking to obey (sometimes not very well) God's Word as I understood it, I would be a very weak Christian today, if I would even be recognizable as a Christian.

I have often said to Judy and to myself that the two greatest tangible gifts I have ever received from God are the Holy Scriptures and Judy herself. With the Bible I read and even experience God's revelatory activity while I meditate in it; with Judy I see and even experience God's revelatory activity while I live with her daily. Concerning God's written revelation, I believe that the wisest people in the world are those who have a personal knowledge of God based upon a broad, deep, and balanced knowledge of the Bible.

2. Gerald F. Hawthorne, *The Presence and the Power* (Dallas, TX: Word, 1991), 150–52, 199–225.

They understand clearly the words of the apostle Paul that the "foolishness" of God is wiser than human wisdom, and the "weakness" of God is stronger than human strength (1 Cor 1:25).

The Writings of Others

Another category of gifts from the God of all grace that he has used mightily to shape me is the large quantity of written materials—books and articles especially—that I have read and studied. Through these, my mind, heart, and will have been informed, nourished, and inspired beyond measure to understand God, God's written Word, God's world, how to live in this world, and especially how to love God and love my neighbor as myself. In addition, these materials have given me thousands of hours of reading pleasure far beyond the so-called pleasures of this world.

I have enjoyed and benefited from both fiction and non-fiction. Most of my fiction reading (outdoor adventure novels especially) has been done in my childhood years and in the more recent years of my life. As my life has become more and more difficult, reading fiction has been one of my primary ways of escape from the trials of life.

Between my childhood and my later life I consumed textbooks (both those I was assigned as a student and those I assigned as a teacher), reference works (in part, of course), biographies, autobiographies, book reviews, and a truckload of books on biblical studies, history, apologetics, ethics, spiritual theology, systematic theology, historical theology, pastoral theology, world religions, and alternative religious movements. When I wander among the (now greatly thinned) stacks of my library, my heart is often warmed as I note some special connection with perhaps every other book. These items are among my dearest (non-human) friends on earth.

Professional journals in theology, biblical studies, and ethics have helped me greatly in keeping up with developments in my fields. In a good journal, the book reviews alone more than justify the annual subscription price. Popular periodicals have also contributed significantly to my development both professionally and personally. *Christianity Today, Mission Frontiers, Priscilla Papers, Prism, Mutuality, The Christian Century*, and numerous other publications have been invaluable in my life and service for God. With both journals and popular-level materials, I have subscribed to some that I largely agreed with and some that I regularly quarreled with. Both classes of periodicals have been beneficial in helping me to remain alert to all sides of developing issues. In addition, all of my life I have been a daily reader of a major big-city newspaper. This has been no small part of my total education.

Grace

Following people, churches, schools, the Word of God, and the writings of others, the one remaining category of God's gifts that has made me who I am today is, very simply, the grace of God.

As mentioned earlier, I have found that grace is the most important word in the Bible (at least to me) except for the names of God. It is fitting, therefore, that this book has been all about grace. And it is very fitting that I mention here that, above all the gifts I have ever received, the highest, purest, and most magnificent is the grace of God: the Almighty himself loving and giving to his creation his divine favor, power, and presence to all who cry to him out of their need and helplessness. He searches for us and woos us by his grace and, in that mysterious dance of love involving God's quest and our response, he draws us to himself. He graciously changes us by his kindness and strength and gives us a new heart.

In his ongoing quest he then leads us as a shepherd leads the sheep. It is for good reason that Psalm 23 is the most beloved of the psalms ("The LORD is my shepherd"), and that John 10 is such a strong comfort for the children of God ("I am the good shepherd").

One of the highlights of my life, from the standpoint of listening to preachers and other speakers, was hearing W. Phillip Keller present a series of talks on Psalm 23 in the mid-1960s. Keller was a man of God who for years had been a shepherd in British Columbia, Canada. He traveled from time to time to Alberta to visit the Prairie Bible Institute, where his daughter Lynn was a classmate of Judy and me. He visited Prairie not only to see his daughter but in response to the invitations he regularly received to speak at the Prairie Tabernacle.

As Phil Keller moved clause by clause, verse by verse, through Psalm 23, several thousand listeners, including me, were mesmerized by Keller's detailed knowledge of raising sheep and the close correlations between his explanations and the corresponding elements of the psalm. In 1970 these talks were published as *A Shepherd Looks at Psalm 23*. About twenty years after hearing these talks I read this book, and was every bit as enthralled then as when I first heard Mr. Keller's talks.

This rugged outdoorsman who grew up among the herders of East Africa surely writes with authority when he says that sheep "require, more than any other class of livestock, endless attention and meticulous care. It is no accident that God has chosen to call us sheep. The behavior of sheep and human beings is similar in many ways. . . . Our mass mind (or mob instincts), our fears and timidity, our stubbornness and stupidity, our perverse habits are all parallels of profound importance."[3]

I will never again read Psalm 23 as I did before hearing and especially reading Keller's fascinating material. In fact, I have tried to obtain and read all of his books. Keller writes very simply but by no means simplistically. In some of my darkest hours the Lord my Shepherd has used the writings of this plain-spoken, rough-hewn man to comfort and encourage my soul greatly along the journey of life.

I will bring this book to a close by stating several Scripture passages on grace that have been among the most instrumental Bible texts in over a half-century of my life under the care of the Good Shepherd. Because of his wise shepherding, his loving and patient care, his discipline, and his relentless quest after me to this day, I have found truth and hope in my lifelong pursuit of salvation, spirituality, and the grace to suffer well.

> Let us then approach God's throne of grace with confidence, so that we may receive mercy and find grace to help us in our time of need (Heb 4:16).

> It is good for our hearts to be strengthened by grace. . . . (Heb 13:9).

> But by the grace of God I am what I am, and his grace to me was not without effect. No, I worked harder than all of them—yet not I, but the grace of God that was with me (1 Cor 15:10).

> But he said to me, "My grace is sufficient for you, for my power is made perfect in weakness" (2 Cor 12:9).

> And God's grace was so powerfully at work in them all that there were no needy persons among them (Acts 4:33).

> But he gives us more grace. That is why Scripture says, "God opposes the proud but shows favor to the humble" (Jas 4:6).

> And the God of all grace, who called you to his eternal glory in Christ, after you have suffered a little while, will himself restore you and make you strong, firm and steadfast. To him be the power for ever and ever. Amen (1 Pet 5:10–11).

---

3. W. Phillip Keller, *A Shepherd Looks at Psalm 23* (Grand Rapids, MI: Zondervan, 1970), 21.

The above Scriptures display a confidence-building blend of grace as favor and grace as power. As we read them we may be inclined to think of grace as a substance, especially when the text is focusing on grace as power. I have done that at times as I have tried to grasp this truly amazing and mysterious concept. Yet grace is not something tangible. It is not a substance or a thing. It is, rather, the very presence of God himself living and flowing within us and allowing us to experience his face shining upon us, his mercy consoling us, and his energy strengthening us for every task and situation we face.

I will be forever grateful for the God of all grace and for all those he has used along the pilgrimage of my life to assist me in my still-ongoing grace quest. I desire to say, at the end of my earthly journey, as Paul said when the time for his departure was nearing: "I have fought the good fight, I have finished the race, I have kept the faith (2 Tim 4:7)." If I can say this, it will truly be by God's grace and for God's everlasting glory.

Epilogue

IF, IN THE PASSING of years, you should travel through Spring Lake Park in Minnesota and ride by the white house on the corner—the one with the big cottonwood tree by the door—you may see Judy and me standing at the window or sitting on the front steps. Or perhaps someone else will be living here.

However the future unfolds, the God of all grace—the God of the Quest—will never cease reaching out to us and to all who are weary, hungry, suffering, lost, and searching. It is this God—the One who died on a shameful cross 2,000 years ago—who said, "And I, when I am lifted up from the earth, will draw all people to myself."

Recommended Books on Suffering and Loss

Carmichael, Amy. *Rose from Brier*. Fort Washington, PA: Christian Literature Crusade, 1973; first published 1933. 200 pages.

> This is a book unlike any other I have read on physical suffering and the inevitable, accompanying sufferings of mind and spirit. The author was a missionary to India who experienced a terrible fall that resulted in her being an invalid for the last twenty years of her life. The book is a compilation of her letters concerning her life, pain, thoughts, moods, and relationship to God during her constant sufferings following the accident. This work strengthened me most due to the author's very honest telling of her struggles, her remarkable insights into the mental and spiritual side of severe chronic illness, and her simple yet profound way of encouraging the reader in every letter. I can't imagine, for my own life, a more valuable companion in suffering.

Dawn, Marva J. *Being Well When We're Ill: Wholeness and Hope in Spite of Infirmity*. Minneapolis, MN: Augsburg, 2008. 278 pages.

> Theologian and educator Marva Dawn has written the most theologically substantive, most comprehensive, and most helpful volume on living with chronic illness that I have ever read. The list of her chronic afflictions is very long, and includes diabetes (for over 50 years), a kidney transplant (leading to serious side effects from the immunosuppressant drugs she must take for the rest of her life), and a disabled leg that requires her to use crutches and orthotics. She struggles daily with physical pain and psychological pain, and on some days spiritual pain. She works at a very high level with key biblical and theological materials in discussing her issues.

Greene-McCreight, Kathrn. *Darkness is My Only Companion: A Christian Response to Mental Illness*. Grand Rapids, MI: Brazos, 2006. 176 pages.

> The subtitle describes the book well. This is a very honest, fascinating, and encouraging account of one person's serious mental health issues (bipolar disorder) and how, through God's mercy, she found (and finds) life worth living. Because the book includes serious theological reflection it differs significantly from most books on suffering.

Piper, Don, with Cecil Murphy. *90 Minutes in Heaven: A True Story of Death and Life*. Grand Rapids, MI: Revell, 2004. 206 pages.

> Piper's book is very helpful, not (to me) because of the author's two chapters describing his visit to heaven, but because of the other 16 chapters relating his recovery from a truly awful car accident. Because of Piper's very detailed and very honest account, I can relate to many of the problems *and moods* he experienced (and still experiences) in his long (since 1989) recovery. He lives in constant pain even now. The book's main contribution to me has been in assuring me that someone else knows almost exactly how I have thought and felt in the very difficult years since my heart transplant. The title is misleading, and does not really indicate how valuable the book is to chronic sufferers. However, this work has no doubt helped many, probably none more than me.

Sittser, Gerald D. *A Grace Disguised: How the Soul Grows Through Loss*. Grand Rapids, MI: Zondervan, 1996. 181 pages.

> This is a truly remarkable and revealing first-person account from a professor of religion whose wife, mother, and daughter were killed in a horrific nighttime car crash. The other driver was drunk, traveling at 85 miles per hour, when his car jumped his lane and smashed head-on into Sittser's minivan. The subtitle is well-chosen. This is a book for those who have experienced any kind of loss in their lives. The author's aim "is not to provide quick and painless solutions but to point the way to a lifelong journey of growth." This work helped me substantially with my major losses of health, career, and social life.

Wangerin, Walter Jr. *Letters From the Land of Cancer*. Grand Rapids, MI: Zondervan, 2010. 199 pages.

> The widely-acclaimed author, during the last days of 2005 and the first days of 2006, learned that he had lung cancer. He then began writing a series of letters to family and friends, explaining in considerable detail his physical, psychological, and spiritual journey of survival. He is brutally honest about his pain, wild mood swings, and thoughts regarding life, dying, and death. His deep trust in Christ pervades the book. As an account on chronic illness from the sufferer himself, this work is superb. It is truly hope-engendering.

Other Publications by the Author

Books Edited or Authored

Readings in Christian Ethics, Vol., 1: Theory and Method. Edited with David K. Clark. Grand Rapids, MI: Baker, 1994.

Readings in Christian Ethics, Vol. 2: Issues and Applications. Edited with David K. Clark. Grand Rapids, MI: Baker, 1996.

Serving by the Spirit: Spiritual Gifts and Spiritual Preaching, 3rd edition. Quezon City, Philippines: CGM Press/Action, 2004.

Sirviendo por el Espiritu: Los Dones Espirituales y la Predicación Espiritual. (Spanish edition of *Serving by the Spirit*; publishing information confidential.)

Heart Cries: Praying by the Spirit in the Midst of Life. With Jane E. Spriggs. CreateSpace, 2010. This is a slightly revised edition of *Praying by the Spirit: Cries from the Heart in the Midst of Life*, with Jane E. Spriggs. Quezon City, Philippines: CGM Press/Action, 2008.

Contributions to Works Edited by Others

"Lord's Supper" and other articles. In *Nelson's Illustrated Bible Dictionary*, general editor Herbert Lockyer Jr. Nashville, TN: Thomas Nelson, 1986.

"Clark H. Pinnock." In *Baptist Theologians*, edited by Timothy George and David S. Dockery. Nashville, TN: Broadman, 1990.

"New Dimensions in the Study of Angels and Demons." In *New Dimensions in Evangelical Thought: Essays in Honor of Millard J. Erickson*, edited by David S. Dockery. Downers Grove, IL: InterVarsity, 1998.

"Benediction/Blessing." In *Dictionary of Christian Spirituality*, general editor Glen G. Scorgie. Grand Rapids, MI: Zondervan, 2011.

Articles in Academic Periodicals

"John Wesley as a Theologian of Grace." *Journal of the Evangelical Theological Society (JETS)* 27:2 (June 1984) 193–203.

"Human Rights and Liberties in the Political Ethics of John Wesley." *Evangelical Journal* 3:2 (Fall 1985) 63–78.

"The Contribution of John Wesley Toward an Ethic of Nature." *The Drew Gateway* 56:3 (Spring 1986) 14–25.

"James 2:14-26: Does James Contradict the Pauline Soteriology?" *Criswell Theological Review (CTR)* 1:1 (Fall 1986) 31–50.

"Ethical Choices: A Case for Non-Conflicting Absolutism." *CTR* 2:2 (Spring 1988) 239–67.

"Evil and the Goodness of God: Some Definitional and Existential Considerations." *Bulletin of the Evangelical Philosophical Society* 11 (1988) 82–101.

"Clark H. Pinnock: A Theological Odyssey." *Christian Scholar's Review* 19:3 (March 1990) 242–70.

"The Persistent Vegetative State and the Withdrawal of Nutrition and Hydration." *Journal of the Evangelical Theological Society (JETS)* 35:3 (September 1992) 389–405.

"Becoming Like God: An Evangelical Doctrine of Theosis." *Journal of the Evangelical Theological Society (JETS)* 40:2 (June 1997) 257–69.

Popular-Level Writings (partial list)

"The Question Box," bi-weekly question and answer column for *Red Deer Advocate* (principal daily newspaper for central Alberta), Red Deer, Alberta, Canada, January 1973 to January 1975.

"Why God Permits Suffering," *The Standard* 78:9 (October 1988) 8-11. Reprinted in *Pulpit Helps* 15:12 (September 1990) 1-4. Also reprinted in booklet form by Action International Ministries, Bothell, WA (1991).

"When Does Death Come?" *The Standard* 81:10 (November 1991) 24-27.

"When Suffering Continues," *Christian Reflection* 7 (2003) 26-35.

"Matters of the Heart," *Heart and Mind* (Fall 2005) 2-4.

Blog Postings

Popular-level pieces, mostly on issues of the Christian life, in "The Benediction Project" http://bobrakestraw.blogspot.com/ (2007-2013) and "The New Benediction Project" http://newbenedictionproject.blogspot.com/ (since 2013) (Both blogs are in transition.)